"It is my pleasure to commend Dr. Eric Redmond's expositions as an essential companion for preachers and students of the Bible! It's rare to come across a commentary that perfectly marries exegetical depth with concrete practicality. No academic aloofness here; Dr. Redmond's work evidences a preacher with his feet on the ground. His page-turning expositions amplify the priority of the pulpit and refuse to cower from naming the relevant individual, communal, and societal idols of our time. The distinctive of Dr. Redmond's work lies in its ability not only to educate but to equip the preacher to boldly declare, 'There is a word from the Lord for our time today!'"

Emmanuella Carter, director of women's ministries, Progressive Baptist Church, Chicago

"Redmond's commentary succeeds in its goal—to draw out the meaning of the text of these biblical books and to apply their meaning to a contemporary world. Although Judges and Ruth were not written in a modern context, they speak clearly to the church in the twenty-first century in a post-pandemic world. The author demonstrates how both books foreshadow and typify the coming of Jesus the Christ, the hope of all peoples. Written in an engaging style with clear and practical applications, this commentary's focus on the exegetical and literary focus of the author and implications for the contemporary church makes it particularly helpful for preachers and teachers."

Glenn R. Kreider, editor in chief of *Bibliotheca Sacra*; professor of theological studies at Dallas Theological Seminary

"Dr. Redmond's commentary is a fabulous resource. He models the essential elements for faithful exposition of the Scriptures:

(1) careful attention to the textual messages in Judges and Ruth;

(2) clear, text-guided applications for today; and

(3) consistent adoration of the Risen Christ.

I highly recommend this book to help the preacher and the everyday disciple hear and heed what the Spirit speaks through the books of Judges and Ruth."

Ronjour Locke, instructor of preaching and urban ministry and director of the Center for Preaching and Pastoral Leadership at Southeastern Baptist Theological Seminary

"The unique contribution of Eric Redmond's work to the Christ-Centered Exposition series is rooted in his desire to see believers properly taught and his rich devotion to the orthodoxy of the Christian faith. Writing with the heart of a pastor and the eye of a scholar, Redmond offers balance, with a palatable theological perspective coupled with clear and portable application. This book and series are a complement to any library and very useful tools for discipleship. Pastors and laymen alike will be blessed by this well-written and accessible resource."

Zion McGregor, pastor, Mission City Church, Grand Prairie, Texas; contributing author to *Urban Apologetics*

"With a scholarly eye and pastoral impulse, Dr. Redmond's exposition of Judges and Ruth bridges the world of the biblical text with the world of the contemporary Church. This interplay makes his work a valued asset in the library of every expositor."

Eric Rivera, assistant professor of pastoral theology, Trinity Evangelical Divinity School; lead pastor, The Brook, Chicago

"Dr. Redmond's work is a much-needed pastoral voice for the American church. His clear, concise, and engaging writing style draws together deep exegetical work with hymn lyrics, historical and current events, and bold application that will encourage, challenge, and strengthen faith. This is a master class in written form for how to preach and apply Old Testament narrative texts. The study questions pinpoint key and pressing issues facing churches and individual Christians today, motivating a courageous and grace-filled resolve to follow Jesus in ever-growing faithfulness. Pastors, students, Bible-study leaders, and lay Christians will all benefit from having this commentary as a guide for studying Judges and Ruth."

Megan C. Roberts, assistant professor of Old Testament; Bible/Theology program director, Prairie College, Three Hills, Alberta, Canada

CHRIST-CENTERED

Exposition

OT / COMMENTARY · FEATURING · CSB

AUTHOR Eric C. Redmond

SERIES EDITORS David Platt, Daniel L. Akin, and Tony Merida

CHRIST-CENTERED
Exposition

EXALTING JESUS IN

JUDGES AND RUTH

HOLMAN®

REFERENCE

NASHVILLE, TENNESSEE

SERIES DEDICATION

Dedicated to Adrian Rogers and John Piper. They have taught us to love the gospel of Jesus Christ, to preach the Bible as the inerrant Word of God, to pastor the church for which our Savior died, and to have a passion to see all nations gladly worship the Lamb.

—David Platt, Tony Merida, and Danny Akin
March 2013

AUTHOR'S DEDICATION

To Pamela, my autumn,
who, in fields of brook and wind,
in lands of ham and places to sing novel carols by the ton,
in the dales of meadows dwelling,
and wherever an Adirondack might unfold,
has given me the pleasure of being by your side,
like two gazelles prancing in the forest,
for thirty years,
and with anticipation of much more fun to come.
I love and adore you.
The remote is on your side.

And to the Moody Bible Institute Classes of 2020–2024,
who did college through the COVID-19 pandemic,

go be the Othniels for the evangelical church in America,
in the power of the Holy Spirit given by Christ Jesus our Lord.
I am praying for you to do so.

And to the Moody Bible Institute Task Force on Race, 2020–2021,
thank you for your humble, faithful service,
in the hopes that many like Ruth will enjoy being welcomed
in our Bethlehems.

TABLE OF CONTENTS

Judges

Ruth

PREFACE

Judges is a fascinating book. You are now embarking on the reading and studying of a book that teaches that *Israel's moral relativism Canaanizes them, bringing them closer to destruction than to securing the promised land.* Every chapter shows the path and outcomes of "everyone [doing] whatever seemed right to him" (Judg 17:6). The assembly that led the conquest of the promised land makes choices that keep them from obtaining the land fully.

Ruth is equally exciting. In Ruth's pages you are reading about *the providential working of God to fill the emptiness of Naomi and Ruth.* On that subject, Ruth teaches that *the Lord orders their lives in his mercy such that they find favor in the eyes of Boaz, their kinsman redeemer.* Reading every chapter of Ruth with these ideas in mind will help the meaning of each chapter unfold for you. In Ruth one reads about how a sovereign God loves his own by means of tragedy.

I am grateful to the Spirit of God for giving Judges and Ruth to the church as part of the canon of inspired Scripture. Wading through Judges's and Ruth's writer-editor's selection of postconquest stories deepened my knowledge of God, his Word, his will, and his ways. I hope the same will become true for you and every reader of Judges and Ruth. As you are reading through these books, I pray that the Spirit of God will open the eyes of your heart to know in a great way the hope, riches, and power the Lord provides to us in Christ (Ps 119:18; Eph 1:19-23).

To that end, I have provided a commentary that seeks exegesis—*to draw out* the meaning of the text. This work is not what the academic and publishing guilds identify as an "*exegetical* commentary," for it is not an advanced, scholarly discussion of paratextual and introductory matters, original languages and textual-critical concerns, structural patterns, historical milieu, and theological teaching and positions of Judges or Ruth. However, it is exegetical in terms of providing a means for the reader to see what the author intends to communicate through the combination of the words, tone, structure, and theology of each passage in its historical context. It is exegetical in terms of demonstrating the relevance of what the author intends to communicate for a contemporary audience. This is a commentary for believers who wish to discern the voice of God in passages of Scripture, as are all the commentaries in the Christ-Centered Exposition series.

I want you to fall in love with God as he reveals himself in the pages of Scripture. Therefore, I must allow each text to tell us what its central idea is and how that idea is meaningful to the obedient walk of believers individually and corporately. As we let each text show us what it is saying, we will be taught, rebuked, corrected, and trained in the righteousness that pleases the Lord with respect to the central idea in each passage. We do not know what those ideas are until we work through each passage. Therefore, expect to be surprised and challenged in every chapter of Judges and Ruth. I was.

Some readers might find it odd that someone with a PhD on a New Testament (NT) passage has produced a commentary on a book of the Old Testament (OT). But this should not seem odd, for my undergraduate, graduate, and pastoral tenures have given me opportunities to explain the full canon of Scripture and not simply one Testament. My thirty years of ministry have led me to emphasize *scholarship* in one discipline of the NT. However, those same thirty years have been spent studying and teaching the *interpretation* and *communication* of both Testaments of Scripture. Explaining the meaning of OT passages is something I love to do. I have enjoyed writing previously on Jonah for this commentary series. I hope to follow this commentary with commentaries on Mark and Acts, as well as works to help believers read Proverbs, biblical narrative, and the Fourth Gospel.

I was working through this commentary during the painful period of the deaths of George Floyd and Ahmaud Arbery and their aftermaths. Even more than after the deaths of Eric Garner (2014), Jamar Clark (2015), Freddie Gray (2015), Philando Castile (2016), Alton Sterling (2016), DeJuan Guillory (2017), Michael Brown (2018), Stephon Clark (2018), and Botham Jean (2018), my heart and mind wept with the families of Floyd and Arbery. I still weep for them, along with the families of Breonna Taylor (2020) and Sandra Bland (2015)—families still awaiting justice for racial injustice to materialize in forms greater than financial settlements. I could not escape my reality of writing about the wickedness of a nation of people who thought they were pleasing the

Lord while rejecting his lordship for a relativistic morality. I do not wish to escape this reality; I wish to preach the Word of God to the people of God and to pray for and call for repentance, righteousness, and revival within the Lord's church.

As I agreed to write this commentary many years before the adoption of Resolution 9, "On Critical Race Theory and Intersectionality," at the 2019 Annual Meeting of the Southern Baptist Convention, I decided keeping my word was more important than breaking a contract to make a statement of protest; examining the narratives of Barak and Jephthah cautioned me against speaking rashly. Yet I applaud the bold responses by pastors Dr. Ralph West, Rev. William Dwight McKissic, and Dr. Charlie Dates—the latter two of whom are personal friends I hold in high regard. Their actions help expose the blindness many evangelicals have with regard to their own paucity of efforts to call the church toward the full justice demands of the gospel, even while the church goes about attempting to be faithful to the Great Commission. We do not need *theory* to see this; we only need texts like Judges 21.

Three significant works related to much of the content of Judges were published when I had completed more than 85 percent of this commentary. Therefore, I was unable to take advantage of them: Willie James Jennings's *After Whiteness: An Education in Belonging* (Eerdmans, 2020), Carl Trueman's *The Rise and Triumph of the Modern Self: Cultural Amnesia, Expressive Individualism, and the Road to Sexual Revolution* (Crossway, 2020), and John Piper's *Providence* (Crossway, 2021). I look forward to seeing how these works influence the renewal of Christ's church and her faithfulness to the gospel as their research appears within the writing of others.

It takes a great supporting cast of people to complete a commentary. I have done the reading and writing, but others pushed me, encouraged me, prayed for me, and gave me the allowances needed to bring the work to fruition. Many thanks go to Sarah McCaffrey for leading a dedicated team of prayer warriors behind every effort that went into the final year of the work. I can imagine Sarah's joy-giving smile and warmth as I think of her holding this book in her hands.

Many of my past and present students gave hours of prayer support, too. I had many students giving me a "You're almost there; you can do this!" cheer in the final months of the work. Gretchen Douglas (MBI class of 2023) and Leah McDonald (MBI class of 2023 and one of my faculty assistants) asked weekly about the progress of the commentary and spoke of how eager they were to read it. The Four Friends from Houghton 9 (and 10)—Adda Frick, Nikki Stansford (soon to be Mrs. Tabor), Gabby Gonzalez, and Tehilla Wasserman—frequently gave similar inquiries and words of encouragement, as did their RA and my lead faculty assistant, Karie "Mouse" Anderson. Yes, Annie Huie, mom of Cod, you too greatly supported this work.

My division chair, Dr. Steven Sanchez, gave me grace as I kept speaking of the commentary in the same breath I would speak of my faculty duties. My longtime friend Professor Ronjour Locke of Southeastern Baptist Theological Seminary helped me think about the meaning of some passages when I was not sure I had captured the author's main idea. Ronjour, your friendship has been a treasure to me in many ways, and I lose buttons on my shirt like a big brother when I see the works of your ministry.

Dave Stabnow and the team at B&H Publishing Group showed great patience and kindness toward me as my family experienced the death of a family friend and became overwhelmed by grief for an extended time—an experience of grief that was complicated by the COVID-19 pandemic and quarantine. I appreciate their understanding and grace as my writing was delayed while properly addressing grief. They knew that faithfulness to this commentary should not mean faithlessness to my family's increased need for care. Dave, it has been a joy to work with you and your team as you offered Christ's love toward me. Thank you, too, for the additional weeks of patience when I lost work on five edited chapters due to my own user errors that I originally thought to be a glitch.

Finally, as in all my works, none of this would be possible without the finite person in this world who brings me the greatest joy I could ever know. Pam, we have shared thirty years of married love together in Christ. That love is in every word of this commentary. Maybe our first reading together of the commentary will be on a beach in Spain after the COVID-19 crisis has long passed. In the meantime, may these few words sing of your praises in the gates.

ECR
Winfield, Illinois
Good Friday, 2021

SERIES INTRODUCTION

Augustine said, "Where Scripture speaks, God speaks." The editors of the Christ-Centered Exposition Commentary series believe that where God speaks, the pastor must speak. God speaks through His written Word. We must speak from that Word. We believe the Bible is God breathed, authoritative, inerrant, sufficient, understandable, necessary, and timeless. We also affirm that the Bible is a Christ-centered book; that is, it contains a unified story of redemptive history of which Jesus is the hero. Because of this Christ-centered trajectory that runs from Genesis 1 through Revelation 22, we believe the Bible has a corresponding global-missions thrust. From beginning to end, we see God's mission as one of making worshipers of Christ from every tribe and tongue worked out through this redemptive drama in Scripture. To that end we must preach the Word.

In addition to these distinct convictions, the Christ-Centered Exposition Commentary series has some distinguishing characteristics. First, this series seeks to display exegetical accuracy. What the Bible says is what we want to say. While not every volume in the series will be a verse-by-verse commentary, we nevertheless desire to handle the text carefully and explain it rightly. Those who teach and preach bear the heavy responsibility of saying what God has said in His Word and declaring what God has done in Christ. We desire to handle God's Word faithfully, knowing that we must give an account for how we have fulfilled this holy calling (Jas 3:1).

Second, the Christ-Centered Exposition Commentary series has pastors in view. While we hope others will read this series, such as parents, teachers, small-group leaders, and student ministers, we desire to provide a commentary busy pastors will use for weekly preparation of biblically faithful and gospel-saturated sermons. This series is not academic in nature. Our aim is to present a readable and pastoral style of commentaries. We believe this aim will serve the church of the Lord Jesus Christ.

Third, we want the Christ-Centered Exposition Commentary series to be known for the inclusion of helpful illustrations and theologically driven applications. Many commentaries offer no help in illustrations, and few offer any kind of help in application. Often those that do offer illustrative material and application unfortunately give little serious attention to the text. While giving ourselves primarily to explanation, we also hope to serve readers by providing inspiring and illuminating illustrations coupled with timely and timeless application.

Finally, as the name suggests, the editors seek to exalt Jesus from every book of the Bible. In saying this, we are not commending wild allegory or fanciful typology. We certainly believe we must be constrained to the meaning intended by the divine Author himself, the Holy Spirit of God. However, we also believe the Bible has a messianic focus, and our hope is that the individual authors will exalt Christ from particular texts. Luke 24:25-27,44-47 and John 5:39,46 inform both our hermeneutics and our homiletics. Not every author will do this the same way or have the same degree of Christ-centered emphasis. That is fine with us. We believe faithful exposition that is Christ centered is not monolithic. We do believe, however, that we must read the whole Bible as Christian Scripture. Therefore, our aim is both to honor the historical particularity of each biblical passage and to highlight its intrinsic connection to the Redeemer.

The editors are indebted to the contributors of each volume. The reader will detect a unique style from each writer, and we celebrate these unique gifts and traits. While distinctive in their approaches, the authors share a common characteristic in that they are pastoral theologians. They love the church, and they regularly preach and teach God's Word to God's people. Further, many of these contributors are younger voices. We think these new, fresh voices can serve the church well, especially among a rising generation that has the task of proclaiming the Word of Christ and the Christ of the Word to the lost world.

We hope and pray this series will serve the body of Christ well in these ways until our Savior returns in glory. If it does, we will have succeeded in our assignment.

David Platt
Daniel L. Akin
Tony Merida
Series Editors
February 2013

Judges

Compromising Our Calling

JUDGES 1

Main Idea: The path from compromise to powerlessness should help the people of God think carefully about our own calling.

I. **Compromising Starts by Helping God (1:1-3).**
   A. A prayer to God (1:1)
   B. A promise from God (1:2)
   C. A plan without God (1:3)
II. **Compromising Still Achieves Successes before God (1:4-18).**
   A. Success over a great king (1:4-7)
   B. Successes over great territories (1:8-18)
III. **Compromising Sadly Results in Limited Triumphs in Spite of God (1:19-36).**
   A. Limits of technology (1:19)
   B. Limits of territory (1:20-21)
   C. Limits by treachery (1:22-26)
   D. Limits for every tribe (1:27-36)

In June 1978, Aleksandr Solzhenitsyn famously pronounced the following during his Harvard University commencement address:

> It would be retrogression to attach oneself today to the ossified formulas of the Enlightenment. Social dogmatism leaves us completely helpless in front of the trials of our times. Even if we are spared destruction by war, our lives will have to change if we want to save life from self-destruction. We cannot avoid revising the fundamental definitions of human life and human society. Is it true that man is above everything? Is there no Superior Spirit above him? Is it right that man's life and society's activities have to be determined by material expansion in the first place? Is it permissible to promote such expansion to the detriment of our spiritual integrity? ("World Split Apart")

While Solzhenitsyn was addressing the social and moral self-destruction of societies, his three questions about our view of the greatness of man, the priority of material expansion, and the sacrifice of spiritual integrity equally could be addressed to the modern church. While seeking to live for Christ, we can live as if man were superior to God, that this life is the kingdom of God, and that it is appropriate to sacrifice our spiritual integrity to achieve (seemingly) the things of God. None of us intends the destruction of the church and her witness in society. But akin to an unhappy family hidden behind the facade of a plush home, on so many fronts it would appear that we have settled for compromise in accomplishing the will of God, and it is masked by the facades of material and spiritual successes.

Judah, apparently unknowingly, thinks lightly of how she will accomplish the will of God. The resulting God-wrought success masks the slow journey to spiritual and moral self-destruction. Judah's story is informative for all that we will see in the book of Judges, the compromising decisions we make as believers, and the power of success to hide the dangerous consequences that come from such compromise. Judah's story reveals three things about compromising our calling as a church: compromising starts by helping God, compromising still achieves success before God, and compromising results in limited triumphs in spite of God.

Compromising Starts by Helping God
JUDGES 1:1-3

Israel experienced victory in the promised land under Joshua. Now that he has died, certainly they will want to continue in that success.

A Prayer to God (1:1)

Rightly, therefore, they seek the Lord in prayer. They are seeking the will of God. It would seem that they want to honor the Lord in the manner by which they accomplish what he has called them to do—that is, to acquire all their allotted territories in the land of promise. They want to fight to secure the land. Inherently, they recognize that the victories in their history come as a result of following the Lord's voice—the words of God. It is right for them to ask the Lord to specify his choice of tribes to lead in the absence of a new leader being appointed in place of Joshua.

A Promise from God (1:2)

The Lord will speak and make his voice known. The Lord decrees two things in his speaking. First, *Judah alone is the tribe he appoints to go up first to fight the Canaanites on behalf of Israel.* This would be in keeping with the Genesis 49 prophecy of Judah's hand being on the neck of her enemies and the scepter remaining with Judah (Gen 49:8-12). This would agree with the Deuteronomy 33 prophecy of the Lord's contending for Judah against her enemies. Judah's going up first is consistent with the priority of Judah among the tribes in redemptive history, for Judah is the tribe from which the Messiah will come. Judah alone is the tribe he appoints to go up first to fight the Canaanites on behalf of Israel.

Second, *the Lord decrees victory with certainty for Judah.* The Lord already has determined that the Canaanites will experience defeat at the hands of Judah. The Lord calls Judah on behalf of Israel. All that Judah and the rest of Israel have to do is trust the voice of God—that he will be true to his word. The Lord has decreed victory for Judah, and they are to secure it alone.

A Plan without God (1:3)

What happens next is a travesty, even though there is no outcry in Israel and no comment by the editor of Judges:[1] *Judah invites Simeon to join their tribe in the fight against the Canaanites in a quid pro quo agreement that offers to secure Simeon's allotment the same way.*[2]

Apparently, Judah finds the word of the Lord to be insufficient in providing the guidance for victory over the Canaanites. What seems to be an innocent invitation is laden with rebellion against the Lord and maybe reveals fear—or at least a lack of faith—on the part of Judah and all Israel. I suspect that no one thought the words of God augmented

---

[1] That Judges is edited is beyond question. The contents of Judges span a period of more than 350 years. Also, it would seem that one editor is responsible for compiling the historical works so that they tell one story up to the day of the Babylonian conquest. On editing and inspiration, see Grisanti, "Inspiration, Inerrancy, and the OT Canon."

[2] On what basis does Judah make this overture? In keeping with the development of the narrative of the failures of the tribes below, it seems that the decree of God assigned Judah to fight without any mention of Simeon or another tribe. That same voice of God assured Judah victory without any suggestion that victory would require more than what the Lord spoke. This might appear to be an argument from silence, but I am suggesting that this is the pattern of the narrative.

with Judah's practical reasoning was a problem. No one in Israel shouts in opposition; no one stands against the plan.

Whenever we go beyond the Word of God to achieve what we aspire to accomplish, we are compromising the voice of God and thus compromising our faith. Judah should have known this is a path to self-destruction, for disobedience to the Lord's word to give the land to Israel resulted in forty years of wilderness wandering for the first generation of Israel. Anytime we augment the words of God in order to accomplish our desires, it is a compromise with promised destruction, even if it is as seemingly innocent as asking Simeon to help accomplish what the Lord has promised to accomplish.

In our sensate culture in which subjectivity rules over objectivity, asking the people of God to allow the Word of God to have absolute authority in their lives is a challenge. A 2020 Pew Research Center poll revealed that half of Christians say casual sex—defined in the survey as sex between consenting adults who are not in a committed romantic relationship—is sometimes or always acceptable (Diamant, "Casual Sex"). This means that for half the church, God's Word on premarital or extramarital sexual encounters has no authority in determining what is right before the Lord. In effect, that half is saying, "Yes, the Lord said no sexual relations outside of marriage. Now who will have sex with me outside of marriage, for God's way of doing relationships and sexual intimacy is not sufficient?"

It is not simply with respect to sexual ethics that we make such choices. We work longer hours in order to keep our jobs while asking our families to understand. But the Lord promises to provide for his own. We hear what the Word teaches on marriage, divorce, and remarriage, but we will place the desire for happiness—"The Lord wants me to be happy"—above his voice. The product of the Spirit working in us is meekness, but we convince ourselves that we must be brash and forceful at work if we will survive. These and many other decisions are just as compromising as Judah's invitation to Simeon. They are plans made without God's Word in mind.

Compromising Still Achieves Successes before God
JUDGES 1:4-18

Following their choice to work with Simeon, Judah's encounters with the Canaanites result in several solid victories. This includes victories for

Caleb, Othniel, Achsah, the descendants of Moses's father-in-law, and the tribe of Simeon. But the cracks in the foundation formed by their disobedience are forming.

Success over a Great King (1:4-7)

The Lord does not need the help of Simeon to give victory to Judah. The Lord gives ten thousand warriors of the Canaanites and Perizzites into the hands of Judah. Functioning as instruments of the Lord's justice, Judah defeats Adoni-bezek, the king of the Canaanites and Perizzites. The Lord uses Judah to repay the wrongs of Adoni-bezek, and Simeon is nowhere to be found in the description of these victories.

Successes over Great Territories (1:8-18)

Judah then captures Jerusalem from its inhabitants, defeats the Canaanites in the hill country and the lowlands of the Negev, and defeats the Canaanites living in Hebron, including the sons of Anak.[3] Via the leadership of Caleb and the warring of Othniel, Judah will capture Debir, and Othniel will gain a wife for his efforts. The account of the victory previously recorded in Joshua makes an appearance in our chapter on Judah's compromise as a flashback story of success achieved under Joshua (Josh 15:13-19). Yet Achsah's securing of the springs goes beyond what Caleb promised to Othniel in a fashion similar to Judah's going beyond what was promised to them. The decisions of the corporate people of God are reflected in the lives of individual worshipers of the Lord.

After Achsah's incident, the talk of Judah's being victorious changes. Judah works with the descendants of the Kenites as they approach Arad. Surely this should not be a problem, for Moses's father-in-law was a friend of Israel who helped guide them. But it is a problem, for this will be the first time Judah does not secure a solid victory. The compromise with the Kenites reveals a lack of the presence of the power of God to drive out the inhabitants of Arad, as Judah and the Kenites are forced to live among the people of Arad. Their settling with the people shows contentment with failing to do all that the Lord commanded.

---

[3] See Num 13:22. The writer will return to reference the defeat of these three sons of Anak in v. 20.

Afterwards, in what looks like obedience to the commandment to destroy the peoples of the land, Judah defeats Zephath with the help of Simeon. This only looks like full obedience; they are doing what the law commands, but Judah is doing it while inviting the help of Simeon. The Judges writer alerts his readers to the subtle ways in which one might compromise. Even so, Judah will capture Gaza, Ashkelon, and Ekron without any mention of help from another tribe. Their success seems to keep them from recognizing little compromises.

Many leaders with glaring miscues have large and successful ministries, if one measures according to membership numbers and media influence. One observing these leaders and their influence might wonder how the Lord could allow success through people embezzling funds, abusing authority, practicing immorality, or proclaiming false doctrine. Answer: The Lord allows us to make poor choices and reap the consequences. The consequences should act as warnings to turn away from sin and toward Christ and his body. The Lord will not force obedience or compliance to his rule.

Compromising Sadly Results in Limited Triumphs in Spite of God
JUDGES 1:19-36

From this point forward, the reader will witness a change in the tone of the story and the outcomes of the campaigns to take possession of the land. There now will be limits to how much land is conquered by the various tribes—if any is conquered at all. The writer intends to show that what began as an inquiry into God's will becomes a tour through hearing God's voice, choosing to compromise, obtaining initial victories, but then watching society deteriorate as the tribes fail at their calling. When they were having victories over the thumbs and toes of Adoni-bezek and conquering hill country and lowlands, no one could foresee the damage done by one simple compromising act. The successes hid the impending danger from the people's reasoning. But disobedient chickens always come home to roost. In this case, the disobedience to God's word manifests in an absence of the power to accomplish the will of God—to completely drive out the inhabitants of the land. There will be success, but God's people will face limits as to how much success can happen apart from following God's word fully.

Limits of Technology (1:19)

Verse 19 is informative for us theologically when recognizing the limits caused through compromise. First, *victories come at the hand of the Lord.* The power of God is present with Judah, enabling the tribes. Both the presence and the power are important. The Lord did not leave them when they compromised; neither did he draw away his power completely.

Second, *the presence of the Lord to enable them victory in one place does not guarantee continual victory elsewhere.* Keep in mind that Judah has compromised, which is sin. Thus, their access to God and his power is broken in a relational sense.

Third, *the compromise resulted in a limit related to technology.* The people of God are stopped in their conquest because the enemy has greater technology—i.e., iron chariots, which apparently Judah did not have and whose power Judah could not overcome. Had Judah not compromised, the Lord would have smashed those iron chariots to bits for his people or given Judah greater ones than those had by her enemies. Instead, the power of Judah without God is no match for the technological advancement of their enemies. If the power of God were still present, the iron of the chariots would not have mattered (see Josh 17:17-18; Judg 4:13-16).

Limits of Territory (1:20-21)

By reviewing Caleb's acquisition of Hebron and defeat of the sons of Anak, the writer reminds us about the success brought about by faithfulness to the voice of God. In contrast to the rest of Judah in the hill country, Caleb does drive out those occupying the territory belonging to him. The great Anak sons are individuals who are comparable to the Canaanites' iron chariots. Yet in this case Caleb succeeds where Judah failed.

Benjamin will follow in the footsteps of Judah. They will capture only part of Jerusalem and will fail to accomplish the Lord's will for them to drive out the inhabitants. Instead, the Jebusites become their neighbors and thus their coworkers, soccer coaches, competitive business owners, alternate religion providers, and girlfriends, brides, boyfriends, and grooms for the children of Israel.

Limits by Treachery (1:22-26)

The reader of OT history might be tempted to think the insertion of Joseph, next, would be another successful exception against the pattern of failure. It is when they capture a resident and put the town of Luz to the sword. But then, rather than obeying the command to destroy the peoples of the land completely, they let the captured man and his family go as a gift of kindness for helping them enter the town.

The people of Joseph did not have the right to offer this man kindness when the Lord had declared destruction. Only if someone were accepting terms of peace with Israel should they have been spared. Based on the man's actions after his release, he is not at peace with Israel. If he had been at peace, he could have stayed in Joseph's territory, served with them, and followed the God of Joseph. Instead, the man goes to the territory of an enemy of Israel, and there he builds a city. Thumbing his nose at his captors, he names the new city after the town Joseph destroyed, almost as if he is saying, "You and your God will not own the territory of Luz!" This is a move of betrayal in response to the kindness of Joseph. The man from Luz takes their unauthorized kindness and stabs them in their backs with it. At the time of the writing of the history of the period of the judges—which may have been anywhere from four hundred to eight hundred years after the events themselves—the backstabber's city still is standing. The consequences of the small compromise spans generations.

Limits for Every Tribe (1:27-36)

The remaining verses in the chapter read like a dystopian novella about the lives of Manasseh, Ephraim, Zebulun, Asher, Naphtali, and Dan. Most of the tribes cannot drive out the inhabitants of their lands but instead force them into labor as slaves. The Amorites will maintain a huge swath of land that should have been Israel's. Can you imagine the testimony of the tribes and the Lord in the eyes of the Canaanites? Project these decisions and failures across the breadth of the story of the judges, and the moral decline that characterizes this period makes sense.

Application

The path from compromise to powerlessness should help the contemporary people of God to think carefully about our own calling. Here are five things we should consider.

First, *our calling is to be a holy people who give witness to the resurrection of Christ to point people to the kingdom of God.* Therefore, we must fight the pull to be worldly in our bodies, minds, talk, leisure, spending, aspirations, ethics, and friendships. This means we should beware of subtle encroachments of unholy ideas influencing our lifestyle choices.

Second, *some compromise is inevitable.* Therefore, we should be sober and vigilant in our strivings for obedience. We should think of every sermon and every reading of Scripture as being something that points out where we are not honoring the Lord.

Third, *the cause of compromise is both a lack of knowledge of the Word and lack of love of the Word.* Therefore, we must pursue the Word of God in earnest. This includes developing plans for reading Scripture daily and obeying whatever Scripture says. We cannot look into the mirror of Scripture and say, "Yes, Scripture says 'X,' but I still plan to go against 'X.'"

Fourth, *compromise is not simply a matter of doctrine.* It also is a matter of deeds. Therefore, we must be willing to confess and repent when the Word shows we err. We should have loving, trusted friends within our local assemblies with whom we can share our misdeeds and find guidance, grace, correction, and companionship.

Fifth, in striving against compromise, *we must not make an idol of striving against compromise,* lest we pride ourselves in being uncompromising while actually compromising. We must strive in grace.

Close

Certainly, grace is what we need to live in this world without compromising our calling. Only the grace of God in Christ Jesus our Lord will give us the fortitude and zeal to be a peculiar people who fulfill the Great Commission, for in our own strength we are too fragile to follow the Word fully. As Charles Spurgeon has said,

> Our natural tendencies and corruptions, our sinful habits and lustings, and the warping and bending of our spirit towards evil—all this has to be overcome; and we shall not possess the land so as to enjoy undivided tranquility until sin is utterly exterminated. What Joshua could not do our Lord Jesus shall fully accomplish; the enemy within shall be rooted out, and then shall dawn the day of our joy and peace, when we shall sit every man under his own vine and fig-tree, and none shall make us afraid. That perfect victory shall be ours; but not yet. ("Chariots of Iron")

Spurgeon is right: To accomplish all the Lord has called us to be, do, and have as the church, we rely on the victory of Christ. Christ shall address our enemies; Christ shall provide our peace; Christ alone—without needing help from us—will make us successful until the day he comes.

Reflect and Discuss

1. What might have happened if Judah had not invited Simeon to join them in battle? What does this suggest about the smallest act of disobedience toward the Word of God?

2. What are some examples you have experienced of believers making excuses for disobeying the Word of God? What happened the last time you justified disobedience to Scripture?

3. Why are believers tempted to help bring about God's will with our own resources rather than trusting his Word?

4. When Judah is defeating the kings initially, all seems well. How does this story address the question, If that person is a false teacher, why is the ministry thriving? What does this story teach about using outcomes to measure spiritual vitality?

5. Why does the writer insert the story of Caleb from the book of Joshua?

6. What masks Judah's compromising in this story? Why would Simeon be content to disobey the instruction that Judah secure its territory on its own?

7. Why did the nation turn to compromise so quickly after Joshua died?

8. How does the judgment of the tribes' compromise finally materialize? What warning does this give you concerning obedience to God's Word?

9. What is the problem with the tribes of Joseph allowing the one resident of Luz to leave with his family? What might the generation of Israelites who read this during the exile have learned from the Benjamin episode?

10. What resources has Christ provided the church to promote faithfulness to him rather than compromise?

11. What commitments can members of a small group, Bible study, Sunday school class, or ministry team make concerning the effort to be uncompromising in obedience to the Word of God?

12. Upon finishing this first chapter, it would be good for the reader to set aside a period of two hours to read Judges 1–21 (preferably in the CSB) from start to finish in one sitting with minimal interruption. It would be best to read without referring to Bible reference notes or any other helps. The reader will gain a context for placing each chapter within the full story of the book. I encourage the reader to make a second full reading of Judges after finishing reading through the commentary on Judges 1–12. The same encouragement is offered for making a full reading of Judges 1–21 and Ruth 1–4 in one sitting after finishing reading through the commentary on Judges 13–21, and then reading Ruth 1–4 after completing the commentary reading on Ruth 1–4. Reading whole books multiple times increases the understanding and significance of every chapter for the reader. The full readings allow the reader to make links between earlier and later chapters in each book.

The Distress of Disobedience, Part 1

JUDGES 2:1-15

Main Idea: The church will experience the distress of her disobedience to God until she walks in his armor to obey the Great Commandments in the present world.

I. **Distress Begins with the Lord's Tiring of Our Disobedience (2:1-5).**
   A. The movement of the angel of the Lord (2:1a)
   B. The speaking of the angel of the Lord (2:1b-3)
   C. Responses of weeping and worship to the angel of the Lord (2:4-5)

II. **Distress Reveals Stronger Discipleship Could Minimize Disobedience (2:6-10).**
   A. Faithful disciples under and after Joshua (2:6-7)
   B. Faithful disciples to Joshua and the Lord (2:8-9)
   C. Unfaithful disciples arising after the faithful disciples (2:10)

III. **Distress of Our Idolatries Brings Wrath for Disobedience (2:11-15).**
   A. The choice of idols over the Lord (2:11-13)
   B. The wrath for following idols rather than the Lord (2:14-15)

In his well-known article, "The Evangelical Persecution Complex," Alan Noble writes,

> Persecution has an allure for many evangelicals. In the Bible, Christians are promised by Saint Paul that they will suffer for Christ, if they love Him (Second Timothy 3:12). But especially in contemporary America, it is not clear what shape that suffering will take. Narratives of political, cultural, and theological oppression are popular in evangelical communities, but these are sometimes fiction or deeply exaggerated non-fiction—and only rarely accurate. This is problematic: If evangelicals want to have a persuasive voice in a pluralist society, a voice that can defend Christians from serious persecution, then we must be able to discern

accurately when we are truly victims of oppression—and when this victimization is only imagined.

. . .

In the United States, evangelical values have often been in tension with public policy and cultural mores, especially in the last several years; this includes recent debates over contraceptives coverage, abortion rights, and the rise of same-sex marriage. Some Christians anticipate major restrictions to religious liberty in the future as a result of these tensions, a concern that is not unfounded. But in anticipating such restrictions, it is easy to imagine, wrongly, that they are already here. ("Evangelical Persecution Complex")

While Noble's article focuses on the evangelical fetishizing of suffering and recognizes real persecution believers face, it also allows us to think about how we view our place in society when the church faces hostile disagreement from the world.

In our common, popular discussion of anything opposing our cherished positions, the church is under attack. The world wants to stop us from gathering for worship during a global pandemic, and it wants to remove "Christ" from Christmas. The world wants to destroy the family and marriage, and the world intends to force their LGBTQ+ views on our children. Everything against us is framed as the work of the enemy, spiritual warfare, a battle for souls, or hatred of the church. But rarely do we frame what we perceive to be persecution as distress caused by our own lack of faithfulness to Christ as we live within the culture. That is, rarely do we frame the hostility toward our beliefs to be a result of our lack of (1) loving the Lord with all our heart, mind, soul, and strength, (2) loving our neighbor as ourselves, and (3) making disciples among the nations—the mission to which Christ has called the church in this modern age.

Much like what one sees in Judges 2:1–3:6, I propose that some of the distress the church experiences at the hands of the world in modern culture is the result of our disobedience. I also propose that such distress can be mitigated as we disrupt and end a pattern akin to the Israelites' covenant-breaking cycle of sin for which they receive distressing judgment throughout the book of Judges. We can reverse the pattern and habits that bring the distress of disobedience.

The length of this passage invites me to consider it in two parts.[4] In this first part, I will explain 2:1-15, especially examining the role idolatry played in Israel's distress. In the second part, I will explain 2:16–3:6, giving priority to the cycle of sin and deliverance that develops in Judges 3:7–16:31.[5] This first examination explains how this distress begins, what the distress reveals, and what form the distress takes.

Distress Begins with the Lord's Tiring of Our Disobedience
JUDGES 2:1-5

The Movement of the Angel of the Lord (2:1a)

This passage opens with the angel of the Lord moving from Gilgal to Bochim. The title *angel* indicates that the figure is a messenger from God. Yet it is evident in the totality of the appearance of this personality in the OT that this figure is divine. The angel of the Lord is an OT appearance of God, also known as a "theophany." More specifically, we would say this is a "Christophany" because the divine messenger sent by God is not God the Father and he is not the Spirit. Instead, this is the preincarnate—the prebodily—appearance of Christ. Christ—the angel of the Lord—is going to speak to the people.

The movement from Gilgal to Bochim seems like simple geography. However, the naming of "Bochim" in 2:5 indicates more is taking place than provision of mile markers on a road trip across the promised land. Gilgal is the place Israel lands when first crossing the Jordan River. There Israel deposited twelve stones of remembrance from the Jordan to tell later generations that the Lord had dried up both the Jordan

---

[4] The subject that unifies Judg 2:1–3:6 is the Lord's fulfillment of his word to turn away from driving out the nations due to Israel's disobedience to the commandments toward the nations. Separately, Judg 1:1-36 catalogs the remaining territory for Israel to possess. Judges 3:7 begins a narrative cycle of judges appearing to rescue Israel—a cycle that begins with the raising of Othniel, Ehud, and Shamgar and ends with Samson's burial in 16:31. Judges 2:1–3:6 supplies historical and covenantal background to the cycle of 3:7–16:31 in addition to the background information of 1:1-36.

[5] Here I am distinguishing "cycle of sin and deliverance" from a "narrative cycle of judges." The two cycles are different yet related in our understanding of the editor's strategy of telling the story. Israel falls into a pattern of sin, judgment, deliverance by a judge, and peace in the land. The judges toggle back and forth between judges who have long narratives and judges who have short narratives.

River and the Red Sea in order for Israel to cross over on dry ground (Josh 4:19-24).

In that same episode at Gilgal, the children born to those who came out of Egypt were circumcised. The writer of Joshua tells us, "The LORD then said to Joshua, 'Today I have rolled away the disgrace of Egypt from you.' Therefore, that place is still called Gilgal today" (Josh 5:9). At Gilgal they kept the Passover, the manna stopped falling because they could eat the produce of the land, and the "commander of the LORD's army"—the angel of the Lord—met Joshua to reveal who would be providing victory for Israel (Josh 5:14).

Gilgal is a place of victory and blessing that celebrates the faithfulness of the second generation of Israel. In contrast, *Bochim* means "weeping." The angel of the Lord's movement from Gilgal to Bochim vividly portrays the Israelites' movement from an obedient people whose reproach has been removed to a disobedient people whose failure in sin would bring about their weeping.

The Speaking of the Angel of the Lord (2:1b-3)

The words of the angel of the Lord review Israel's breaking of their suzerain-vassal treaty with the Lord. As the one who redeemed them from Egypt, the Lord freely chose to act as overlord, or suzerain, for the nation of Israel. As his vassal, they had stipulations to keep in the covenant with him.

The Lord had established that he would keep his covenant forever to give Israel the land of Canaan, communicating the promise through Abraham, Isaac, Jacob, and Moses (Gen 17:7-8; 26:6; 28:13; 35:12; Exod 6:4; Deut 31:6; Ps 105:11). To make sure Israel would secure the land, the Lord would be the one to drive the inhabitants from the land, using Israel as his tool (Lev 18:24; Deut 4:38; 9:4-5; 11:23). Israel's responsibility was to wage war against the nations and completely destroy them from the land. This included refraining from making any covenant with those nations, from giving their children in marriage to those nations' children, and from worshiping their gods. However, as Judges 1 revealed, Israel failed to keep their covenant responsibilities.

As a result, the Lord keeps the word of his covenant and refuses to drive out the nations going forward. The words "But *you* have not obeyed me. What have *you* done?" lay the fault of the coming distress at the feet of Israel.

Responses of Weeping and Worship to the Angel of the Lord (2:4-5)

Hearing that they have brought on themselves the Lord's refusal to secure the land for the disobedient generation, the people weep in grief. They memorialize the place as "Bochim," meaning "weepers"; every time they pass this location, they will have a reminder that they were brought to weeping by the revelation of their disobedience and the Lord's judgment. They also make sacrifices in their weeping, but the sacrifices are not such that the nation turns from their disobedience, as Judges 3:6 will show immediately. At Bochim, the angel of the Lord shows Israel that she has caused the coming distress.

In my village in the suburbs of Chicago, we have weekly street sweeping from April 1 to November 30. Signs are posted on every residential street in the neighborhood telling all residents what day to expect the sweeping on their side of the street, the requirement to remove all vehicles from the side of the street 8:00 a.m.–4:00 p.m. on the day of sweeping, and the enforcement of a penalty for failure to obey the street sweeping law.

Our police department does not ticket violators each time one fails to move a vehicle in time. This probably is due more to the sheer volume of streets and violators than it is to grace. The good part of this is that if you forget to move your car to the opposite side of the street the night before your sweeping is due, you might not have a ticket on your windshield at 8:30 a.m. The bad side of the police inaction is that the fear of the fine, which helps one to remember to move one's vehicle in a timely manner, might disappear until a ticket shows up on the windshield. I have groaned to the Lord a handful of times for what seemed like his failure to remind me to move my car in time! Truthfully, however, the four signs on the four blocks on my side of the street are contracts that have bound me to move my car if I want my street swept and do not want to incur a fine for my disobedience.

In the same way, our sovereign King has given us responsibilities both to live as salt and light in the world and to be vocal in proclaiming who he is and the salvation he offers. When we do not, like Israel failing to drive out the nations, we are not providing a means for would-be enemies to become allies and for persecutors to become friends. Instead of looking only at the *fact* of hostility, we should consider that the reality of the *distress* from those who are hostile indicates that we are not reading rightly the signs reminding us of our responsibilities to the world and of the results of our failure to be faithful.

Distress Reveals Stronger Discipleship
Could Minimize Disobedience
JUDGES 2:6-10

The faithfulness of the Joshua generations—the generations who had seen all the great work of the Lord on behalf of Israel—to the commands concerning securing the land gives way to a third generation who does not know the Lord or his works. The editor of Judges reviews the previous faithfulness of the Israelites. The review provides an implicit comparison to the faithless activity of the generation that does not drive out the nations.[6]

Faithful Disciples under and after Joshua (2:6-7)

Under Joshua, the second generation of Israelites worked to secure the inheritance of the tribes as prescribed by the Lord. They were faithful during Joshua's lifetime and under the elders of Israel even after Joshua's passing. Although that generation had not seen the plagues and Red Sea crossing, they had seen the Lord split the Jordan, bring down the walls of Jericho, defeat great nations, and make the sun stand still (Josh 3:14-17; 6:15-21; 10:12-14; 11:1-9).

Faithful Disciples to Joshua and the Lord (2:8-9)

That same generation of Israelites honored Joshua as the Lord's servant. They were not merely obeying because they thought Joshua had a popular following or power to harm them. Instead, they had hearts for the Lord, recognizing Joshua as God's appointed steward to lead them. Following the word of the Lord, they buried Joshua at the place the Lord had commanded the Israelites to give Joshua an inheritance (Josh 19:50).

---

[6] Daniel Block writes, "The narrator offers a retrospective look at Israel's past commitments in light of which the pattern of apostasy and infidelity described in this book are to be interpreted" (*Judges, Ruth*, 120).

Unfaithful Disciples Arising after the Faithful Disciples (2:10)

However, a noted shift takes place with the generation that lives after Joshua. Seemingly, these are the grandchildren of the generation that served Joshua.[7] The writer traces that generation's faithlessness to not knowing the Lord—his identity—and not having seen his works on behalf of Israel. The writer is inviting us to ask, "Why did this generation fail to know the identity of the Lord if their parents and grandparents knew the Lord and served him faithfully?"

The intentionality required to prioritize and sustain making disciples of our children for three generation takes great prayer and discipline. Staggering is the number of children raised in faithful Christian homes who walk away from the faith as teens and young adults. We all know, "Kids from wonderful gospel-centered homes leave the church; people from messed-up family backgrounds find eternal life in Jesus and have beautiful marriages and families. But," as Pastor Jon Nielson writes, "it's also not a crap-shoot. In general, children who are led in their faith during their growing-up years by parents who love Jesus vibrantly, serve their church actively, and saturate their home with the gospel completely, grow up to love Jesus and the church" ("Why Youth Stay in Church").

Nielson, a former youth pastor and university campus minister, finds three common factors in the lives of twenty-somethings who continue in the faith in which they were raised: (1) they experienced true conversion, (2) they have been equipped to do ministry and not simply entertained in their church youth groups, and (3) their parents preached the gospel to them. These factors recognize the role of the Lord, the church, and parents in raising a generation of youth to become faithful beyond the years in which they observed their parents' generation's faith.

For a local church body as a whole, this means our priority is not on best performances on Sunday; neither can we give lip service to youth being our future without every member seeing younger generations as the main focus of our internal ministries. As adults, we will have to set

---

[7] Elihu Schatz proposes that Joshua led Israel for fifty-two years ("The Length of the Rule of Joshua," 32). That would have been enough time for all those over twenty years old to have raised children to adulthood and possibly to have witnessed some of those children raise children of their own. My assumption here is that the children of those serving Joshua saw the work of God and the securing of the land as they were growing up. The children of those children, not born during the time of the conquest of the land, did not see the works of the Lord firsthand.

aside thinking of what makes worship and church ministry likable and comfortable for us, glorying in the past while complaining about what we don't do now. With Philippians 2:3-4 in mind, considering younger generations better than ourselves is a project of everyone in the body. We sustain our efforts year after year with commitments with one another and our grandchildren for more than twenty years by embracing humble membership in our congregation. In such membership, we should have an eye on seeing our grandchildren and other members' grandchildren faithfully worshiping Christ and proclaiming the gospel we love and cherish.

Distress of Our Idolatries Brings Wrath for Disobedience
JUDGES 2:11-15

Israel's abandonment of the Lord for the Baals and Ashtoreths provokes the Lord's anger. As a result, he gives Israel over to plundering and terrible distress by the surrounding enemies, according to his sworn word.

The Choice of Idols over the Lord (2:11-13)

The people make a choice to do what is evil in the sight of the Lord—an idea to which we will return repeatedly in Judges (3:7; 4:1; 6:1; 10:6; 13:1). The Baals were not one false god but several idols that had "various manifestations of the high god Baal in the various Canaanite worship sites" (Butler, *Judges*, 42). That the Israelites are abandoning the Lord for the Baals is more than a simple violation of the first two commandments. They are depending on these false gods the way they should have been depending on the one who redeemed them from Egypt. They bow their faces to the ground in submission and fear to these idols.

Twice the writer says the people of Israel provoked the Lord to anger by their acts. One notes this even before the author adds that Israel also worships the Ashtoreths, the consorts of Baal in Canaanite literature. They were goddesses of fertility and of war (Butler, *Judges*, 44). To worship them was to say that procreation and victory in war were acts of the Ashtoreths.

The Wrath for Following Idols Rather than the Lord (2:14-15)

It is little wonder the Lord responds with great anger. On the Lord being provoked to anger, John Stott notes,

They did not mean that Yahweh was irritated or exasperated,
or that Israel's behaviour had been so "provocative" that his
patience had run out. No, the language of provocation expresses
the inevitable reaction of God's perfect nature to evil. It indicates
that there is within God a holy intolerance of idolatry, immorality
and injustice. Wherever these occur, they act as stimuli to trigger
his response of anger or indignation. He is never provoked
without reason. It is evil alone that provokes him, and necessarily
so since God must be (and behave like) God. If evil did not
provoke him to anger he would lose our respect, for he would no
longer be God. (*Cross of Christ*, 124)

The Lord is not brushing off their idolatry as innocent ignorance. He
views it as unrighteousness.

In the modern world, we should think of idols as what non-Christians
depend on as the source of life, strength, joy, provision—the things that
are ultimate for their happiness. For what we are saying in following the
Lord is that he is ultimate for our happiness; he is ultimate for health,
strength, provision, peace, righteousness, salvation; he calls the shots.

If political victories drive you more than anything else, no matter
how much you pray, they are idols. The same goes for being seen on
social media, if getting views drives you. The same could be said of working so as to never experience poverty (again), or to be in a position in
which no one ever can take advantage of you.

The same can be said of living to make people grovel at your every
command (often cloaked in "You don't have to like me, but you do have
to respect me"). Your idol could be outsmarting everyone, having the
family that proves your parents were wrong about you, or getting published in the top outlet for your field or awarded by the top organization
or with the top prize in your field. For some, an idol might be living in
safety apart from the vices of broken neighborhoods and getting your
children into neighborhoods with the top-rated schools. Yes, there is
good in every one of these endeavors, and they can be had from good
motives. But idolatries of our day take subtle forms. There is not necessarily a Buddha in our yard, a turret behind our house, or a sacred cow
walking through our streets. But the idols are there, wielding rule over
us rather than the Lord's ruling.

One of the biggest idols tempting each of us to bow our faces to it is
the need to be liked and to keep our jobs; it can eclipse our obligation

to share the gospel or even to admit to being a Christian. It is easy to be a Christian in a place like Prince George's County, Maryland, where the school system is flooded with teachers who attend local churches. It is much harder to do in Oak Park, Illinois, where a Young Life group has less traction than an LGBTQ+ society in a local school.

On idolatry, John Calvin writes,

> When [Moses] relates that Rachel stole her father's images, he speaks of the use of idols as a common vice. Hence we may infer, that the human mind is, so to speak, a perpetual forge of idols. There was a kind of renewal of the world at the deluge, but before many years elapse, men are forging gods at will. There is reason to believe, that in [Noah's] lifetime his grandchildren were given to idolatry: so that he must with his own eyes, not without the deepest grief, have seen the earth polluted with idols—that earth whose iniquities God had lately purged with so fearful a Judgment. (*Institutes*, I.11.8.)

Calvin recognizes that Noah possibly was distressed over seeing his grandchildren embrace idolatry. We have our hands full with work to do if we wish to avoid being distressed by the departure of our posterity from church.

Application

What, therefore, are our first steps in addressing the distress of disobedience? First, we each need to be faithful to practices that review and reinforce the gospel as a message of God as our only Savior. I am especially thinking of being present when your congregation holds baptism services because baptism rehearses the salvation of God in bruising and raising Jesus, in burying our sin with Christ and raising us from the dead in Christ, and in the promise to raise our mortal bodies from the dead. Each of these is a work of God alone: God poured out his wrath on Christ, God raised Jesus from the dead, God revealed our need for him in the preaching of the gospel, God granted us eternal life, God promises hope when we die, and God alone will raise us from the dead without any help from us. Baptism reviews the saving work of God so that we do not think that we saved ourselves or that there is another Savior.

Our children and grandchildren should be present with us in baptism services, and we should review the message of God's salvation with them regularly and repeatedly when we learn of an upcoming baptism. Without drawing out false confessions of faith, we should encourage our children and grandchildren to pursue baptism, encouraging them to explain the salvific work of God in their own words and to confess Jesus alone is God. The same holds true for our corporate and family participations in the Lord's Supper.

Second, we need to renew our commitments to revere the Scriptures. The problem with Israel began when they disregarded the words of the Mosaic covenant. I am speculating, but I suspect their choice not to drive out the nations came as the intention to be faithful met strong challenges from the nations. That is, the word of the Lord became a hard word to obey because they lacked personal resolve to follow the word when doing so was not easy, cozy, comfortable, or peaceful. It took great courage, might, fortitude, and steadfastness to drive the Canaanite nations out of the territories they saw as their own. Israel had the promises of God in their favor. They did not know the promises demanded faithfulness even when it was difficult.

Like you, I am saddened when people turn away from following the Word of God when life's challenges make faithfulness hard. It is not that God is not faithful; it is that we assumed God's Word promised a haven of peace or a life with practical success in all areas at all times. But life in the fallen world obliterated our fantasy ideas about married life, having and raising children, the climb up the corporate ladder to the corner office or golden parachute, having perfect health, having faithful friendships, and even—for many of you—finding a church in which you could trust others to be loving, gracious, and welcoming.

At these points of revelation, we should not disregard God's Word on enduring suffering, turning the other cheek, putting away all bitterness and malice, loving our neighbors as ourselves and our wives as Christ loved the church, not exasperating our children, giving faithfully to the Lord of our finances, showing hospitality, praying for our enemies, living in holiness in our bodies, and fleeing sexual immorality. We do not, then, get to put forth the "But God must want me to be happy" sign to excuse rejection of the Word of God.

Instead, we need commitments to humble ourselves under the preached Word of God, to meditate on the Word of God daily, to read through the Word of God annually so that we hear all God's words to us, and to participate in small-body settings in which we can learn from gifted teachers, be accountable to fellow members, and ask questions about living out the Word of God. Put Sunday morning, your daily reading and meditation times, and your study group times in your digital planner with reminder alarms. Add a Bible app to your phone. Tell your closest Christian friend to ask you weekly about your faithfulness to revere God's Word over the previous week.

Third, we need to keep committing ourselves to one another's children and grandchildren. Put the names of three of your friend's children and grands on your personal prayer list and pray for them as if they were your own children and grandchildren. Pray that they will not leave the church and that they will grow and have positive experiences at home and in church. Pray for them to yield to Christ early in life, and if they are already past early life, ask the Lord to arrest them to himself in whatever stages of life they now find themselves. Ask the Lord to have mercy on them and to give them rich, abiding friendships with believers and mentors in their occupational fields who can show them how to work as Christians in their occupations. And when you see these children and grandchildren, be gracious to them rather than frown at their multicolored hair, endless tattoos, abundance of body piercings, and clothing styles that differ greatly from yours. Those externals do not matter; what matters is that they love Christ. Show them what loving Christ looks like.

Reflect and Discuss

1. What stands out in Alan Noble's opening quote, and how does it feel with respect to your idea of the persecution of Christians?
2. In addition to the example the present author gives, what are some examples of conflicts with secular culture that believers are quick to identify as warfare against the church?
3. Why might believers be slow to make self-examination when we experience pushback against our beliefs and values from the broader culture?
4. What is the significance of the angel of the Lord appearing to speak to Israel in the midst of their disobedience?
5. What human and divine factors contributed to Israel's failure to secure the remainder of the promised land, and what might this say about the church's failure to have greater influence in modern society?
6. If you had been living in Israel at the time when the angel of the Lord spoke to Israel from Gilgal, after you had finished weeping

with the rest of the country, what would you have prayed for Israel to do?

7. What is the writer doing by revisiting the Joshua episode, and what response might he be seeking from the sixth or fifth century BC Jews who would be reading this insertion?

8. In your own words, explain the respective responsibilities of the Lord, the local church body, and parents to work to keep believing children faithful to Christ as they become young adults.

9. Other than prayer, what practical, faithful role should you have toward families in your congregation in order to work with them to see their children continue in the faith as they reach the end of high school? Write down one new commitment you will make, and put that commitment before the Lord in prayer daily for the next two weeks.

10. How do our Christian cultural values become idols, and what cultural values are you most unwilling to let go of?

The Distress of Disobedience, Part 2

JUDGES 2:16–3:6

Main Idea: The church will experience the distress of her disobedience to God until she walks in his armor to obey the great commandments in the present world.

I. **Distress Tests Our Faithfulness to God's Appointed Leaders (2:16-23).**
   A. The role of the judges as deliverers (2:16)
   B. The response to the judges with disobedience (2:17)
   C. The limitations of the judges' victories (2:18-19)
   D. The anger of the Lord for the testing of the nation (2:20-23)
II. **Distress Forces Us to Use Spiritual Weapons or Embrace Spiritual Defeat (3:1-6).**
   A. The testing of the nations for war (3:1-4)
   B. The embracing of the nations for defeat (3:5-6)

At age twenty-nine, pop star Kelly Clarkson put to music the famous dictum of Fredrich Nietzsche, "That which does not kill us makes us stronger." For Clarkson, pain of the departure of a former lover, rather than making her weak, vulnerable, and feeling a need to return to the departed partner, turns her into a fighter who stands with her back straight and head held high. Unlike so many who fall apart at the point of becoming alone again, Clarkson's alternative universe exhorts the listener to view the pain like the pressure of weights in powerlifting: *The increased pressure builds rather than harms.* It gives her perspective to see herself as alone but not lonely, as one who gets the last laugh rather than being the victim of such laughter, and of seeing good when it looks like all good has departed with the lover. For Clarkson, the breakup did not kill her emotions or esteem; instead, it strengthened her resolve and made her see her life as better than before, with lighter steps, not heavier ones.

The lyrical musings of Clarkson find expression in many arenas in which we need to tell ourselves that defeat is not the end of us. Team gets crushed in a game? "What doesn't kill you makes you stronger," says a well-meaning coach. Wrongly fired from a job? "What doesn't kill you makes you stronger," says a friend who is trying to encourage you to immediately look for more work. Overlooked this time for participation in an outstanding local endeavor as you watch people younger but less talented get selected? "C'mon, now. Dust yourself off and try again the next time. You know what doesn't kill you only makes you stronger," your successful friend tells you.

Even as you feel the above comments to the broken ones are insensitive and out of place, we must recognize that there are times when the harsh thing in life that does not kill does not always serve to make you stronger. It can physically cripple you, hampering your past athleticism or your ability to enjoy leisurely activities. It can traumatize, causing you to spend years in therapy, self-doubt, avoidance, and self-criticism. It can make you suspicious of small oppositions, even when people are being genuinely kind to you, because you think you have seen such overtures of love before in the mouths of those who now are your enemies.

Nevertheless, it is possible for challenges we face and survive to make us even stronger for the next challenge. It is possible that having hard parents prepares you to endure a hard marriage and that hard jobs in your young adult years build you so that harder jobs in your middle ages seem doable. It is possible that surviving a toxic environment in one job gives you the experience and skills you need to navigate an even unhealthier environment in a newer job. *And it is possible that challenges we face as believers for our faith are working to force us to go to the Lord for even more strength to be found faithful before the greatest temptations to embrace the ways of the world.* It is possible that the distressful offenses to our faith will lead us to maturity in Christ rather than to failure before him.

Review

Judges 2:16–3:6 is the second portion of one unified passage in 2:1–3:6. The full passage explores the distresses caused by our own lack of faithfulness to the Lord's words in Scripture. In the first portion, we considered three thoughts within 2:1-15. First, in 2:1-5 one sees that *distress begins with the Lord's tiring of our disobedience.* That is, the angel of the Lord put Israel in the distressing position of facing opposition in the promised land without his help to secure the inheritance allotments. The angel of the Lord brings this word of judgment because Israel failed to keep the covenant stipulations to destroy the nations.

Second, in 2:6-10 one sees that *distress reveals that stronger discipleship could minimize disobedience.* Ancient Israel had holes in their discipleship programs. The generation of Joshua's peers, and the generation that outlived him, buried him, and served the elders who served with him remained faithful to the covenant. But their children did not, for while one generation secured the land, their offspring were enjoying the fruits of the inheritance without meeting the Lord for themselves. This led to Israel's breaking of the covenant. If only they had paid attention to the Shema and made talking about the Lord's words and work part of the rhythms of every aspect of their lives, then their children would have seen the Lord as indispensable rather than nonessential.

Third, in 2:11-15 one sees that *the distress of our own idolatries brings wrath for such disobedience.* The Lord's response to Israel's choice to take the easy road of idolatry rather than the hard road of obedience is to make the road even harder. Since they want the Baals and Ashtoreths, the Lord lets them fall into the hands of the enemies who worship those gods. The editor of Judges is explicit in saying, "Whenever the Israelites went out, the LORD was against them and brought disaster on them, just as he had promised and sworn to them. So they suffered greatly" (2:15).

Distress Tests Our Faithfulness to God's Appointed Leaders
JUDGES 2:16-23

In the remainder of chapters 2–16, a pattern emerges. The Israelites, as covenant breakers, follow other gods rather than faithfully following the judges the Lord raises in mercy. This provokes the Lord's anger, making him refuse to drive out the nations for the generations to follow. The presence of the nations tests the faithfulness of Israel's walk with the Lord as they face the choice of following him or the gods of the nations.

The Role of the Judges as Deliverers (2:16)

In response to the nation's suffering, God raises up judges. These judges are not officers of a governmental court system. Except for Deborah in Judges 4, none of the judges sit in judgment of the affairs of people. Instead, these judges are military leaders sent to be deliverers of the people from their oppressors. "They gained power and authority from Yahweh for a soteriological, not a legal purpose, delivering Israel from external enemies rather than settling internal disputes" (Butler, *Judges*, 46). In the chapters to follow, every judge we meet acts to rescue Israel from enemies—from "marauders" or robbers who used their oppression of the Israelites to steal from them.

The Response to the Judges with Disobedience (2:17)

The raising of judges as saviors did bring Israel out of the hands of their oppressors. But it did not keep Israel from self-sabotage through disobedience to the Lord's commandments. When it came to a choice between listening to the God-appointed leader who came to save them or bowing down to the gods of the nations, Israel chose the gods. They prostituted themselves both by participating in the immoral practices of the nations and by forsaking their husband—the Lord—for other lovers.[8] While the judges were attempting to steer Israel away from the idols, offering deliverance from enemies without and poor spirituality within, the nation would not heed the judges' words.

The judges had no inherent power to compel the people to obey. Following the leader appointed by God to rescue them was a choice. Seemingly, the people followed in order to be liberated from the power of the outside oppressors only so that they could have the freedom to live as they pleased once the subjugating nation had been defeated. The people did not look for the judge to provide full deliverance but only enough deliverance to allow them to live apart from the proximate judgment of God.

The Limitations of the Judges' Victories (2:18-19)

Thus, the judges were limited in their ability to lead the people to secure the entirety of the land promised to them. The acquisition of the full inheritance depended on Israel's obedience to the law of the Lord under the stewardship of the judges. But the people rejected the leadership of the judge, thus also rejecting the leadership of the Lord and his blessings.

The real issue in the people's response to the judges is their heart toward the Lord: the Lord raises each judge, the Lord stands with the judge in power and presence, the Lord saves Israel through the judge's leadership, and the Lord is moved to pity when Israel suffers oppression for rejecting him. The one who has revealed himself to Israel as "a compassionate and gracious God, slow to anger and abounding in faithful love and truth" (Exod 34:6), gives mercy to Israel by sending judges. The Lord hears their cries of distress from the judgment against their disobedience, and the Lord acts to save them.

---

[8] Although the formal charge of the forsaking of the Lord as Israel's husband awaits the coming of the prophets, the concept of Israel's spiritual adultery is evident here.

However, the peace experienced from deliverance was temporary. The death of each judge was for Israel like the absence of the boss from an office for a workday or the absence of the normal grade-school teacher for a school day. Israel immediately returns to the idol worshiping exploits that would lead eventually to their oppression. Each generation would outdo the idolatrous corruption of the previous generation.

This cycle is evident with all twelve judges in the book. The Israelites will embrace sinful practices, most often in the form of idolatry. The Lord will bring the judgment due to their sin in the form of an oppressor and subjugation. Israel will cry out to the Lord in her distress, and the Lord, moved with pity, will raise a judge to defeat Israel's oppressor and deliver Israel. The land will have peace through the lifetime of the judge. Then the judge will die, and Israel will repeat the cycle. See Fig. 1.

Solitude
The land has rest during the life of the judge.
(3:11,30; 5:31; 8:28)

Stewardship
The Lord promises to give Israel the inheritance
of the land with Israel having the responsibility to
destroy the nations and their idols and to refuse
to covenant with them.
(1:2; see also Deut 7:1-5,23; 9:1-3; 11:8-12;
Josh 1:2-6; 23:5-8)

Sin
Israel does what is evil in the
Lord's sight,
most often idolatry.
(3:7,12; 4:1; 6:1; 8:33;
10:1,6; 13:1)

Salvation
In mercy, the Lord hears Israel and
raises up judges to deliver them.
(3:9,15,31; 4:3-6,24; 6:7-8,11;
8:28; 10:10,16; 11:11,33)

Slavery
The Lord sends Israel into slavery to judge their rebellion.
(3:8,12; 4:2; 6:1-2; 10:7; 13:1)

Fig. 1: Cycle in Judges

This cycle repeats in the book of Judges from 3:7–16:31 with minor nuances within the cycles.

The Anger of the Lord for the Testing of the Nation (2:20-23)

Rightly, the Lord punishes Israel for her rebellion throughout the cycle of sin. Israel's turn toward idolatry both fails to keep her part in the covenant with the Lord and disobeys his voice. The covenant breaking and disobedience to God's voice are the same thing; together they result in the Lord's turning from dispossessing the remaining Canaanite nations from the land.

In the providence of God, the failure of Israel and resulting judgment still serve the Lord's purposes under the judges. The Lord uses the nations to test Israel's faithfulness to walk with him as the generations surrounding Joshua did. The intent to test the nation partially reveals why the promise to gain all the land was not accomplished in Joshua's day. The Lord left challenges that would provide opportunity for Israel to grow in their faithfulness toward him. The incomplete work sets the stage for the Lord to raise judges as his appointed delivers.

Much like the children of Israel regarding Joshua and the judges, members of a local assembly can think to themselves that they are wiser to give direction to God's people than are God's appointed pastor and elders. Challenges to pastors and elders often appear to be innocent inquiries about the so-called biblical direction of the church. But such inquiries are attempts to mask simple desires for personal preferences and/or agendas to gain power to set direction for the church. A person, a set of families, a group of members with long-standing ties to the church, or those who are large tithers become frustrated with a change in their musical preferences, the defunding of a cherished missions project or the support of a nontraditional missions work, the addition or firing of a staff member, or too much emphasis on racial or gender equality, justice, or unity in the pastor's sermons. In order to reverse what they perceive to be an ungodly turn in the body, they speak against the pastor, first privately and eventually publicly. Soon, meetings are held in people's homes or small business shops after work hours to coordinate plans to make formal motions in business meetings. Yet through the entire process, rarely does any one of the persons feeling zealous for the truth enough to challenge the pastor or elders see that he/she is not being zealous about submitting oneself to God's ordained leaders.

Paul Alexander, speaking specifically of churches with congregational governance forms, writes,

> Biblical congregationalism includes leadership and spiritual oversight by congregationally recognized elders. Congregations are responsible for the doctrine they listen to, the disputes they allow to fester, the discipline that must be carried out on unrepentant members, and the regenerate quality of their church membership. But the congregation is also responsible to obey its leaders and respect their authority (Heb 13:17). God has given elders to the congregation as a blessing, and they must be free to exercise their God-given authority for the health of the church and the purity of its corporate witness in the surrounding community. Every church member is responsible to obey their authority so that their work will be a joy and not a burden, and so that they may give account to God with a clear conscience. Elders do function most biblically in the context of congregationalism; but congregationalism also functions most biblically under the godly, wise, loving authority of biblically qualified elders. Biblical congregationalism also recognizes that the congregation is not the infallible guide to faith and practice (2 Tim 4:3). That role is reserved for God's Word. Even though we have been raised up with Christ, we are still fallen. ("Is Congregationalism a Democracy?")

Israel did not simply run after idols. They chose idolatry over listening to the leadership the Lord had appointed. Local congregants can do the same when choosing to make a priority of holding their interests and comforts over following the direction of the congregation's pastor and elders. It is not that pastors and elders are infallible, for they are not. Only the Word of God is infallible. But the pastor and elders are appointed to their tasks by the Lord through the process of a congregation recognizing and affirming that these leaders have been called by the Lord. It is then the Lord's job to remove the disobedient leader; it is the people's job to "obey your leaders and submit to them" (Heb 13:17).[9]

---

[9] On the mutual role of pastoral care by elders and submission to elders by the congregation, see Acts 20:28; 1 Tim 5:17-20; 1 Pet 5:5. The NT reveals a relationship between

An unwise decision to challenge God's leader has ramifications for a church's health. Any success in swaying a congregation or a portion of a congregation to disobey its appointed leaders when there is not a question of sin or ethical breach, but only a question of preferences and tradition, is a pyrrhic victory at best; it might be a defeat if the church takes a black eye in public (cf. 1 Cor 6:7). The stress from the confusion, infighting, disruption, and division that often surround the rebellion of members of a congregation is the direct result of failing to follow God's leadership properly.

Distress Forces Us to Use Spiritual Weapons or Embrace Spiritual Defeat
JUDGES 3:1-6

The Lord's leaving nations in the land intends to test Israel's obedience to Moses's commandments as the untested generation learns to fight wars. Yet this still results in Israel's giving away their sons and daughters to the peoples of the nations.

The Testing of the Nations for War (3:1-4)

Having come from slavery in Egypt, Israel did not have a standing army or previous need for one. Even in leaving Egypt and escaping the Egyptian army, they did not go to war against Egypt. Instead, the Lord went to war on their behalf. Thus, Israel's experience in confronting standing armies only came as they faced one nation after another *en route* to the land of Canaan and upon their attempts to secure the land.

Yet in order to face the nations in war, Israel had to agree with the Lord on his word to destroy the inhabitants of Canaan. The opposing nations resident in the land of promise provided a means to improve Israel's fighting skills and an opportunity to choose to follow the Lord.

---

shepherds and congregants that requires meek and gentle Christlikeness on the part of shepherds in their care and meek and gentle Christlikeness on the part of congregants in their response to the shepherds. Shepherds should not be authoritarian even though they must lead the members, and members should not allow for unqualified shepherds to maintain elder offices even though the members are to obey and submit. Both shepherds and members must trust the sovereign hand of a good God when there is disagreement on decisions in the church in which moral or ethical breach is not a factor.

The Embracing of the Nations for Defeat (3:5-6)

However, once the nation had some victories in war under Joshua, the writer of Judges reveals a growing *comfort* with the Canaanites, the Hethites, the Amorites, the Perizzites, the Hivites, and the Jebusites, along with a growing *disobedience* toward the Lord. Instead of refraining from exchanging their children in marriages to the people of nations, they accepted marriage of women outside the covenant to their sons and gave away their daughters to marry the sons of the nations they were supposed to destroy. In facing the reality of war, rather than choosing the path of obedience leading to victory, they chose the path of disobedience leading to defeat. Their choices reveal a lack of faith in the Lord's ability to defeat the nations, a disregard for the word of God, a fear of the people of the nations, a love for the ways of the nations around them, and a lack of discernment about what was at stake in going to war.

The church faces war as testing in the same vein as Israel's warfare. The war is spiritual in nature, even though it manifests itself in the earthly realm of human beings. When the apostle Paul says, "Our struggle is not against flesh and blood," he is indicating that what takes place in our conflicts in the human realm is coordinated, fueled, and run by invisible evil forces (Eph 6:10-12). This is consistent with Moses's writing about the ongoing conflict between the human offspring of the woman and the offspring of the serpent (Gen 3:15). The human offspring do not fight the ethereal; they fight the ethereal as manifest in human forms of real people—people like Cain, Ham, Abimelech, Ishmael, Esau, and Pharaoh. We face this same spiritual war in the form of human opposition against us for our faith and against the church for its message of the truth.

This war, however, is not a cultural war, even though it takes place over cultural artifacts and issues. We might turn it into a cultural war, but we are not in a fight to maintain Judeo-Christian cultural norms. Instead, the war is about making disciples among all people and loving the Lord with all our being and loving our neighbor as ourselves in order to carry out the disciple-making mandate.

The challenge posed to the church by pro-LGBTQ+ forces should not be framed as a concern over providing single-gender bathrooms for our children's safety, a matter of the definition of marriage, or a matter of the rights of churches. Instead, the pro-LGBTQ+ platform is a matter of making disciples of people who are currently sympathetic to a pro-LGBTQ+ position.

In this war we need faith to believe the Lord can do the impossible. We have to stand on all the Lord's Word says about the order of creation and showing mercy and kindness to all. We cannot choose people-pleasing or loving the acceptable position of secular culture. We must be discerning about seeing that lives—not comfort—are at stake in the war. Our hope in being tested by workplace policies, changes in laws about marriage, trainings on understanding gender orientation, media that promotes same-sex relations, and the choice of some of our own children to declare themselves gay or allies of the same is that the Lord will strengthen our resolve to trust him, declare his truth, and demonstrate his love, and that he will turn the hearts, minds, and souls of many to see Christ's power for overcoming confusion, struggle, and choice related to all that is pro-LGBTQ+.

Application

How do we gain both the meekness to follow the Lord's leaders and the resolve to live out the gospel in a culture whose message is opposite both of these ideas? First, we need to yield our rights: we need to yield the right to be in charge of church and the right to be in charge of the culture. In the West, especially in the US, we have religious freedoms that allow us to think in terms of legal rights afforded to us. The rights are afforded to us as citizens of free nations. We especially claim them as believers, for we champion liberty as a human right.

But what if we live in a scenario like the early church, one in which the government and citizens of Rome turned hostile against the church? Or what do we do when we live in a state without rights of freedom afforded to the free church, as is the situation in some socialist nations and under some Islamic states? Do we then get to claim rights, or do we follow Christ without rights, trusting him to rule the hearts of the kings and keep his own to himself? With no rights to demand, we still would worship faithfully, raise our children to love Christ, work faithfully under the authority of non-Christian managers, and proclaim Christ is Lord, because rights are not a promise of Scripture. We should strive for the things that are just, but there is no guarantee they will be gained in this life. Even where they are not gained, we have to obey the words on being loving and submitting to authorities.

The same holds true in a local assembly. We are slaves of Christ in our memberships with one another. We have servant ownership in our congregations, not absolute ownership. We take ownership to be responsible *servants*, not to be riot starters who will secure mob justice. We do not own the church, the pastor, the staff, or the elders; neither does the church own the members absolutely. When we cannot be servants who follow the Word of God and God's appointed leadership, we are allowing rights to trump what is right.

Second, seek counsel outside of your own echo chambers. Both the approval of disrespect of leadership and love for the things of the world often bathe in the warm waters of people who are entrenched in their positions—positions that agree with our own positions on an issue. Instead of inviting winsome, credible, solid arguments against our position for us to consider in wisdom, we listen to echoes of our position in the voices of others. Then we feel justified in doing what is wrong because no one is in our circles to help us see that we might not be infallible in our practices and thoughts.

Each of us needs a God-fearing objector in our lives who will help us think beyond our seemingly unchangeable positions. We need many voices of maturity and wisdom to speak to us so that we do not love the world when following Christ becomes difficult for us.

Close

Israel's cycle reveals just how fickle the nation was when it came to following the Lord, his chosen leaders, and his word. One nation showed up on their doorstep—offering alternative gods, providing beautiful options for their children to marry, and threatening war—and they quickly forgot the covenant of God. When the resulting oppression came, they would cry for help, the merciful God would raise a deliverer and rescue them, and they would follow the deliverer in peace until his death. Then the nation would turn away from God and find their security and happiness in the hands of the nations that were supposed to be rejected. They were fickle.

Israel's cycle also reveals a need. As we read of Israel's endeavors, with the coming of each judge, we are hopeful that Israel will remain faithful even after the death of the judge who delivers them. Maybe they will continue following after Shamgar dies? No. Maybe they will remain faithful when Deborah dies? No. Maybe after Gideon? Not a chance. Certainly after Samson? That's not the way the last five chapters of the book end this story.

What hope, then, does Israel have of securing the land? When will they understand that the judge is the instrument to lead them to follow the Lord continually? What judge's defeat of Israel's enemies will establish wholehearted commitment from Israel to obey the covenant of the Lord? Israel's hope lies in a judge who is powerful enough to command powers and principalities in the heavenly realm. We all need Jesus as the final judge.

Reflect and Discuss

1. What is right about Nietzsche's "stronger" dictum, and what is wrong about it?
2. How has the Lord used one incident involving the harshest and most distressful pain to both weaken and humble you and also strengthen you to be wiser and more faithful in future difficult challenges?
3. What painful experiences still influence you to be hesitant, skeptical, or fearful in life, even as a believer?
4. In the book of Judges, what is a "judge," what do judges do, and how does Deborah's role as a judge differ from that of the other judges?
5. What forms did Israel's disobedience take, and what might this say about heeding the words of pastors and elders in our local congregations?
6. Read Acts 20:17-35. How do Paul's warnings to the elders at Ephesus reflect the warning of the Judges 2:1–3:6 story?
7. How were the judges limited in their efforts to help Israel secure the promised land, and how does their limitation point to the need for Christ to act as the true Judge—"Judge" in the sense of military leader and not weigher of righteous edicts?
8. What is the cycle that will characterize the Israelites' experiences under the judges?
9. When people wrongly challenge a faithful and good leader in a congregation, what might be their motivation behind their opposition?
10. How can congregational privilege and accountability go awry, and what do you need to do personally to make sure your assembly's congregational voice and/or voting freedom does not become weaponized to harm a congregation and its leaders?
11. What do you need to do today to begin escaping Christian forms of echo chambers that only allow you to hear opinions that agree with your own? Why is leaving an echo chamber an act that could lead to greater love of one's neighbor?

Resourceful Church Leadership for Oversized Oppressors in a Time of Cultural Bondage

JUDGES 3:7-31

Main Idea: The Lord's giving of Israel into the hands of oversized enemies because of their evil gives way to deliverance at the hands of three warriors who each use the tool available to him to secure victory, even as Israel cries out to the Lord.[10]

I. **Confronting the New Sexual Revolution: A Spirit-Filled Leader to Defeat Double Evil (3:7-11)**
    A. An older generation forgot God (3:7).
    B. An older generation experienced severe discipline from God (3:8).
    C. An older generation wisely cried out to God (3:9-10).
    D. A younger generation gave them hope in God (3:11).
II. **Confronting Self-Infatuation: A Sharply Trained Leader to Make Dung of Puffed-up Emperors (3:12-30)**
    A. Shrewd in his preparations (3:15-18)
    B. Cunning in his execution (3:19-25)
    C. Swift in his demolition (3:26-30)
III. **Confronting Bondage on the Horizon: A Swiftly Tooled Leader to Street Fight a Perennial Enemy (3:31)**

Readily the contemporary church recognizes that a cultural idolatry seeks to bring God's people into bondage in its grip. Whether we identify that bondage as "worldliness," "secular worldview," "liberalism,"

---

[10] In each of the episodes, the hero—Othniel, Ehud, and Shamgar—simply uses what is available to him to secure victory: *the Spirit of the Lord, a sword on a right thigh, and a cattle prod*. In all three of the stories, we see the deliverance of Israel: "The Israelites cried out to the LORD. So the LORD raised up Othniel son of Kenaz, Caleb's youngest brother, as a *deliverer* to save the Israelites" (3:9; emphasis added); "Then the Israelites cried out to the LORD, and he raised up Ehud son of Gera, a left-handed Benjaminite, as a *deliverer* for them" (3:15; emphasis added); and "After Ehud, Shamgar son of Anath became judge. He also *delivered* Israel, striking down six hundred Philistines with a cattle prod" (3:31; emphasis added). Moreover, each of the enemies is *oversized*: *double evil* (3:8), "extremely fat man" (3:17), "six hundred [warriors]" (3:31).

or "humanism," we are attempting to label the results of the evidence of the church's embrace of idolatrous ideas and practices. "Idolatrous" is an appropriate term, even though we do not have statues of wood, silver, or bronze in our homes to which we bow down, nor do we run to hills to worship carvings of false gods set on poles. Because we do not see carved or engraved artifacts, we often do not identify many idols. However, the effects of idolatry are all around us, which can only be accounted for by the presence of idols and our embracing of them—our *worship* of them. We, therefore, must turn away from idols and turn repeatedly to the cross of Christ and to his empty tomb for grace to adhere to the promises of God amid a godforsaken culture.

The challenge is not small. When we expose the dark sides of their lures, the entertainment industry, sports industry, modern universities, Silicon Valley, and Wall Street all seem to have the upper hand on dictating the direction of society and on painting the church as out of touch with modern times. As a result, many believers give in to the air of the age rather than fight a war in which we seem outmatched and outgunned. At this point it would appear that the war cannot be won in this life unless we control the White House, the courts, and all general assemblies, make our own grade schools, create our own TV networks and shows, and live mostly among ourselves rather than among those who do not know Christ.

What if, however, defeating this oversized enemy did not require cultural withdrawal or cultural war but the raising of some savvy leaders in the church? What if the resources needed are not seats in the Senate but the use of tools of this life that are available at one's disposal?

When idolatrous Israel faced oversized enemies that could keep her in bondage, the Lord raised three leaders who used familiar, available resources to confront and defeat their enemies, freeing Israel from their oppression. Together, the three judges provide us with a picture of resourceful leadership to confront oversized oppressors in a time of cultural bondage.[11]

---

[11] The three divisions recognize that 3:7-31 are one unit marked out by the same pattern of characteristics: Israel needs deliverance from bondage (due to idolatry in the first two scenes and the rest of the book but not explicitly stated in the third scene of v. 31); the enemy ruler is exceedingly great in some form of his threat and rule; the Lord raises an unlikely hero who acts as judge among the people; and the hero is uniquely resourceful in his victory over the enemy. These three episodes follow the larger pattern in Judges 3–16,

Confronting the New Sexual Revolution: A Spirit-Filled Leader to Defeat Double Evil
JUDGES 3:7-11

In this first judges cycle, God's people face the worst enemy in the entire book, and it is Othniel who comes on the scene as the deliverer. Four things in this episode instruct us on defeating such enemies and escaping cultural bondage.

An Older Generation Forgot God (3:7)

Forgetting God and *serving the Baals and Asherahs* are the same act. To forget God is a rejection of his covenants, his deliverance from Egypt, his commandments (especially the first two and the eighth), his promises to be with them, and their inheritance.[12] Israel throws all this away to run after Asherah, the consort of Baal and fertility goddess. Thus, the Israelites become disciples of Baal and Asherah, and Israelite society then reflects the worship of these gods. Israel follow a fertility religion—a religion of sex, or rather, sex as religion. Their choices to follow the gods of the Canaanite nations bring about the societal evil they are about to experience.

An Older Generation Experienced Severe Discipline from God (3:8)

Rightly, the Lord responds to their rebellious idolatry with wrath. It would be unloving for the Lord to see Israel love gods that are not God, look the other way, and do nothing. It is *loving* for him to do all to help them see for themselves that they are missing out on their own blessings by following after other gods.

The passage speaks of the Lord's anger burning, as if someone has lit a bonfire. God then makes a sale to the nations and says in effect, "Here, she's yours now. Do to her as she desires because she wants to be with you rather than with me." This is strong discipline, but strong discipline of his people is needed when we do wrong and depart from him.

The Lord makes Israel fall into the hands of Cushan-rishathaim of Mesopotamia. The name of this king means "Cushan of double-wickedness" (Block, *Judges, Ruth*, 153). Daniel Block notes,

---

in which Israel is gradually *demoralized* through a cycle of idolatry, bondage, deliverance, and temporary peace that *Canaanizes* them (2:10-23).

[12] Hb *sakah* is "to disregard, not to take into account" (Block, *Judges, Ruth*, 151).

He was the most powerful of all the enemies of Israel named
in the book. For him to extend his tentacles as far as Judah in
southern Canaan meant he was a world-class emperor, who held
Canaan in his grip for at least eight years. (*Judges, Ruth,* 152)

Israel now faces huge moral oppression. If there was a means to be
wicked, twisted, amoral, immoral, unjust, abusive, vile, heinous, hateful,
or godless—from government, to campus, to temples of worship, to the
home of the private individual—evil was a regular occurrence in Israel's
daily life for eight years.

Would God discipline his people in this extremely harsh way? In his
commentary on Judges, Dale Davis muses,

> We are so accustomed to our secularized, nonrevelatory view of
> history that depicts events as resulting from various observable
> causes, conditions, and factors, and, paradoxically, we are so
> familiar with biblical historiography that we fail to recognize
> how strange biblical (prophetic) history is. Not a tame natural
> process but blazing supernatural wrath explains Israel's
> servitude. Yahweh is the God who makes and orders history.
> And "who considers the power of thy anger, / and thy wrath
> according to the fear of thee?" (Ps. 90:11 RSV). (*Judges,* 49)

So for Davis, believers should consider the role of a God who is sovereign over history when we see God's people being overrun by evil forces.
Davis continues by saying,

> Yet even here, in Yahweh's anger, is hope for Israel, for
> his anger shows that he will not allow Israel to serve Ba'al
> unmolested. Yahweh's wrath is the heat of his jealous love by
> which he refuses to let go of his people; he refuses to allow
> his people to remain comfortable in sin. Serving Cushan-
> rishathaim may not sound like salvation to us—and it isn't,
> but, if it forces us to lose our grip on Ba'al, it may be the
> beginning of salvation. We must confess that Yahweh's anger
> is not good news nor is it bad news but good bad news. It
> shows that the covenant God who has bound himself to his
> people will not allow them to become cozy in their infidelity.
> "Steadfast love" pursues them in their iniquity and is not above
> inflicting misery in order to awaken them. The burning anger
> of Yahweh is certainly no picnic, but it may be the only sign of

hope for God's people, even though they may be yet unaware of that fact. (*Judges*, 49)

It would be wise to ask how and why we live in such a morally confused culture that works hard to erase Christian standards from all society and make laws that intend to intrude on the church's ability to accomplish the mission of the gospel. It should not seem too far-fetched to think of cultural pushback as God's discipline. As many theological thinkers have noted, modern secularism is curing the church from thinking we can be seeker sensitive to the culture and give people a nice religious setting that is good for advancing oneself in a Judeo-Christian society. Modern secularism—which the church helped create—with its cultural pervasiveness and its idolatrous temptations, is a wake-up call for the church to be the distinct people of God.

An Older Generation Wisely Cried Out to God (3:9-10)

The solution to Israel's dilemma seems so obvious! Keep praying for mercy, for revival, for justice, for salvation of souls, and for the Lord to beautify his people. As Israel prays, the Lord raises Othniel to be a judge of his people. Two things are important to notice about Othniel. *One is that God raised him to "save" Israel.* The judges were military leaders and led troops to win a war, and then they returned home to be head of state, like Washington or Eisenhower. We will see them in this role throughout the book of Judges.

A second thing to see is *Othniel's detailed description.* He is "son of Kenaz," so he is a Kenite proselyte to Israel. Kenites, like Moses's father-in-law, were of the line of Esau and migrated to Israel.

He is called "Caleb's youngest brother." Caleb is revered by the people as an accomplished leader. Othniel was in the shadows of Caleb the rock star. But apparently Othniel was watching Caleb walk with God, for when it came to taking Kiriath-sepher (also known as "Debir") for the reward of Caleb's daughter's hand in marriage, Othniel stepped up and defeated the city.

Also, Caleb is "son of Jephunneh," an appellate mentioned twelve times in Numbers 14–Judges 1. But Othniel, as just said, is "son of Kenaz," so noted five times in Judges and 1 Chronicles. Joshua and Judges identify him as the "brother" or "younger brother" of Caleb (Josh 15; Judg 1:13; 3:9), but it is more likely that he is a nephew. Therefore, 1:13 is not a scene of an uncle marrying a niece.

Third, *the Spirit of the Lord comes upon him*, which Block says "signals the arresting presence and power of God, often [on] individuals who are unqualified for or indisposed to service for him" (*Judges, Ruth*, 154). The Spirit of the Lord brings Othniel to meet double evil head-on.

Othniel represents *a younger generation*—i.e., Caleb's *younger nephew*—that wishes to continue in the vein of Joshua in obediently following the Lord and conquering the land. He is doing what is right in the eyes of Caleb and Joshua, which is to do right in the eyes of the Lord. Or should we say he was *discipled* by Caleb and Joshua? And now, as the first judge, filled with the Spirit of the Lord, this member of a younger generation of Israelites sets a pattern that should have been followed by all. This young man is the tool of God to rescue Israel.

A Younger Generation Gave Them Hope in God (3:11)

Othniel goes to war, and the Lord delivers double evil to him for defeat. He brings in forty years of peace—*forty years of keeping the covenants, following the commands of God, remembering the Lord who delivered them from Egypt, trusting his promises, and looking forward to inheriting the land.* Israel experiences a revival and renewal that affects two generations; two generations of families live in a society that remembers God. All this comes about as the Lord raises up one young nephew who watches an older generation walk with the Lord and who then conquers portions of the promised land as the older generation's young disciple.

Confronting Self-Infatuation: A Sharply Trained Leader to Make Dung of Puffed-up Emperors
3:12-30

After two generations of peace from bondage, it seems unbelievable that Israel would go back into evil following the death of Othniel. However, they do, so the Lord raises up the mighty Eglon of Moab, along with the Ammonites and Amalekites, to take possession of the City of Palms (or Jericho).

The rearing of Moab, the Ammonites, and the Amalekites is an indicator that the idolatry and resulting judgment are sending Israel backwards as a society. They have become enslaved to the offspring of the daughters of Lot that came about from living in Sodom and Gomorrah—the Moabites and Ammonites (Gen 19:36-38). They are enslaved to the children of Amalek—the first nation they defeated after crossing the Red Sea (Exod 17:8-16). They have lost the city of Jericho, which was conquered under Joshua (Josh 6). Backwards to Sodom and Gomorrah's same-sex society, backwards across the Jordan where they feared their children would be destroyed by the nations, and backwards across the Red Sea to the place where the king commanded children be killed— backwards they go for eighteen years! Finally, in year eighteen, they get enough sense to stop their evil ways and to call on the Lord. In mercy he hears them.

Whom does God raise this time, but another unlikely hero to take on this oversized oppressor named Eglon? God raises up Ehud, a sharply trained warrior.

Shrewd in His Preparations (3:15-18)

Ehud was a "left-handed" man from Benjamin, meaning he was ambidextrous. Equipping himself with a two-edged sword on the thigh opposite the one used by right-handed warriors allows him to seem harmless, as does the claim that he is coming to present tribute to the king. He acts with shrewdness as he takes on the king of self-infatuation. "Eglon" is a word for a young bull, indicating that he was a very fat man. He is sated with his large self and rule—self-infatuated. Ehud anticipated the best way to confront this size of evil.

Cunning in His Execution (3:19-25)

Sending away those carrying the tribute, turning back at the idols, and claiming he had a "secret message" from God for the king allows Ehud to gain the audience of the king without raising suspicion. Escaping by way of the porch and locking the doors to the king's restroom chambers behind him allows him time to execute the rest of his plan without being caught in the king's palace. We often wade into confrontation with the culture's spirit of self-infatuation without planning with Ehud's level of cunning. We attack the outward expressions of self-infatuation—the self-promotion, the bling bling, the obsession with selfies, the makeovers and nips and tucks. But Ehud prepared to go much deeper—literally into the belly of the sated king—and get at the center of self-infatuation. We may need to rethink how we get to the real issue of self-infatuation—a heart in love with self—before we try to take on the culture and industry of self-infatuation. We need to teach our children, by example, that it is OK to be seen in public *slightly imperfect.*

We need to emphasize cultivating a righteous heart. If we only emphasize the external, we devalue our inner selves and reduce people to their looks. And if we are just the sum of our looks, selfies, TikTok videos, clothes, hair tracks, and expensive athletic shoes, human lives are cheap, and we can traffic them or murder them without feeling guilty at all. Like Ehud confronting Eglon, we need to go inside the self-infatuated to show that behind all the fatness, tribute, and palms is nothing but a pile of dung. (Apparently the servants can smell Eglon through the chamber doors; 3:24-25.)

Swift in His Demolition (3:26-30)

Now Ehud can enlist others in confronting the evil oppressing Israel. If he defeats Eglon but does not take advantage of the Moabites' being down, they could rise up against Israel again. Instead, the enemy is subdued. God is giving us a picture of hope. This is important, for we cannot push back the tide of cultural idolatry from overrunning the church by winning against evil in only one corner of society.

Confronting Bondage on the Horizon: A Swiftly Tooled Leader to Street Fight a Perennial Enemy
JUDGES 3:31

Shamgar's appearance as a judge raised up by the Lord means Israel has again reverted to a course of evil. They need deliverance because the Lord has returned them to oppression in an act of judgment. Shamgar is the Lord's tool of mercy and deliverance.

The evil that Shamgar faces is undefined other than noting that there are six hundred Philistines. This description is enough to tell the reader the problem facing Israel. The Philistines are perennial enemies of Israel. They will appear in the latter part of the book of Judges and throughout the history of the monarchy in Israel. Shamgar seems aware of the threat they pose and will push them back—at least during his lifetime.

But how does one man take on six hundred enemy warriors when there is no mention of the Spirit of God empowering him and he is not a left-handed sword wielder? He, like Othniel and Ehud, uses the resource available to him—in his case a nearby oxgoad. In what amounted to an all-out fight in the streets, that wooden cattle prod in the hands of one man who was yielded to the Lord became enough to take down hundreds of enemies who were enslaving Israel. That was some oxgoad! It was not a sword, but it was a tool in the hands of one the Lord called to confront the evil of his day for the sake of rescuing the Lord's people.

Application

What should we do as a church to stand against modern oversized oppressors? First, individual bodies of believers must keep gathering to pray for the children, grandchildren, and great-grandchildren of your fellow church members. Pray that they might walk with the Lord and serve him and that the Lord might bring about revival through them even if we do not see it in our lifetimes.

Second, older believers should consider serving in middle school, high school, and college ministries at your church, and/or support these ministries. Ask your student pastors and campus ministry workers how you can help them in their weekly tasks.

Third, put the names of ten students on your prayer list and cry out for them daily. If you need help populating your list, ask the youth leaders in your congregation for names. Include all your pastors' children's names on your list.

Fourth, make it your habit to find godward, encouraging things to say to student-aged members of your assembly every time you run into them. Make it your habit to run into them, to speak to them, and to ask them how life is going. Keep your criticisms at bay.

Fifth, if you are a student-aged believer, pray daily for the Lord to use you to be an instrument of revival and redemption within our culture. Ask the Lord to fill you with his Spirit so that you can stand against the encroachment of evil on the church. Ask him to fill you with wisdom and make you resourceful for the sake of the kingdom of God.

Sixth, if you still have children ages ten and under, consider catechizing your children in the standard catechisms of the faith as part of your family devotions or family worship. *The Baptist Catechism,*

Westminster Shorter Catechism, Heidelberg Catechism, or *New City Catechism* need to become part of their daily existence so that we have the upper hand on telling them what to believe as the culture wages war against them for the souls of all people.[13]

Seventh, do not be naïve about your children's and grandchildren's exposure to sexual images and experiences. Talk to them directly and frankly about their exposure, and do not accept anything like "I don't know what you're talking about" or "I don't want to talk about that." Remember that the world speaks to them about sex directly, frankly, boldly, unashamedly, wrongly, and regularly.

Eighth, do not underestimate the power of sex in our culture, for it is everywhere. Go to extreme measures to stay free of sexual immorality's tempting power. Rid your home of anything pornographic, and use filters to keep it from coming into your house. Invite your children to do the same.

Ninth, whether married or single, bind yourself to single and married friends with strong, mature Christian commitments and *conversation* and disassociate yourself from close ties to single and married friends with little or no moral standards—even those claiming to be believers. Otherwise, you risk walking according to their standards, and you will not demonstrate the holiness of the call of the gospel to them. Christ died to make us holy.

Tenth, in your circles of influence, speak boldly when topics about sexual sin come up, including conversations about the evils of Internet pornography, the exploitation of women in music and music videos, and sex trafficking. All those demonstrate high forms of idolatrous worship. We are trying to rescue a culture and individuals within that culture. If people are not shown their and society's sinfulness, they will have no need for a savior.

---

[13] Jeff Robinson, "Are Catechisms a Baptist Thing?," *9Marks* blog (Oct 2018) https://www.9marks.org/article/are-catechisms-a-baptist-thing, accessed May 28, 2021, provides helpful insight and practical resources for using catechism. See also, J. I. Packer, *To Be a Christian: An Anglican Catechism* (Wheaton: Crossway, 2020); Gary Parrett and J. I. Packer, *Grounded in the Gospel: Building Believers the Old-Fashioned Way* (Grand Rapids, MI: Baker Books, 2010); John Piper, "A Baptist Catechism," *Desiring God,* https://www.desiring god.org/articles/a-baptist-catechism, accessed May 28, 2021; Carl Trueman, *The Creedal Imperative* (Wheaton: Crossway, 2012).

Close

In the end, Othniel, Ehud, and Shamgar, like the rest of the judges, have their reigns ended by death. Each time that happens, the people of God quickly revert to their evil ways. This pattern intends to tell us that the real hope in the book of Judges is not in Othniel, Ehud, Shamgar, or the like. Instead, the real hope is that the Lord will later raise up a Judge who will live forever and bring eternal peace to the land. He finally does this in Jesus, who battles the fullness of evil and our evils on the cross and in the grave, rises victoriously over death and evil, and reigns as King with the promise to return to get us.

In him we hope, even as we look to him to raise up a generation of Othniels, Ehuds, and Shamgars to confront the evils of our contemporary culture. May the Lord Jesus be gracious to us.

"Little children, guard yourselves from *idols*" (1 John 5:21; emphasis added).

Reflect and Discuss

1. Why are modern idols difficult to discern?
2. The present writer mentions "the entertainment industry, sports industry, modern universities, Silicon Valley, and Wall Street" as venues of modern idolatry. What idols do each of these entities cast toward us, and in what ways have you and your church embraced any of these idols?
3. What ties the stories of Othniel, Ehud, and Shamgar together? What do the three judges do that is similar in the way they attack the evils confronting them?
4. Why might the writer have placed the defeat of Cushan-rishathaim first in the cycle of judges? What should the placing of this story tell the reader both about living as a Christian in an evil society and what to expect in the remainder of the book?
5. What is the fallacy of equating senior ages with Christian maturity?
6. Why do you think it took eighteen years of oppression for Israel to cry out to the Lord under Eglon? What might they have been doing during that time?
7. Where and how does self-infatuation invade the Christian life and the church? Give some concrete, personal examples.
8. From start to finish, using your imagination, express verbally what would have been involved in Shamgar seeing the Philistines attack

Israel, grabbing an oxgoad lying in nearby grass, and killing six hundred of those warriors. What character elements did Shamgar display in his victory?

9. Of the suggested list of applications, which one will you do immediately, and why? How will doing this help the church push back against the oversized evil of our day?

10. From the suggested list of resources above, begin reading one of the catechisms daily. Think of how you could invite your children and/or grandchildren to join you in reading the catechism.

Men Who Win

JUDGES 4

Main Idea: Men's compromising of God's Word concerning the way to lead the church to accomplish its mission still brings about the successful advancing of God's kingdom but transfers to women the honor of the power and authority role God gives men.[14]

I.   **Men Who Win Run with the Prophetic Word (4:1-10).**
  A. Sisera's harsh oppression (4:1-3)
  B. Deborah's distinctive judgeship (4:4-5)
  C   Deborah's calling of Barak (4:6-7)
  D. Barak's courting of Deborah (4:8-9)
  E. Barak's command of ten thousand (4:10)
II. **Men Who Win Rout with Powerful Might (4:11-16).**
III. **Men Who Win Recognize Potential Danger (4:17-22).**
  A. Flight of Sisera (4:17)
  B. Trust of Sisera (4:18-20)
  C. Death of Sisera (4:21)
  D. Shame of Sisera and Barak (4:22)
IV. **Men Who Win Lead a People to Win (4:23-24).**

Edward VII's abdication of the throne as king of England remains one of the most shocking events of the twentieth century and the history of the British Empire. Edward VII intended to marry American divorcée Wallis Simpson in 1936. Yet as the head of the British Empire

---

[14] I have shortened the main idea to remain consistent with the format of the series. However, my fuller statement representing the author's intended meaning is, *The church's male leadership's compromising of God's Word concerning the way to accomplish its mission still brings about the successful advancing of God's kingdom in accomplishing the mission of the church but transfers to women the honor of the power and authority role God has given men as the church's men, like men in secular leadership roles, give leadership away to women for superficial reasons.* I derive the application statement from this statement of meaning for Judges 4: *Barak's compromising of God's prophetic promise of victory for Israel by his hand still brings about Israel's destroying of Jabin and Sisera but transfers honor of victory to Jael as both Barak and Sisera trust their lives to women for security.* The statement intends to reflect the words, structure, tone, genre elements, and theology of Judges 4. This passage criticizes a failure in male leadership. It is not a direct critique of the role of women (e.g., Deborah) among the people of God.

and nominal head of the Church of England, marrying a divorcée was out of bounds for the monarch. Moreover, British intelligence rightly thought that marriage to Simpson posed a risk to the security of England.

Yet, as made famous to contemporary audiences by the 2011 movie, *W.E.*, and as depicted with embellishment by Netflix's series *The Crown*, Edward VII seemingly intended to pursue love (or lust) over the responsibility of the throne.[15] Eventually he made a formal Instrument of Abdication in which he relinquished the throne to his younger brother, Albert; then he married the now twice-divorced Simpson.

Edward VII, afterwards known as the Duke of Windsor, remained married to Simpson for thirty-five years. But his relinquishing of the throne forever tarnished his name and removed him and his descendants from ever obtaining the throne of England. While the monarchy continued relatively successfully, being restored to a place of honor by the rule of Queen Elizabeth, the appropriateness of Edward VII's choice has been a topic of political, academic, and popular debate ever since. Many simply cannot believe that he relinquished his responsibilities as king for the superficial reasoning of what he saw in the American woman.

Lustful monarchs are not alone in abdicating their responsibilities. Throughout history men have had superficial reasons for abdicating our responsibilities as men and passing them to women. We think this is inconsequential to what happens to men and women of the church in society—that is, that society will find success despite the abdication. We believe, too, that the hope for success in accomplishing the Great Commission will be unaffected by our abdication.

For example, it is common in contemporary society to leave the giving of affection and religious instruction of our children to Mom— an idea similar to the phenomenon of yielding grade-school teaching largely to women. We hand off ministry to teens, young adults, and women so that men can do "men" things like providing physical upkeep to the church edifice and to members' homes and cars. Even a trend we see in Bible college education is that families are willing to send their daughters to training at our Bible schools, but they send their sons to schools where the future men can major in subjects that will generate wealth. We do this approvingly, as if ministry's sacrifices are for girls only

---

[15] *W.E.*, directed by Madonna, Semtex Films and I. M. Global, 2011; *The Crown*, Season 4, Netflix, 2020.

(or maybe some parents suspect that their daughters are guaranteed to find a good husband among the few men still going to such schools).

Raising the question of men's abdication of responsibility is not a concern about women's occupational abilities, intelligence, class, savvy, creativity, worth, greatness as leaders, or fitness as executives. It is only a matter of certain divinely ordered responsibilities for men in society, the ways we fail at them, and what we can do to prevent such failures. Rather than be men who *abdicate and fail*, from Barak and Sisera's story we should learn about *men who win*. From the negative example of this chapter we will learn five things about men who win—men who do not abdicate their male responsibilities by giving them to women.

Men Who Win Run with the Prophetic Word
JUDGES 4:1-10

Sisera's Harsh Oppression (4:1-3)

We are back in a cycle of doing evil and gaining oppression as judgment. That cycle of captivity is analogous to contemporary cultural captivity— our being surrounded by the world and its rule of the philosophy that turns society. This time Israel meets Jabin and his general, Sisera. Sisera must be a warrior of notoriety, for the writer remarks about his nine hundred iron chariots. With the help of Sisera's military policing, Jabin oppresses Israel for two full decades. This, however, is not your garden-variety oppression. The Hebrew term *chozqah* indicates that the oppression was done with force. This helps the reader understand why translations modify the oppression with "harshly" (CSB), "cruelly" (ESV, NIV), "severely" (NASB), or even "ruthlessly" (NLT). Sisera's army used the might of their chariots to make the worse kind of oppression for the people of God. The images of American chattel slavery and of the concentration camps and kilns of the Jewish Holocaust probably approach the experiences of Israel under Sisera.

Deborah's Distinctive Judgeship (4:4-5)

The severity of the oppression also might be the reason there is no record of Israel's crying out to the Lord for rescue in this episode. When we expect Israel to pray, we have nothing. The absence of the supplication could indicate despair or defeat on the part of Israel. Yet the Lord acts as King—as the one who subdues us to himself, rules and defends us, and restrains and conquers all his and our enemies (*Keach's Catechism*, Question 30). He strategically places Deborah into the role as judge in this particularly dark time of Israel's history.

The appearance of Deborah walks the modern reader into much debate about the role of women in ministry. The Lord used Deborah in the role of judge in a manner similar to how he used Othniel, Ehud, and Shamgar before her, and Gideon, Jephthah, Samson, and the like after her. For some, this simple comparison is enough to draw conclusions toward contemporary church offices and roles. As Nijay Gupta writes,

> In a time and place where women were not considered to be suitable for leadership (the ancient Near East in the time of Israel's settling into the land of Canaan), with Deborah we have a woman who was already serving as leader and judge over Israel (Jud 4:4). Could this have been a bad thing? Could it be that Deborah shouldn't have been the national judge . . . ? Did Israel worry about a woman leading the nation in this way . . . ? I don't think Judges promotes gender equality as a primary point. However, Deborah makes all the difference by *implication*. She is a reliable prophet (who speaks from the wisdom of God), and a trustworthy teacher—as the Song of Deborah proves. In a sense, she becomes one of the "authors" of Scripture (with her teaching inscribed into Judges 5), and by implication an authoritative evangelist through her testimony. . . . What we do know is that it was the Lord's will to use her as a leader of God's people to deliver them (with Barak's help as general). Judges does not offer a command to promote women, but it only takes one example like Deborah to show that women are just as capable in leadership as men. ("Why Deborah Makes All the Difference"; emphasis in original)

For Gupta, the fact of Deborah's judgeship provides an analogy to the NT preacher or evangelist.

This exposition does not intend to address all the issues of the complementarian versus egalitarian views of the roles of men and women, for that is not the point of the passage. However, the passage does imply that Deborah's judgeship is unique rather than normative to the period of the judges. As such, it does not lend itself to a pro-egalitarian position but rather will argue for men not abdicating the roles of men.

First, *the passage identifies Deborah as a "prophetess."* She had a role as an authoritative speaker in Israel on behalf of the Lord in the same way as David, Isaiah, or Malachi. In Israel, she spoke oracles on behalf of God that were the voice of God to the people.

Second, *she is identified as "wife of Lappidoth."* Therefore, she is married, and she is acting in her role in agreement with her husband. Her husband is not shutting down her role as judge for her to be at home; neither is Deborah acting independently of her role as wife.

Third, *unlike all the other judges, Deborah acts in the role of a court judge rather than a military leader only.* Her work of settling disputes resembles the work of Moses and the leaders of Israel who settled the people's disputes (see Exod 18:13-27).

Deborah's Calling of Barak (4:6-7)

Instead of reading about the Lord raising up Deborah to save Israel, one now reads about Deborah, as a prophetess, summoning Barak to rescue Israel. When Deborah calls Barak, she speaks on behalf of the Lord, giving Barak every assurance that victory is at hand for him.

First, God has commanded him to go, which should be word enough for him to go get the victory to which Deborah summons him. The command calls him to lead men from his own region of tribes.

Second, God will both draw Sisera and his chariots to battle at the river Kishon and deliver them into Barak's hand victoriously. The picture is reminiscent of the Lord's hardening Pharaoh's heart to send his army into the Red Sea. One who hears these words should anticipate the deaths of Sisera and his entire army.

Barak's Courting of Deborah (4:8-9)

For Barak, however, the word of the Lord through the prophetess is not sufficient for victory. In the vein of Judah's courting Simeon for help after the Lord pronounced victory, Barak turns to Deborah for help, establishing conditions by which he will obey the word of the Lord: he will not take on Sisera and Jabin in war without the help of the prophetess; his refusal to do as the Lord has said is absolute.

Deborah does indeed condescend to Barak's rebellious requirements. However, Barak's decision to augment the plan of God is not without consequence. For his disobedience, rather than the general's being given into his hand—as said in 4:7—Sisera will be given into the hands of a woman.

The *woman* is unspecified at this point. The writer is emphasizing gender. The writer does not say, "Into the hands of another warrior," "Into the hands of a civilian," "Into the hands of a friend," or "Into the hands of a stranger"—the latter three all being possible descriptions of Jael. Neither does the writer say, "Into the hands of [name of a woman]," which would have been easy to do since the writer names Deborah, and since Deborah, as a prophetess, could have revealed the name if the Lord intended it. Instead, the writer specifies a gender. In the matter of obtaining honor from winning the battle to which he has been called to lead and be victorious, the honor that should be Barak's will go to a *woman*, says Deborah.

Barak's Command of Ten Thousand (4:10)

Apparently satisfied both with what Deborah has prophesied to him and her agreement to come with him, Barak summons his troops and goes to war, Deborah going with him. He has no hesitation about abdicating his calling to go to war as the singular leader ahead of the troops from the tribes.

As men who are appointed by Scripture to lead the church in its calling to proclaim the gospel to all peoples, we must be satisfied with the authority of God's Word and what it says about our roles as men. Our satisfaction with the authority rests on the infallibility of the Scriptures as words breathed out from the mouth of God. As the *Baptist Faith and Message 2000* states,

> The Holy Bible was written by men divinely inspired and is God's revelation of Himself to man. It is a perfect treasure of divine instruction. It has God for its author, salvation for its end, and truth, without any mixture of error, for its matter. Therefore, all Scripture is totally true and trustworthy. (Article 1, "The Scriptures")

Since God has spoken and has given the Scriptures to us as the "prophetic word strongly confirmed" (2 Pet 1:19), we are bound to obey the voice of God in Scripture on all matters of life and faith.

Specifically related to this passage, the Scriptures consistently give the highest leadership roles in the church to men. This is true of elders and shepherds who must demonstrate faithfulness to a "wife" (1 Tim 3:2; Titus 1:6) and of men who should not be under the authority and teaching of women (1 Tim 2:12). To augment this in any way would be to say that the Lord's Word is not sufficient. To suggest that a woman also is needed in this role to help men accomplish the work to which they are called would be akin to Barak's asking Deborah to go with him into battle. However, this is not to suggest that the wise input of women should be rejected. God-fearing leaders who lead with pastoral care will embrace the wisdom of women.

Men Who Win Rout with Powerful Might
JUDGES 4:11-16

One of the things Barak cannot see but that he would have benefited from by faith is the movement of an ally of Israel to a place that will be on the escape route for Sisera. The descendants of Moses's father-in-law already are in position to aid Barak even though he does not know it. If he had accepted the initial prophetic word, the people of Heber could have held the fleeing Sisera without stealing any honor from Barak. Or they could have turned the fleeing Sisera back into the hands of Barak.

Sisera will come to battle with his nine hundred chariots of oppression. Deborah, observing Sisera's approach, commands Barak to go to battle with his troops as one into whose hands the Lord will give Sisera. The reference is to victory rather than capture, as the narrative shows.

Barak, wielding ten thousand warriors as the instruments of the Lord, routs the army of Sisera.[16] The entire army of Sisera falls. Not one chariot driver is left to oppress the people of Israel. Sisera is the temporary sole survivor of Barak's conquest. All of this is the Lord giving Sisera's army into the hand of Barak. Barak is successful at his campaign through the blessing of the Lord. However, Sisera still manages to escape the edge of the sword and attempts to escape on foot.

---

[16] The word translated as "routed" in the CSB could be translated as "threw into panic." The sense is the same in either translation: Barak so overwhelmed the armies of Sisera that they were thrown into a panic.

Men Who Win Recognize Potential Danger
JUDGES 4:17-22

Flight of Sisera (4:17)

The focus of the story now shifts from Barak to Sisera. The writer repeats Sisera's fleeing on foot. Seemingly the author wants us to understand that Sisera is running and not fleeing in a chariot.

With the aid of the adrenaline rush of a flight response, Sisera will race from Barak's pursuit as hard as he can run and will run to someone he hopes will be an ally in his escape. This lands Sisera in the tent of Jael.

Trust of Sisera (4:18-20)

Jael is the wife of Heber the Kenite. The writer expands our understanding of Heber as one who has a peaceful accord with Jabin, even though he has come from within the boundaries of Israel and has a distant relationship with Israel's great lawgiver, Moses. Because Heber's house is at peace with Jabin, Sisera *assumes* that everyone in the household is at peace with Jabin and that such peace with Jabin will transfer to peace with Sisera.

Thus, when Jael bids the fleeing general to turn aside, he sees no reason not to find shelter in her tent, nor does he suspect that the rug she throws over him is for anything other than hiding him. When he needs a drink, there seems to be reason enough to trust she will only provide him drink, even though she immediately covers him again. Having found shelter and drink—and a rug over him!—he trusts Jael to keep him hidden from any inquiry about his presence in her tent if a pursuing warrior comes to her door.

Death of Sisera (4:21)

However, Sisera's trust in Jael is shortsighted and short-lived. The author will identify Jael as "Heber's wife" to draw out both the gender of Sisera's assailant and the significance of Sisera's wrongful assumptions. A Canaanite should have thought of one identified with Moses as a potential spy or untrustworthy. All of Sisera's reasons for trusting Jael are superficial. The warning signs are evident, but the exhausted, fleeing Sisera is too tired to discern them. While sleeping off his tiredness, he winds up with a tent peg through his head, courtesy of Jael—the Jael he had trusted for safety. He should not have left the responsibility of his own preservation in the hands of Jael. With great irony and wry humor, the passage shows Sisera fleeing men, yielding his safety to a woman, then dying at the hands of a woman.[17]

Shame of Sisera and Barak (4:22)

In the ancient Near East, it was shameful for Sisera to have died at the hands of a woman.[18] But the shame will not be his alone. Barak, still in pursuit of Sisera, hopes to deal the final blow to the general of the army that oppressed his tribes. But as foretold by Deborah—the Deborah he had trusted for victory—honor will not go to Barak. Jael will have honor, as Israel will later sing in the Song of Deborah (Judg 5:24-27).

Imagine what Barak thinks and feels about the decision he made to invite Deborah into war. If he had run with the prophetic word by himself, he could have put a sword through Sisera. He could have had a song in his honor. He could have history record him as a deliverer in Israel. Instead, all history records is his disobedience and lack of honor for turning to Deborah and Sisera's death and shame for turning to Jael. Two men abdicate responsibilities to two women, and both of them go without honor.

The reason Barak trusted Deborah was in contrast to the prophetic promise, and the reason Sisera trusted Jael was based on a relationship that meant nothing in wartime. They are both superficial reasons for abdicating their responsibilities to women in that *both are rooted in a sense of security in the two women characters that is false.*

---

[17] Barry Webb notes the way in which the writer designs the literature to emphasize the woman in the role to remove the honor of men: "That dénouement is reached with the ironic juxtaposition of victor and vanquished in the tent of Jael, the woman who has in effect conquered them both: Sisera, by depriving him of his life, and Barak, by depriving him of the honour that should have been his as the chosen deliverer" (*An Integrated Reading*, 135). Similarly, Gale Yee writes, "Through his emphasis on Deborah's gender at her introduction, through her reminder to Barak of God's command, through Barak's reluctance to enter the battle without Deborah, and through her foretelling of Barak's loss of honor, not only in his inability to kill Sisera but also in witnessing a woman accomplish what he has failed to do, the author cumulatively throws into relief Barak's shaming by the female" ("'By the Hand of a Woman': The Metaphor of the Woman Warrior in Judges 4," *Semeia* 61 [1993]: 116; cited in Butler, *Judges*, 107).

[18] One only needs to read Judg 9:54 to see that a man dying at the hands of a woman was shameful.

In the contemporary church, men abdicate their male responsibilities and give them to women for superficial reasons. Such reasons include the following:

- Women show themselves to be as competent or more competent than men in executive leadership roles, both in society and in the church.
- Women are just as educated as men, both secularly and in divinity training.[19]
- There are few, fewer, or no men in the local assembly from whom to select leaders.
- Women need representation in the elder and/or pastoral leadership of church body.
- Women have a preference to hear from, or greater receptivity to hear from, other women.
- Men do not lead in the church and in spiritual matters, but women do.
- Women express a calling to ministry, too.
- We exist in an increasingly matriarchal-led society and church.

Men Who Win Lead a People to Win
JUDGES 4:23-24

The Lord remains the hero of this story, as in all the victories accomplished over the Canaanite nations in Judges. Through the hands of Deborah, Barak, and Jael, the Lord defeats Jabin. But the author writes the narrative to show that the people follow Deborah and Barak to secure complete victory over Jabin. This victory was prophesied by Deborah, appointed to Barak, but carried out by Deborah, Barak, and Jael. Barak was the military leader, so he would have been the face of the victory others would have followed, even though honor for victory went elsewhere. But Judges 5 indicates that the people followed Deborah (Judg 5:1,9,16).

---

[19] This is not a statement against the education of women or the important role women play in education of all persons. Neither does the statement propose that there is something wrong with better education for women worldwide, nor that there is a problem with women being better educated than men. It only is indicating that as a reason for reversing roles in the church and society, it is superficial. Similarly, the statements to follow should not be misread as criticisms of the progress modern societies are making toward the betterment of life for women in all areas.

Real, Christ-loving, God-fearing male leaders in the church should be worthy of the rest of the Lord's people to follow to victory. If male leadership alienates anyone from serving the Lord for reasons other than sinfulness, it is not leadership that can lead the church to honor the Lord in society.

Conclusion

Judges 4 teaches the *opposite* of what many in the modern church suggest it supports: it is not a passage supporting women in preaching, shepherding, or leadership (authority) roles over or equal to men. Instead, it fully instructs men to take the responsible and divinely given role of leading in the church and in society, like taking the divinely given role of leading troops to a promised victory.

Reflect and Discuss

1. Besides her gender, what indicates that Deborah has a role as judge that is unique among the judges?
2. Early in the story, what elements break the typical pattern of stewardship-sin-slavery-salvation-solitude seen in the previous stories and the stories to follow?
3. What is at stake when Barak invites Deborah to join him in battle?
4. Why does this passage cause controversy in the modern church?
5. Why is it right to see the Lord as the hero of this story?
6. Why do Christian men abdicate their responsibilities to the church?
7. What are differences—real or perceived—in the way people respond to the leadership of men and women?
8. How can a local assembly disciple men in a way that they can both act with courage to follow the Word of God in the face of hostility to God's people and be sensitive to the identity and needs of women?
9. In what sense is Jael a hero in the victory over the forces of Jabin? What is admirable about Jael's actions?
10. What do you think Barak felt when he saw Sisera lying dead?

Celebrating Women's Leadership

JUDGES 5

Main Idea: Believers' celebration of God's triumphs—through leaders willing to follow during unique times of women's leadership—invites church leaders to bless the Lord both for divine intervention to make ministry successful and for the men with courage to follow, while casting down those who refuse to offer the gospel to a fearful and restless society.[20]

I. Deborah Blesses God for His Intervention (5:1-5).
II. Deborah Recognizes a Societal Occasion (5:6-11).
III. Deborah Specifies Men Who Act as Companions (5:12-22).
IV. Deborah Proclaims Hope for a Mother's Frustration (5:23-30).
V. Deborah Offers Rest to a Victorious Nation (5:31).

The Southern Baptist position on the role of men and women in the home and the church is well known. On marriage, the *Baptist Faith and Message 2000* states,

> The husband and wife are of equal worth before God, since both are created in God's image. The marriage relationship models the way God relates to His people. A husband is to love his wife as Christ loved the church. He has the God-given responsibility to provide for, to protect, and to lead his family. A wife is to submit herself graciously to the servant leadership of her husband even as the church willingly submits to the headship of Christ. She, being in the image of God as is her husband and thus equal to him, has the God-given responsibility to respect her husband and to serve as his helper in managing the household and nurturing the next generation. ("The Family," Article XVIII)

---

[20] The full historical statement of meaning is, *Deborah and Barak's postvictory song of Israel's leaders' willingness to following her rise to victory invites the kings of the earth to share in blessing the Lord both for his cosmic intervention as the God of Israel and for his friends' courage, casting down the enemies who failed to follow and will perish, and preceding the land's rest for forty years.* Important to the meaning is to remember that rest for the land follows victory in the other narratives.

On the church, it says, "Its scriptural officers are pastors and deacons. While both men and women are gifted for service in the church, the office of pastor is limited to men as qualified by Scripture" ("The Church," Article VI).

These statements are controversial in modern society, yet they represent God's ideal for the family and the church. The Scriptures teach that men and women complement each other in the roles they have, yet the Scriptures also give honor and dignity equally to both of them.

The complementarian position has come under attack because it seems that it is chauvinistic at best, bigoted at worst. Many people think these views do not allow women to have a role in society that recognizes the leadership gifts of many women. Women who lead schools, small businesses, hospitals, nonprofits, think tanks, and corporate companies and boards seemingly are not allowed to exercise their leadership gifts in a local assembly or in the home, ever. It would almost seem that some churches would rather have poor male leadership than competent and gifted women's leadership and that men would prefer not to follow a woman leader even if she represents a chance for rescuing a society desperately in need of solutions to the spiritual and social ills it is facing.

Contrary to the patriarchal portrayal of complementarianism, we see something different in Judges 5. In the absence of male leadership, it is not wrong for women to step up and lead. In fact, it may be absolutely necessary for women to lead where biblically *qualified* men do not step up and lead in the church if we are going to have a society that is safe and in which all people can thrive. Such faithful leadership by women should be celebrated by all as God's gracious and providential hand to care about society's need for the gospel. We should *celebrate* rather than hold to ideological positions for the positions' sakes themselves.

Judges 5 is the mirror of Judges 4. Chapter 5 fills out details that are absent in chapter 4. In this chapter we will see how Deborah was exalted by men who chose to follow her when Barak would not lead. This sort of submission needs to be celebrated if we are going to honor God and honor women. Five things are evident in this celebration.

Deborah Blesses God for His Intervention
JUDGES 5:1-5

Chapter 5 is an invitation to bless *God*. Judges 5 points us beyond any idea that it is about the simple or patronizing celebration of the victory of a woman. It also is *not* about the pushing of feminism or a feminist agenda. Judges 5 recognizes *God's* hand upon a woman to bring about victories in ancient Israelite society. It is the celebration both of Deborah and of God's providential and supernatural working for, with, and through a woman. Just as Deborah invited the leaders of the earth to bless God for this working, and just as this song would have been sung by the generations of Israel (and by Jesus), so too we all need to bless God for his working in Deborah and the lives of other women leaders.

Deborah blessed the Lord because the leaders in Israel led willingly. Later in Judges 5, we will see that what they willingly do is follow Deborah's leadership. But just the fact that they lead willingly on their own accord is to be celebrated here. There was not a resistance to lead or to step up to leadership when leadership was needed.

Deborah invites the leaders or the kings to *sing*. This celebration is in song. It's something that would have been remembered in Israel as part of their worship practices. As a song, it was a pleasurable, emotional, and memorable act of celebration.

Deborah celebrates other leaders. In our culture people celebrate themselves and often fail also to celebrate those who are coleaders or followers with them. Then the coleaders feel like they have been dishonored, that no one is thankful for the work they have done, or that the honor is only going to one person, as if victory came about through one person's efforts. Deborah, in contrast, celebrates the leaders who followed her and invites everyone to sing and celebrate them with her.

Deborah acts with great wisdom. In ancient Near Eastern societies, honoring men was significant, and being put below a woman was dishonor, as seen in Judges 4. It is right for Deborah to invite the people to sing in order to honor all the leaders, all of whom would have been men except for her. Then later, when she celebrates herself, she is just one of all the other leaders who have been celebrated.

Deborah Recognizes a Societal Occasion
JUDGES 5:6-11

We are celebrating a woman because of a unique occasion. The special occasion is that no one feels safe to go on the highways or even to live in this locale in Israel. The male leadership had not been making it so that people felt safe by rising up against their enemies. As a review of the events behind Judges 5, this also is the only time in Judges when a male leader called to lead shrinks back from leading. People are scared to travel, go to the store, venture out to see grandma, or go on vacation. It is as if every road were covered with bandits and oppressors who would do harm to the people of Israel, and no male figure could marshal armies of men behind him to lead against the evil in society. It is right then that Deborah will arise at this time and offer some needed solutions.

"In the days of Shamgar" (v. 6) takes us back to the last of the three judges recorded in Judges 3, the second minor judge after Othniel. Deborah's story is relative to Shamgar's story. Even though he was a great champion who had mowed down six hundred Philistines with an oxgoad, the people of the nation still lived in fear of going out in public. No one would travel the highways or roads. No man fought alongside Shamgar. But Deborah provided leadership that led the country into war to defeat her enemies. Deborah and Barak then arose in that day as the new leaders in Israel (v. 8 NIV).[21]

There are victories that women bring about that should be celebrated even though they are not accomplished by men or even normally would be accomplished by men. That is the point of the celebrating in Judges 5. We are celebrating victories in society for *all people* at the hands of women or female leadership.

More significantly, we are celebrating as the people of God. This passage points forward to unique times in the church. When there is an absence of men's ability to provide leadership to the church or accomplish a task beneficial for the ministry of the church and toward society, God, seeing the need, in mercy raises up a woman all can follow. Doing so does not establish a precedent or pattern; it offers leadership *in mercy*. As byproducts, it also might provide encouragement to all women who are part of the body and make all women feel included and honored. But the intent is to provide leadership so those in the assembly and our members' spheres of influence might accomplish and experience God's victories.

Tamar Manasseh and Shannon Watts never saw themselves being activists. Both just saw themselves as mothers. Tamar describes herself by saying, "I'm just a mother. I used to think my greatest accomplishment was raising two happy, healthy children in Chicago, where so many other

---

[21] The first line of v. 8 can be translated, "God chose new ones." See Block, *Judges, Ruth*, 226–27.

mothers are denied that right."[22] Similarly, Shannon's "about" page speaks of her time as a stay-home mother.[23] Now Tamar leads the organization, Mothers Against Senseless Violence (MASV),[24] and Shannon founded Moms Demand Action. Both organizations have stepped into modern history to address rampant gun violence that is taking away the lives of many children. While their efforts grew out of love for children, the working of the providence of the Lord is evident: whatever we have been doing to curb gun violence in Chicago has not been working.

Tamar's organization is witnessing the reduction of violence in neighborhoods where MASV has helped organize community meal gathering and mentoring programs and has connected members of the neighborhood to city services. Shannon's organization has helped foster and push through anti-gun violence legislation in several states, even keeping guns out of the hands of students in some public colleges and universities. The Lord has raised up both women and both organizations for violent times like these.

In the same way, in the church, the Lord can and does raise up women to step into roles as leaders when unique opportunities present themselves. This is not a statement against women leading ministries in churches, for those who qualify should lead and use their gifts in such manners. Instead, in speaking of unique occasions where there would normally be male leadership to guide in male-leadership-designated roles in the church, in the absence of such leadership, the church should not sit on its hands until a man—a *qualified* man—is available. Instead, if the Lord raises a Deborah, Shannon, or Tamar to teach, preach, shepherd, or disciple members of a local assembly in that situation, everyone should celebrate.

For Deborah, the celebration means that all persons—rich or poor, small or great—will join the celebration. She offers Singers at the Watering Places record label to publish her song widely (v. 11). In doing so, she intends for all Israel to celebrate what the Lord has done to accomplish his righteousness (noted twice in v. 11). Deborah ascribes

---

[22] See "Our Mission," MASK, https://www.ontheblock.org/about, accessed March 7, 2021.

[23] See "Meet Shannon Watts, Founder of Moms Demand Action," Moms Demand Action for Gun Sense in America, https://momsdemandaction.org/shannon-watts, accessed March 7, 2021.

[24] Sometimes the organization goes by "MASK" (for Mothers Against Senseless Killings) in the media.

leadership victory to the Lord. She only seeks the Lord's name to be exalted and not to change Israel's position on the priesthood or tabernacle servants. No other female judge follows her, and she makes no commotion about that. She is not looking to make women stars who outshine men in their service in the church. She only seeks to make Jesus's work beautiful in the eyes of all.

Deborah Specifies Men Who Act as Companions
JUDGES 5:12-22

Deborah's song of worship now turns to recount actions in the battle. Five times the tune will speak of tribes in Israel marching down to battle behind the leadership of Deborah (whom the song mentions first) and Barak. The mentioning is not because Deborah was singing the song; verse 1 says that Deborah and Barak were singing the song. The mentioning is not making her a lone hero apart from men; each mention of Deborah leading reveals Barak leading with her, assisting her.

Ephraim, Benjamin, Zebulun, and Naphtali all send their warriors to follow behind Deborah in a way they did not offer or follow behind the mighty Shamgar. Noblemen, commanders, and lieutenants all are following her to go into battle against King Jabin and Commander Sisera. Men are following her without reservation in order to clear Israel's highways and villages of their Canaanite oppressors, in order to make Israel's places safe, passable, travelable, and worthy of the prospective home buyers. The Lord calls Deborah to awake and to both lead and sing of the victory the men provide while she leads.

However, men from the tribes of Reuben, Gilead (Gad and the eastern half of Manasseh), Dan, and Asher are hesitant to follow. Eventually none follow when they receive the call to come to battle. This is not a simple matter of not following Deborah because she is female. What they ponder in their hearts is a matter of whether they are willing to risk dying in order to see change for the nation—a risk Zebulun and Naphtali were willing to take (v. 18). So the motivation behind not following is not bigotry, chauvinism, or traditionalism; it is *cowardice*. They do not want to die, and in their selfishness they will remain in their places of comfort rather than seek the good of the whole nation. As Judges commentator Andrew Fausset noted, Dan probably traded with the Phoenicians, and "selfish love of commercial gain kept Dan from making any sacrifice for the nation's independence" (*Critical and Expository Commentary*, 90). But

Deborah and the tribes following her leadership will take risks and make sacrifices for the sake of all God's people.

I propose that cowardice often motivates men's lack of women's advocacy in the public sphere. Naturally, we all understand that in the human, fallen world, those with lesser power will not move into an equal share of the power without the advocacy of those who have power. But offering a share of the pie to those outside the power pie means upsetting some who prefer the status quo, their share of the pie, and their current levels of rule, wealth, and personal serenity. The moral courage needed to advocate for women to have a seat at the boardroom table or in the administration of a company sometimes lags behind the fear of being singled out as soft, weak, whipped, or lacking testosterone. In the church, we must be careful not to allow cowardice to walk in a mask of orthodoxy.

Unfortunately, the men of Reuben, Gilead, Dan, and Asher miss out on what the Lord is doing providentially, mysteriously, and nontraditionally. When the kings of Canaan come against Deborah and her troops, the Lord uses the River Kishon in the Megiddo Valley to sweep away some of the chariots of Sisera into the river forever, just as he did with Pharaoh's army in the Red Sea. The Lord is fighting on Deborah's behalf so that she and her mounted troops can ride to victory. The Lord defeats Sisera, affirming his hand upon Deborah's leadership. The Lord is using this female leader.

Deborah Proclaims Hope for a Mother's Frustration
JUDGES 5:23-30

"Meroz" is a place unknown to us, being mentioned only here in the OT (Block, *Judges, Ruth*, 238). It is a region in Israel from which the tribes should have sent troops to follow Deborah into battle but did not do so. They chose not to help the Lord by fighting with his people. This brings them a judgment of cursing from the angel of the Lord. The angel is siding with Deborah and casting away from God's blessing those unwilling to follow her.

Yet coincidental with the cursing coming to the disobedient, as is the pattern in the OT (e.g., Deut 28), blessings come to Jael because of her obedience to fight against Sisera, siding with Deborah and her troops. Almost as if her verses serve as the refrain in the song, Jael's exploits with Sisera are repeated with intensity. This slowing down of the pace of the song makes the reader focus on the role this *woman* plays in the victory of Israel under Deborah. We get to relive the scenes of deception, heroism, and judgment in the grasping of the peg in the left hand and a hammer in the right hand, crushing the head and shattering part of the skull when Jael strikes Sisera. We are watching in slow motion Sisera sinking, falling, lying dead between Jael's feet; the camera lingers on the scene between her feet, and then it replays to show Sisera again becoming limp as he falls between her feet and lies on the ground in death. For this Jael receives blessing.

Jael's blessing provides hope for women in Israel. But a woman in Canaan, expecting her son, Sisera, to return from war victoriously, is denied that reunion. She has waited patiently, expecting Sisera to return with spoils from having crushed Israel, but he never does. Her shattered expectation could resonate with the shattered dreams of mothers everywhere. The expected victory from a son she raised is far from being realized. You can see that she wails in despair while waiting for him.

The hope Jael provides is not victory by Sisera. Instead, it is that our hopes do not rest in what we paint as successful womanhood: *being a mom who will raise a son who will be a victorious warrior.* Instead, a *female* warrior, in the normal course of life in her tent, arises to provide a victory the male commander of Canaan's armies could not achieve.

If we are going to celebrate women's victories, we are going to have to look at the success of our daughters and slow down to celebrate them rather than waiting on successes that may not come from *some* of our sons. Again, for clarification purposes, this is not to say daughters will be more successful than sons. Instead, it is to look at the juxtaposition of Jael and the mother of Sisera in the text and recognize that we often miss the real tent-peg victories of our own Jaels in our midst while we give so much celebration and expectation to our sons' successes even when signs of their success escape us for long periods of time.

Sadly, Sisera's mother expected Sisera to come home with women to impregnate as part of his spoils. Even in exalting him she is belittling women. As Judges scholar Daniel Block notes,

> One might have expected a refined woman like Sisera's mother to be more sensitive to the vulnerability of women in the violent world of male warfare. At the very least she could have used a more neutral expression. . . . Her preference for this overtly sexual expression reflects the realities of war: to

victorious soldiers the women of vanquished foes represent primarily objects for their sexual gratification, another realm to conquer. Obviously this woman's loyalties to her son and her own people overshadow her concern with the welfare of her gender as a group. (Block, *Judges, Ruth*, 243)

Deborah Offers Rest to a Victorious Nation
JUDGES 5:31

The wishing of different outcomes upon the Lord's enemies and friends ends with forty years of rest for the land. The conclusion about all enemies separates Deborah, Barak, those who followed them, and Jael from everyone else in the passage. Many in Reuben, Gilead, Dan, and Asher perished. Sisera perished. Jabin's army perished. Sisera's mother perished.

The enemies here are not simply the armies of Sisera. At a time when Shamgar is fighting alone, anyone not willing to follow Deborah to defeat Sisera and remove Jabin's oppression is one of God's enemies. The Lord has raised up Deborah to save Israel at this unique time. Those not willing to follow Deborah would thus be the enemies of God. They could have cried "foul" at this point and said, "Moses, Joshua, Caleb, the priests, and the elders of Israel all are male. It is the *sons* of Aaron who are to be priests. Shamgar, Othniel, and Ehud were each male." Under normal circumstances, that argument would have been good. But not at this moment in Israel's history.

Deborah, Barak, those who followed them, and Jael were the friends of God. The promise to them is that they will arise with great strength over their enemies—over *God's* enemies.

Application

It would be good at this point to consider how we can encourage, support, and celebrate what the Lord does through women's leadership. Here are some ideas:

We must be discerning and gracious on matters of women in leadership. This passage's message, which might sound radical and liberal to some evangelicals, will not sound radical enough or liberal enough for our society. Our society promotes an egalitarianism that does not consider the order of creation for roles. Instead, it conflates roles and gender, so that to distinguish roles is to denigrate a gender. But that's just not true.

In our local assemblies, we need to create as many opportunities as possible for women to use their superb range of gifts, skills, experiences, creativity, intellectual capacities, and personalities to bless our congregations. Those who have great freedoms, responsibilities, leadership positions, executive experiences and giftings, and the like should not feel stifled by being in a congregation that believes in male headship. We just have to be much more creative, much more engaging in conversations as a body of both men and women, and much more trusting of the Spirit of God to work in our midst.

We should provide forums in which women can share with church leaders ministry needs they have that are being overlooked by the church. There are items of need men cannot bring to the table of discussion. Yet these needs are real and should be served. Some of these needs can be addressed best by other women members of our congregations. As we watch our sisters lead in service to others, we will celebrate their gifts. Then we will not be hesitant to affirm their gifts of leadership in other areas normally appointed for men when such needs arise.

All believers need to reflect on how the Lord has used women in leadership roles—inside and outside the church—to bless our lives so that we experience success in this life. I learned much about deep, abiding prayer and the resulting power of God from witnessing the prayer lives of many church mothers in my home church—a church in the Afro-Baptist tradition. Hearing them cry out to the Lord in authenticity, in vulnerability, in earnestness, and with resolute faith while yet waiting years for the answers to many prayers greatly helped shape my understanding and practice of prayer to this day. It also continues to influence my trust in the Lord to do what is impossible for man to do. Each of us can think of women managers, teachers, directors, officers in your military chain of command, deaconesses, and instructors in sports, music, and the arts whose leadership is part of who we have become as fruitful believers in life. We have not arrived at places of success because men only were on our paths. In addition to our mothers, grandmothers, aunts, older sisters, and cousins, we each have been shaped profoundly for successes in life by other women. Recognizing this helps us accept the leadership of women when times for such leadership arise.

We should examine whether an instance to withhold women from certain roles in the church is an intention to preserve the truth of Scripture or to maintain an authoritative male presence when such a presence is unnecessary. When the church I currently attend moved to allow laypersons, including women, to distribute the elements of the Lord's Supper to the congregation, I bristled at first. The practice of the Lord's Supper being led by anyone other than pastors, elders, and deacons was extremely foreign to me, and I could not accept this.

However, in the Lord's grace, he showed me that laypersons serving was not the same as pastors and elders examining the congregation, blessing the elements, and performing the ordinances. There was no violation of the order of men and women; neither was there a violation of the responsibility of elders. To limit the distribution of plates to the elders was a theological decision on our part, not something prescribed by Scripture.

Close

In redemptive history, it is apparent that from the time of Adam to John the Baptizer, no man on earth could provide the deliverance the people of this world needed. Noah only could deliver through water but not much further. Abraham, Isaac, and Jacob could get man from the Ur of the Chaldees to Egypt, and then they passed without full deliverance. Moses followed, but sin kept him out of the promised land.

Samuel did not; David, despite all his victories, did not; Solomon's many foreign wives made it so that he could not. The revivalist kings in Judah did not rid the highways of the world of their evils. Evil continued its reign in the streets.

Then, at the end of forty-two generations, a unique leader arose for a unique time. Everyone did not follow this leader when he offered the kingdom of God. But some responded to "Follow me" and joined him in the battle to rescue the souls of men.

Jesus stepped into a role to deliver when no other men would or could save, dying to take the wrath of God due to us, and rising to offer the righteousness that would give us victory over death and joy in the presence of God. Jesus provides hope for every daughter to have success and every son who needs to come home to return. Jesus's exaltation as king will mean rest for his people.

We celebrate Jesus for arising out of Israel for us, and we bless the Lord for giving his Son to us! We celebrate Jesus for raising up women leaders to bless his people, too.

Reflect and Discuss

1. What are your initial feelings when reading the *Baptist Faith and Message 2000* article on marriage, and why do you feel like this?

2. What is your experience with women who are in leadership in their workplaces but are not able to exercise their leadership gifts in a local congregation?

3. In your experience, what are some examples of men holding leadership positions in their workplace but being unable to hold leadership positions in the church?

4. What additional information does Judges 5 give about the historical episode recorded in Judges 4?

5. What does one gain in one's theology of the roles of men and women in church and society by reading Judges 4 and 5 in tandem?

6. What might Jesus have learned from Judges 5 growing up as a child in the Jewish home of Joseph and Mary? How might this learning have influenced the work of his earthly ministry?

7. What are some unique contributions women have made to society that all persons should celebrate?

8. How do you feel about what the writer says about the cowardice of some of the tribes in application to the cowardice of modern men toward women's advocacy, and what experiences (or absence of experiences) have led you to feel this way?

9. How do Sisera's mother's actions reveal a failure often made in culture concerning our sons and daughters?

10. When have you experienced believers hesitating to celebrate the successes of fellow believers?

A Sovereign Hand for Overwhelming Odds

JUDGES 6

Main Idea: God's sovereign hand works in the life of Gideon to empower him to overcome overwhelming odds in defeating Midian.

I.   A Sovereign Hand Convicts (6:1-10).
II. A Sovereign Hand Reveals Mercy (6:11-24).
III. A Sovereign Hand Touches Our Family (6:25-32).
IV. A Sovereign Hand Empowers and Encourages (6:33-40).

After game four of the 2016 NBA Finals, the Golden State Warriors were up 3–1 over the Cleveland Cavaliers. No NBA team had ever come from a 3–1 deficit to win the NBA Finals. The betting odds were strongly against the 57–25 Cavaliers to beat the 73–9 reigning NBA Champion Warriors. Even after a win in game five, few favored the Cavs to win it all. But Lebron James had promised the city of Cleveland that they would win. So something changed after game four.

Their chances were like the odds of the 1972 Pittsburg Steelers beating the Oakland Raiders in the divisional playoff when down 7–6 with 30 seconds to go. Pittsburg had been one of the jokes of the NFL for four decades. Yet we all have seen the replay of Franco Harris's "Immaculate Reception" to know that the impossible can happen. Pittsburg went on to win four Super Bowls by 1980.

As believers, we often face overwhelming challenges to our faith. We have family members closed to hearing the gospel, health issues that threaten our ability to serve faithfully, not to mention preserve our mental stability or life itself, or ministry troubles that are far outside the normal realm. Calming the anxiety over these issues often is more overwhelming than the challenges themselves.

On a broader scale, the church faces a huge challenge posed by the secular age, as the media, business, and college campus rule with intolerance toward Christian theology, ethics, and values. Yet most of us, if not all of us, have walked with the Lord long enough to know that he who is infinite, eternal, and unchanging has the knowledge and power to meet and beat every challenge we face, no matter the size of the opposition or odds.

Gideon and Israel learn that same lesson in Judges 6. Faced with a Midianite coalition that threatens their existence, they will see a sovereign hand help them overcome their overwhelming odds. Israel and Gideon will see four things

A Sovereign Hand Convicts
JUDGES 6:1-10

If we are keeping the pattern in Judges that Israel returns to sin after the death of each judge, Deborah dies, even though there is no mention of her death. When Deborah is off the scene, Israel returns to doing what is evil in the sight of the Lord, doing what is right in their own eyes. In the Lord's judgment, this lands them in slavery to Midian for seven years.

Even though this is not Cushan-rishathaim, this is no trivial enslavement. Midian is so fierce that the Israelites are hiding in caves, hoping not to be seen by marauding Midianites. Combining forces with the Amalekites and the people of the east, Midian makes chumps of Israel at every turn, taking all their crops and their cattle, completely destroying the land.

You think you have a problem with an unbelieving opposition? Imagine if your unbelieving neighbors could just walk over and take your car and make it their own. Some of our brothers and sisters under Muslim states and Communist regimes are in such settings.

This threatening situation brings Israel to lower herself before the Lord. However, the Lord does not immediately send a judge to deliver Israel. Instead, he sends a prophet to declare his word (vv. 8-10). This is a word of *conviction*: the Lord tells Israel that they have failed to honor the one who has redeemed them from Egypt and defended them. They have broken the command not to fear the gods of the Amorites. They have not obeyed the voice of the Lord.

If the Lord had sent a judge immediately, Israel would not have seen their own sin. The overwhelming domination of the nations acts as a mirror for Israel. It places them in a position to hear from the Lord as they look for deliverance. Crushing trials have this sort of sanctifying effect. They send us to our prayer closets on our knees, if not facedown, in prayer. We then are able to lower our hearts and minds before God so that we might learn where we have disobeyed the one who has given us salvation in his Son. The Lord's kindness brings us conviction so that we do not continue in unrevealed sin in our lives.

A Sovereign Hand Reveals Mercy
JUDGES 6:11-24

The Lord does hear the prayers of his people in their Midianite oppression. But the narrative of the calling of the deliverer is much longer than those of the first four judges. The angel of the Lord appears in the calling narrative. The angel of the Lord is the OT appearance of Jesus in prebodily form, just as we encountered in Judges 2:1-5. We conclude that this is Jesus because the OT writers always reveal that the angel of the Lord is God when he appears, as we also will see in this episode.

Also, the Gospel of John and 1 Timothy both reveal that no one ever has seen God the Father, and the Johannine narrative is particular about this (John 1:18; see also 1 Tim 1:17; 6:16). So, if no one has seen God the Father, and the Spirit of God is not visible to the eye, yet God appears visibly in the OT, it is God the Son who appears. He will appear in the first century in the NT in bodily form so that he can reveal the Father to us (John 1:18; 5:17-18; 10:30,38; 12:45; 14:7-9; 17:3-4), suffer and die for our sins, and rise from the dead to provide life to all who believe.

The angel of the Lord appears to a frightened chap named Gideon. Trying to hide from the Midianites, he is threshing wheat in a winepress even though there is no wind in a winepress to blow away the chaff from the wheat. To this scared fellow the angel of the Lord says, "The LORD is with you, valiant warrior," even though we have yet to see any valor in this passage. The words must imply that the might of God is with Gideon, for Gideon responds with questions about the power and faithfulness of the Lord. The first question makes sense in light of Israel's situation (v. 13).

Undaunted by the line of questioning, the angel of the Lord gets to the bottom line of his exchange with Gideon (v. 14). Gideon is to go save Israel, despite feeling weak and small because he—the angel of the Lord—will be with him to defeat the Midianites.

While that word alone should be enough for Gideon to run into battle with only a toothpick in his hand as a weapon, Gideon, scared of the size of the odds against the Midianites, asks for a sign. Gideon and the angel of the Lord work out that he will wait while Gideon prepares food. In presenting the food on the rock, the consummation of the food by a miraculous fire, and the disappearance of the angel of the Lord, that Gideon gets his sign: *he has seen the face of God!*

Now, if we had problems with the Midianites, we really have a problem now, for seeing the face of God while in our human bodies means certain death because we are far too sinful to stand in the presence of the Holy One. Gideon was questioning the Lord to his face about his faithfulness and then further demanding a sign that the ever-faithful God will be faithful—faithful even to a people who have not obeyed his voice—and Gideon lives to tell about it? If some of us had questioned our parents' faithfulness, we would not have made it into adulthood unscarred. But here Gideon, expressing uncertainty about God's word to be with him in battle while standing in the presence of God, yet lives? He lives because the Lord says he will not die (v. 23). That is mercy. An undeserving sinner gets life he does not deserve simply because the Lord says he will yet have life.

All the promises of God come to us packaged with mercy. When the Lord says, "I will never leave you or abandon you" (Heb 13:5), there is mercy, for he should leave us and abandon us, since as sinners we have no right to his presence. When he says, "I am with you always, to the end of the age" (Matt 28:20), it is mingled with mercy, for it would be right for him to say to us, "You're on your own, rebel."

Far more overwhelming than an oppressor like a Midianite-Amalekite coalition, and far more overwhelming than an agnostic or atheistic culture that is hostile to almost any discussion of a Creator, Savior, or final Judge, and far more overwhelming than a visionless church or a city entrenched in cults or vices fueled by greed, and far more overwhelming than any sacred calling—ministry or secular—is standing before the face of the Holy and Almighty God in our own strength, fears, and trespasses. Yet it is to these weaknesses, fears, lawlessness, rebellion, and ignorance that he has shown us mercy in his incarnate angel of the Lord—the Lord Jesus.

If the overwhelming problem of standing before God the Judge as one unrighteous has been answered by God in mercy, what real concern then do we have of the Midianite-Amalekite coalitions before us?

Mercy there was great, and grace was free.
Pardon there was multiplied to me.
There my burdened soul found liberty,
   At Calvary. (Newell, "At Calvary")

The place of God's mercy.

May I say to the reader who has not yet made a decision to give your life to Christ that you cannot solve your own greatest problem; that is, you cannot stand before God when you die and provide cause or reason for him not to pour out his wrath on you for all eternity. Mercy from the wrath of God is found in Jesus, on whom God poured out his wrath on sins in place of us receiving the wrath we deserve. Jesus, after dying for sin, proved that God accepted his substitution for our sins by raising Christ to life over death. Now he can offer mercy *freely*—life over death when you die.

Gideon, certain of mercy, then worships, for the Lord has made peace with him rather than destroy him.

A Sovereign Hand Touches Our Family
JUDGES 6:25-32

Now Gideon is in a better position to listen to the Lord. Obediently he tears down the Baal-Asherah worship site at this father's home. With no permission from his father, who obviously is a Baal and Asherah worshiper, Gideon takes two of his dad's bulls and, with the help of ten men, uses the bulls to pull down his father's altar and the Asherah pole. Then, still without Dad's permission, he sacrifices one of Dad's bulls on the new altar to the Lord, using the wood from Dad's Asherah to fuel the altar's fire. Talk about being in your face about rejecting false religion and following the Lord exclusively! Yet Gideon is not bold, for he works at night in fear of his family's response.

This makes sense. His dad is entrenched in Baal and Asherah worship, and Gideon smashes all the artifacts, makes a financial loss of one of the bulls, and uses Dad's means to get the acts done. He should be afraid.

But look at what happens in God's sovereignty because of Gideon's obedience to be exclusive in his worship of the Lord: when the men of the town call for the execution of Gideon for destroying their altar to Baal, his father steps up to intercede for him! Through Gideon's actions, his dad turns from worshiping Baal and Asherah to recognizing their impotence and to calling for the death of those who defend the false gods (v. 31).

For some of us, our families are the hardest people to have as an audience to the gospel. Our families want to say to us of our faith, "Gideon, what's the matter with you? Just yesterday you used to love Baal and Asherah as much as we did. Now you've found religion and are all Jerubbaal." Or they want to say, "That's nice that the Lord works for you, but I'm fine with my Asherah—my Asherah that I had to cut down, carve and shape, and then lose when someone needed firewood—my Asherah that I am trying to prop up with my good works, and rosary beads, chants, self-meditations, oils, Mass, and the Lord's Supper when Jesus already paid for sin on the cross."

But Jesus is not one option among many. Jesus is the Lord. We, in obedience, cannot back down on this message, even when our families are hard-hearted atheists. In God's sovereignty, he can change the hardest hearts. It does not mean he will, for he chooses to give mercy to whom he will, says Scripture (Rom 9:14-18). Yet the Gideon passage does mean we should keep sharing the gospel.

My mother-in-law is one who has told us not to talk to her about religion, and in response to the proclamation of the gospel by her children, and the conversion of each of them from Catholicism to faith in Christ, she has grabbed a deeper hold onto her Catholic belief. She has no security and now attends Mass daily for her soul to be right before God. My family and my wife's siblings know that we cannot stop praying for their mother and speaking to her about Jesus, even though her Catholicism poses a huge barrier to faith in Christ *alone*.

A Sovereign Hand Empowers and Encourages
JUDGES 6:33-40

The Midianite coalition draws up to Israel's doorstep. Where we expect that Gideon should be afraid, we now find Gideon clothed with the Spirit of the Lord. Gideon gathers the troops for battle, getting many in Israel to come to arms.

But he still is fearful of this massive oppressor at the border. Thus, he asks for two signs. This looks bad to us because he is asking for a sign even though he had one in the fire on the rock. Yet the graciousness with which God responds should give us cause to rethink this episode.

The issue of the fleece is not whether one act is of greater faith than the other or if one is a greater miracle than the other. Instead, this is a passage of simple encouragement: "Gideon, you need another sign to get in the battle? OK, here is your sign. You need a second one in order to trust me? OK, here is another."

How gracious it is for the Lord to give us his Spirit within us to accomplish his will. In this way, we are never alone in our efforts to be obedient. The Spirit of God gives us the grace, mercy, patience, faith, hope, boldness, endurance, kindness, and joy we need to honor God, even when our enemies do not return any of these kindnesses.

How gracious it is for the Lord to give us countless signs of his power to overcome our biggest, most fearful challenges by giving us the stories of Gideon and the record of God's faithfulness throughout Scripture. I hang my hat on the crossing of the Red Sea every day. That is the point of the refrain, "I am the LORD your God, who brought you out of the land of Egypt, out of the place of slavery" (Exod 20:2; see Judg 6:8). In that phrase the Lord reminds us that he poured down plagues and split the Red Sea en route to crushing the Egyptians.

As we faced a move to Chicago two years ago, the Lord split many Red Seas for us, against daunting opposition. Due to a snag between two lending institutions, our securing Chicago housing was in total jeopardy even as we were driving across the county with all our wares in tow on an eighteen-wheeler. We could not go back to our previous house, for it had sold. We could not place everything in storage and search for more housing, for we had no temporary lodging. Instead, with our backs against our own sea, we watched God give us a taste of his faithfulness as he worked out with four hours to spare what my lender said for six weeks would never happen. That was the encouragement that we did not even know we would need for greater challenges after landing our family in Chi-town.

Close

Lebron James said he would bring the championship to Cleveland, and he did. Down 3–1, Lebron led his Cavs to the first three-game comeback in the history of the NBA Finals. Against all odds, the whole city of Cleveland and all the Cavs players, clinging to Lebron's words and power, rose to defeat the record-setting NBA champion Warriors.

The Midianite coalition warriors, with all odds in their favor, met a Gideon empowered by God, transformed by his mercy, motivated by his hand in his family, and encouraged by his faithful word. Our sovereign God is with you in the overwhelming task you face, too.

Reflect and Discuss

1. When you hear that the Lord is "sovereign," what does that mean to you?
2. When has a sermon meaningfully spoken to you in the midst of an experience of severe discipline or distress, maybe in a way it would not have if you had heard it during a period of ease?
3. What does the delay in revealing the calling of a judge do for this narrative?
4. What is important about the angel of the Lord's greeting to Gideon?
5. Why would tearing down his father's idols have been a fearful thing?
6. What might Gideon's boldness in smashing his father's idols say about our bold witness to our immediate family members?
7. What does the presence of the Spirit upon Gideon mean for the ensuing battle?
8. What does the presence of the Spirit of God within the believer mean for struggles against those who oppose the message of the gospel?
9. When has the presence of the Spirit made a huge difference in your outlook on a daunting task?
10. Based on the Gideon narrative, how would you guide someone who is planning to "cast a fleece" to determine the will of God?

A Practical Warrior for the Glory of God

JUDGES 7

Main Idea: Gideon's practical actions as a warrior who trusts the sovereignty of God allow him to defeat the much stronger Midianite army.

I. **Resourceful** (7:1-8)
II. **Worshipful** (7:9-18)
III. **Unpredictable** (7:19-25)

Modern church and nonchurch historians alike have called for the church to be careful in how it sets itself against a culture it perceives to be anti-religious, anti-Christian, antidemocratic, antimoral, antifamily, and antilife. Instead, and rightly so to a certain degree, there are calls to give a greater emphasis to the enjoyment of culture, to winsome apologetics, and to an emphasis on more service, less "preachy," and less "fire and brimstone."

One stark reality we must face is that Christianity is countercultural, and secularism is anti-Christian. Secularism is not necessarily antispiritual or anti-religious, but it is anti-Christian. It does set itself against belief in the objective truth of exclusive monotheism in which the Son of God is the only means to the one true God, that all souls stand in subjection to him for glorification and joy or destruction and misery, and that the moral and ethical implications of the truth of Christ are good and righteous for all people and binding on all persons. To believe the claims of Christ would mean that we would have to say some well-written and greatly enjoyable pieces of literature are wrong in their conclusions about the meaning of life. Perish the thought that I would say Yann Martel's *Life of Pi* is *wrong*!

Another stark reality we must face is that if we are going to survive the onslaught of modern secularism and go on the offense for God, we cannot look to the monastic life or the Crusades for the answer. Doing nothing is not the answer; being practical is the answer. Being a practical warrior for the glory of God is the very thing we see in the life of Gideon as he finally confronts the oppressive forces of Midian. He is a practical warrior in three ways: he is *resourceful, worshipful,* and *unpredictable.*

Resourceful

JUDGES 7:1-8

In one of your favorite Bible passages and mine, the Lord reduces Gideon's forces from thirty-two thousand men to three hundred. He now has 0.9375 percent of the forces he had previously. Everyone shaking in his boots was offered to go home quick, fast, and in a hurry. Anyone who did not lap the water like a dog was sent back to his tent.

Why reduce the troops needed for war? Everything we hear about war concerns the buildup of troops. We may need more troops to recapture a city or win a war. We only reduce troops when others native to the fighting region are able to take over their own warfare and establish or reestablish their own democracies. Yet here we see the reduction of troops for battle. Why? *So that God can get all the glory for victory.*

If thirty-two thousand or twenty-two thousand men went to battle and won, Israel could have said they won by the strength of their numbers. They would not give thanks to God or attribute the victory to him alone. There would be room for speaking of the power of Gideon's strategizing and leadership and of the tactics with which certain battalions fought. The Lord might get a mention in a footnote, but he would not be the special report, headline news, and the lead and only story in every news outlet. However, when three hundred men with a few provisions and some trumpets go to war against a force much greater than thirty-two thousand people and win, everyone will come back speaking only of the power of God to bring victory.

God alone saves us; God alone has made provision for us all the days of our lives; God alone has watched over our children, protected our families, given us the joy of work, opened doors of ministry to the lost, grown our churches, and given all material things to us. All praise should go to God alone.

The huge reduction in forces places Gideon in a position in which he must be *resourceful*—resourceful for the glory of God. Gideon is about to go to war at the command of God but with reduced forces. Fortunately, he has a God-given advantage over Midian, for Midian is in the valley below Gideon (vv. 1,7). So Gideon will use the means at his disposal to battle Midian.

The small-church, rural-church, or planting-church pastor is not the only one with a need for more resources. Neither is a severe lack of resources a phenomenon created only to empty out the pockets of grade-school teachers. Many of the Lord's servants face a reduction in or paucity of resources as they seek to do all he commands us to do. Some will face a loss of income, a shrinking of budget, or a departure of a key employee, benefactor, or extremely faithful volunteer. Some might experience a loss of physical strength or a move to a work or ministry assignment where money, material, people, and advanced technological resources are not as readily available as they were with a previous company or ministry position. Those are not times to lament what was then and is not now; those are times to look to God to see how to glorify him with less. Those are times when we may have to step back so that we might see that we are at an elevation that gives God an advantage even without an abundance of resources. *Be resourceful.*

Worshipful

JUDGES 7:9-18

The Lord offers Gideon an opportunity to alleviate his fears and to strengthen his hands for battle. Gideon may go down to the camp of the Midianites and listen to their words. Something he will hear will make him stronger.

This is not Gideon asking for a fleece. Instead, this is like the Lord giving him two gift-wrapped presents in the days of dew and dryness. That the Lord initiates the actions lets us know that the Lord is up to something. The Lord is at work to bring about an outcome in Gideon.

Gideon and his servant Purah sneak down to camp and see an immeasurable number of men and camels. Whatever they hear better be exceptional information if it is going to make them fight a horde of this great magnitude. What they hear is the telling and interpretation of a parable between two Midianite warriors that indicates that the small Gideon will defeat the Midianites like a small loaf of barley knocking over a tent.

I don't really like camping; I have PTSD from my Webelos experiences. When men at my church say they want to organize a camping trip, I don't even volunteer to take care of the paperwork for them. Therefore, I remain a camping novice. But I do remember enough about pitching a tent to know that if I rolled a Christmas fruitcake down a hill and it hit your tent and knocked it over, either that was one of those typical badly made fruitcakes, or you have a weak tent and poor pitching skills. Either way, the cake is stronger than the tent, and in this parable, the smaller Gideon is going to crush Midian.

Gideon hears specifically that he, Gideon, son of Joash, a man of Israel, will fight, and he hears from a Midianite that God—the God of Israel and not one of the gods of Midian—has given Midian into his hands even though they are like locusts in their numbers across the valley. What now should Gideon do with this exciting news? He should run back to camp, gather the three hundred, race down, and overrun the Midianites like fruitcake rolling onto tents! No. The passage intentionally inserts that Gideon bows to worship. The penultimate goal of God in sending Gideon to listen to the camp is to alleviate his fear, but the ultimate goal of God is to bring Gideon to a place of worship.

The Lord brings Gideon to a place where he understands that all is in the hands of God and God is worthy of praise for victory before the battle even begins! All the Lord had done in the calling of Gideon, reduction in forces, and the perfectly timed hearing of a dream expressly naming Gideon as victor by the hand of God displays the worth of Almighty God. Gideon acknowledges the mighty and sovereign God who wins battles before one finger is lifted to go to war.

It is important that Gideon prioritizes worship because he is going to go back to camp and grab *disciples*. Disciples? Disciples or warriors? Warriors, yes; but disciples also, for Gideon is going to ask them to accomplish their work by mimicking him as he follows the hand of God. Before he can ask disciples to do something totally ridiculous to accomplish an overwhelming task—something as ridiculous as telling disciples to proclaim that a crucified man got up from the dead and offers life to anyone who believes in him—Gideon must be confident that there is a God of the greatest worth leading him and those with him.

The war in which we engage daily is not secular human versus Christian human. We are fighting an invisible, spiritual war in which we are demolishing strongholds and lofty opinions against God, taking every thought captive to obey Christ (see 2 Cor 10:4-5; also 1 Pet 2:11). In that war, God must conquer enemies in an unseen realm for his people to have victory in the visible realm (see Col 2:15; also 1 Pet 3:22). That God—the Lord Jesus—is worthy of praise, honor, and glory for defeating the power and forces that wage war against our souls. As we seek to obey his commission, we should model to those we lead that the priority must be worship before we engage the war of being the Lord's witnesses.

Unpredictable
JUDGES 7:19-25

Unpredictable does not sound like your typical Christian virtue. It's not being loving, treating others as you want to be treated, giving one of two cloaks to him who has none, or not committing adultery. But we are talking about a *war*, a Midianite-Amalekite-peoples-of-the-east war, and talking of wars for the souls of humankind that take place in the human realms of sex trafficking, gang culture, opioid addiction, ransomware attacks, legislation against the God-designed family structure, unequal distribution of material goods, unfair housing practices, and the like. To fight in a predictable manner might mean that we will be met with suspicion or dismissed altogether: "Yeah, yeah, yeah, the Christians are going to try to get their candidate elected, call for a boycott of certain companies, and write a few checks to help with local social programming. We do not have to give any attention to them." Instead, we need to be wise as serpents and harmless as doves, as our Lord Jesus has said (Matt 10:16). We need to use some nontraditional means and methods of ministry for which the non-Christian opposition will not have a reason to dismiss our gospel work.

To be unpredictable gives one a unique advantage. Consider the unpredictable things of this passage. First, they attack at the beginning of the middle watch when the new sentries are not expecting anything to happen. Second, they blow trumpets, smash jars, hold up torches, and shout, using the words of Gideon—words derived from the dream Gideon overheard. That's some fighting strategy when you're outnumbered one hundred to one: *shout your enemy to death.* Yet, because it is the Lord at hand, the strategy works!

As a result of the unpredictable warfare, the Midianites begin to fight one another. Some start to flee. Then more men are called from all over Israel to pursue the Midianites. They capture the princes and the fording places over the watercourses, so Midian and the Amalekites lose their main resource and their main leaders to a people of few resources, and the Lord receives all the glory.

Application

In his book *Christian Worldview: A Student's Guide*, Philip Ryken, commenting on the consequences of the fall of man, writes at length:

The factory, the boardroom, and the cubicle have become places of corruption and oppression, and we all experience the drudgery and dissatisfaction that so often come with working on the job. Like Solomon, the biblical philosopher, we sigh, "What does a man get for all the toil and anxious striving with which he labors?" (Eccles. 2:22 NIV). The curse of the fall extends to the family, where husbands and wives fight to gain the upper hand (Gen. 3:19), and where the woman is afflicted in her unique calling as wife and mother (Gen. 3:16). Men also suffer in their unique calling as husbands and fathers, of course, but God announces a curse to Eve—a curse that refers to the physical pains of childbirth and to much more besides. It refers to childbearing in general and thus to all the frustrations associated with motherhood in a fallen world, including not getting married, not having children, and the heartaches of raising and sometimes losing children. Taken together, the curses that men and women must endure mean that the two most basic tasks of any generation—namely, making a living and raising children—are only fulfilled through suffering. (*Christian Worldview*, 68–69)

Ryken's words are helpful toward us in being resourceful, worshipful, and unpredictable as we try to be gospel effective in the present era.

First, *we should open our homes to others as a place of peace.* Welcome into your home young marrieds and singles, domestic and international college students, and teens of your fellow members so that they can see an example of how one lives for the glory of God in joy in the normal routines of life. Many young people live without ever having seen two people strive to consider each to be better than the other, to prioritize both love and submission, to express forgiveness and grace, and to coexist without speaking in angry and disrespectful voices. Many enter their post-high school and/or post-college-aged years not having the experience of knowing a young adult or middle-aged adult single person who lives contentedly, selflessly, sacrificially, and in holiness. The up-close examples and investment of our time in these others will go further in creating a countercultural community than striving for legislation favorable to Christian ideals.

Second, *if you are the child of a believer, embrace obeying your parents as a happy way to live life without shame.* Can you show the world that obedient children are happy children and grow into happy adults? Can you stop bucking your parents on curfews, choices of friends, clothing, music choices, social media, and web limitations, and instead see your parents setting up parameters for a good life because they love you and want to see you succeed in life? You have enemies, but your parents are not among them. If you embrace obedience as happiness, we will shock the world, and they will have to give a hearing to Jesus.

While you are embracing your parents' authority, in your spheres of influence *speak up on obedience to authority as a means of providing for a civil society.* If you need an argument for making different life choices than many of your peers, speak to them on the realities of the consequences of a heart of disobedience. They have seen the evidence in broken homes, the rise of substance abuse, the increase of abuse and trauma among friends, and the degradation of language and discourse. Those seeking obedience are seeking goodness, truth, integrity, peace, and the righteous treatment of persons; they are seeking to be moral. They are not seeking to deceive or harm others.

Third, *keep fighting for the little guy in the workplace.* I am so grateful for you believers in management positions who take hits for your workers because you are believers. Such sacrifices are foolishness in the eyes of the world because the world would tell us that no one ever gets ahead as a manager doing this. But the dad or mom under you who has to spend one more hour at a child's school sorting out discipline issues for their child thanks you. So does the man who just needed understanding rather than reprimanding while he struggles with a crumbling marriage at home.

Fourth, *keep up the fight for your personal, family, and corporate worship times in your schedule.* Worship concerns God and you personally, your children and spouse, and all members of your corporate assembly. This is the biggest fight we have—to maintain worship within our busy schedule. Nevertheless, this passage is clear that worship preceded the battle against the enemies of God's people, and the priority of worship intones throughout Scripture.

If worship is not a family priority, it will not be a priority for our children when they become adults. If believers do not have a priority to be with the people of God, church will become a victim of our preferences, as evidenced in the slowness of some people to return to corporate gatherings after the pandemic threat passed.[25] Make your God-fearing church grow even more in the grace and knowledge of Christ; plant yourself there and give yourself to faithful corporate gathering with the saints of God.

Fifth, *enjoy your reductions from God as gifts of grace.* Jesus said to Paul, "My grace is sufficient for you" (2 Cor 12:9). From this Paul concluded that when he is weak, then he is strong. Akin to reducing Gideon's troops to three hundred before going to war against thirty-two thousand, Jesus reduces our income, lifestyle, occupational authority, and even our relationships so that he gets all the glory. The world cannot understand joy in reduction, downsizing, and loss because the world's idea of blessing only looks like gain or recovery. Thus, unbelievers might be challenged to inquire of us why we still have joy with *less.*

Then we can tell them that Jesus, alone on the cross, crying out to his Father, asking for forgiveness toward his enemies—all so that he could provide atonement for our sin—was the most practical warrior who ever was and will be. And we follow him. He lived for the glory of God, and we will too.

Reflect and Discuss

1. Why might a monastic approach to living in a hostile culture be unhelpful for a Great Commission witness?
2. Before you read this chapter, what were your feelings about the Lord's reduction of Gideon's troops?
3. Why is it natural to equate reduction with cursing rather than blessing?
4. When has a reduction in your resources brought about growth in your relationship with Christ and faith in his ability to do what seems impossible to accomplish?

---

[25] See more on the slow return to corporate gatherings in Larry Hoop, "The Way Back to In-Person Worship: When to Return? And under What Conditions?," *By Faith,* May 8, 2020, https://byfaithonline.com/back-in-person-worship-after-coronavirus-when -return-what-conditions; accessed June 1, 2021; Sarah Wilkins-Laflamme and Joel Thiessen, "Coronavirus & Easter: Lapsed Christians Unlikely to Return to Church Even in Uncertain Times," *The Conversation,* April 7, 2020; https://theconversation.com/coronavirus-and -easter-lapsed-christians-unlikely-to-return-to-church-even-in-uncertain-times-134302; accessed June 1, 2021.

5. What is something you have done to be resourceful when you have lacked resources for accomplishing ministry?
6. Based on the Gideon narrative, how should we view the casting of fleeces to determine the Lord's will?
7. What is the connection between the reduction in troops and Gideon's coming to a place of worship before battle?
8. In what way are Gideon's warriors his disciples?
9. How does predictability truncate our witness in the public square?
10. How do you think the three hundred and Gideon felt about their chance of success initially, and how do you think they felt after the victory?

Right Estimations

JUDGES 8

Main Idea: Gideon's response to his and his opponents' hostile incorrect estimations of his victories rightfully proportions judgments upon his return, but it also leads Israel into idolatry, the abandonment of the Lord, and the abandonment of Gideon's house after Gideon's death, despite the birth of Abimelech.

I.   Right Estimation Enjoys Grace (8:1-3).
II. Underestimation Experiences Judgment (8:4-12).
III. Wrong Estimation Receives Proportional Vengeance (8:13-21).
IV. Final Estimation Glorifies the Father and Rewards the Undeserving (8:22-35).

We are living in an era when the public expression of anger and the social level of hostility seem unusually high. In late August 2020, as many states entered what they hoped would be the final phases of COVID-19 pandemic quarantine, *Harvard Gazette* staff writer Alvin Powell penned these words:

> Tensions are high about many things right now in America, and health and safety concerns over the COVID-19 virus rank high among them, particularly in families. Many parents are fearful about in-person classes for their children; others are upset that classes will remain remote. Neighbors are irritated by those not abiding by the latest public health guidelines, and by those who are. Some workers can't wait to return to their offices; others resent being forced to. No one wants to get sick or lose their job. ("McLean's Rosmarin Offers Perspective")

You will remember that during the pandemic, airlines reported increased incidents of fighting on flights and in airport terminals. In one incident, a Southwest Airlines flight attendant experienced a violent episode that caused her facial injuries and the loss of two teeth. Southwest Airlines said the passenger "repeatedly ignored standard inflight instructions and became verbally and physically abusive upon landing" (Stankiewicz, "Unruly Behavior").

Unfortunately, the hostility in society turned into a particular form of hatred toward members of the Asian American Pacific Islanders community (AAPI). Chinese Americans became victims of rising hatred due to people's perceptions of China's handling of the outbreak of the coronavirus. Just as "Latino" becomes "Mexican" in the minds of some, "Chinese" became "all Asians" in the minds of some who are racists toward AAPI persons.[26] As a result, many persons of AAPI descent became victims to rising hatred and violence.

The escalating hostility of modern culture also sets it sights on religion. While some might say religion is the *cause* of much hostility, hatred, and violence in the world, religion is an *object* of hostility for many. As writer Ryan Dueck has noted,

> The rise of the "new atheism" is remarkable not for the persuasive nature of its arguments, but for the astonishing degree of its hostility towards God and religion, and the intellectual and moral stridency of its claims—especially in our putative "postmodern" age which is supposed to be characterized by epistemological humility and suspicion toward any claim to know "the truth." ("Angry at the God," 3)

Similarly, Bebe Nicholson speaks of a particular form of angry opposition directed at Christians, saying,

---

[26] For more on "Mexican" and "Latino" being used interchangeably, see Nicole Martinez-LeGrand, "Not All Latinos Are Mexican: The Story of a 1920s Peruvian Steel Worker from Gary, Indiana," IHS Blog, https://indianahistory.org/blog/not-all-latinos-are-mexican-the-story-of-a-1920s-peruvian-steel-worker-from-gary-indiana, accessed June 5 2021; also, as an example, Dennis Romero, "The Worst Slur for Mexican-Americans Is Still a Mystery for Some," *NBC News*, February 1, 2019, https://www.nbcnews.com/news/latino/worst-slur-mexican-americans-still-mystery-some-n959616. On the rise of hatred toward persons of AAPI descent, see "AACC Statement on the Atlanta Massacre and Ongoing Anti-Asian Hate," *Asian American Christian Collaborative*, https://www.asianamericanchristiancollaborative.com/atlantastatement, accessed June 5, 2021; Manjusha Kulkarni, Cynthia Choi, and Russell M. Jeung, "How to Stop the Dangerous Rise in Hatred Targeted at Asian Americans," *USA Today*, March 30, 2021, https://www.usatoday.com/story/opinion/2021/03/30/how-stop-rise-hatred-aimed-asian-americans-column/7044033002; "Statement on Anti-Asian Racism in the Time of Covid-19," *Asian American Christian Collaborative*, https://www.asianamericanchristiancollaborative.com/read-statement, accessed June 5, 2021.

Unbelievers are growing more hostile to faith, and it's become more acceptable to express that hostility openly. . . . When I venture beyond my Christian community of friends, I run into people who blame everything from politics to capitalism on Christians. ("Hostility to Christianity")

Hostility toward Christians—whether in the form of burning a church, murdering missionaries or believers in predominantly Muslim countries, or attempting to silence a Christian perspective in a workspace or classroom discussion—is hostility toward Christ. One might argue that hatred is directed at the way the church and its adherents carry out their forms of Christian practice. The Christian vitriol against LBGTQ+ persons, the failure to address sex offenders in local assemblies, the harm of purity culture, and the associations of Christian practice with nationalism or socialism seem to warrant the hostility in the minds of some. But such a view is naïve to think that the removal of the imperfections of believers would make the hostile opposition embrace Jesus. The Gospels reveal a picture of people hating the perfect, all-loving, always kind Jesus because their own motives were impure.

From his heavenly throne, Jesus exercises great patience toward those who are hostile toward him. However, a day is coming when Jesus will not tolerate hostility toward his will, but he will apportion appropriate judgment to the hostile, and he will discipline his own who sometimes object to doing his will. It is important, therefore, that all persons have the right estimation of the works of Christ so that we each might live in a manner pleasing to him rather than knowingly or unknowingly living with hostility to him. Gideon's encounter with the hostile responses of Ephraim and others reveals the importance of making right estimations toward the war leader as he makes victories for his people. From Gideon's story, a theological line points toward how we should estimate the works of Jesus.

Explanation of Typology

Before jumping into this story, the reader should recognize its typological nature. By *typological*, I mean that this story *prefigures an aspect of the life of Christ*. As a *prefigure*, it looks forward to a correspondence in the *figure*. The story acts as a pattern or type of an aspect of Christ's life. In the age before digital photography, it was commonplace to draw an analogy from camera negatives on film and developed pictures to explain the working of OT *types* and their NT *antitypes*. However, in a digital age an appropriate analogy to explain moving from incomplete to complete might be going from original raw picture to photoshopped publication.

On typology, Aubrey Sequeira and Samuel Emadi write,

> Interpretation of types is an outgrowth of NT authors' textual development of the significance of the persons, events, and institutions across the redemptive-historical epochs in the canon of Scripture. . . . Put another way, typology is not an imposition made on the text by some external interpretive agent (reader, community, tradition, etc.) but a product of biblical-theological exegesis. It emerges from assiduously uncovering an OT text's significance furnished by the rest of the canon. ("Biblical-Theological Exegesis," 18)

When one considers this Gideon episode in light of the revelation of the rest of the canon of Scripture, a picture of Christ emerges.[27] This picture of Christ corresponds to the Gideon story of hostility as people make incorrect estimations. It intends to portray the importance of rightly estimating the work of Christ. Four ideas will reveal themselves regarding rightly estimating Gideon and Jesus.

Right Estimation Enjoys Grace
JUDGES 8:1-3

Upon defeating Oreb and Zeeb, Gideon meets with opposition from Ephraim rather than thanksgiving and victory celebration. Ephraim feels that they were called to the fight too late to participate in the full war and that this prevents them from sharing in the spoils of victory, as evidenced in Gideon's response to their unspoken concern about "gleaning" (8:2). They come at the successful warrior "violently," "vehemently" (NET), or "fiercely" (ESV). Gideon's work to secure victory

---

[27] Mitchell Chase writes, "Gideon was not a king, but he foreshadowed the future king of God's people" (*40 Questions*, 156). Admittedly, the explicit NT antitype evidence is scant for support of my portrayal of Gideon as a type of Christ. But similarly, there is little NT antitype evidence for Job's being a type of Christ. Yet the suffering and restoration of Job and his intercession for his friends who wronged the Lord and his portrayal as one with many of the characteristics of Melchizedek seem to point toward Christ. That is, the narrative develops Job as a type without explicit NT antitype references. I am suggesting similar for Gideon.

without the assistance of the Ephraimites hotly angers Ephraim as they think that absence of participation in the victory will mean an absence of gaining the victors' rewards.

However, Gideon responds to Ephraim's hostility by questioning the true outcome of his victory. The defeat of Oreb and Zeeb and all that belongs to them will belong to Ephraim and not to Gideon. It was Ephraim who gained the heads of the kings even though Gideon led the war and called them to fight. In comparison, therefore, they have far more in spoils of war than Gideon has alone.

As they recognize that they were called to be victorious in the war that Gideon was winning on behalf of Israel, the men of Ephraim lose their anger. The work of Gideon is satisfactory when they realize they have gained reward from his conquest. They have underestimated the true meaning of Gideon's win.

Jesus's work alone as our Victor should silence any and all hostility against salvation by grace alone when one sees the benefits of salvation by grace. Some believers and unbelievers object to the idea that Christ alone has done everything in salvation for us. They think they must work for what they gain. Yet in his atonement, Christ provides for us what we cannot gain because we cannot secure our own victory. Unlike Gideon, Christ does not need to call us to secure victory over his enemies, but he will invite us to share in the final victory over his enemies by grace. Like Gideon, Christ will provide the defeat of his and our enemies and share all his inheritance as Victor with us.

Underestimation Experiences Judgment
JUDGES 8:4-12

Gideon's defeat of Oreb and Zeeb does not complete his stoppage of Midianite aggression. It is one thing to defeat the princes; Gideon must defeat the two heads of state—Zebah and Zalmunna. While pursuing the two kings, much as he did when calling Ephraim to battle, Gideon invites the men of Succoth and Penuel to help in defeating the kings. Only on this occasion he needs food for his troops. He only needs refreshing for his troops, not an unreasonable request considering how few men are with him.

Yet both Succoth and Penuel refuse to provide refreshment, seemingly because they will not be repaid for their kindness. Their concern is for the bread for the army to go to a person already victorious rather than be wasted on one who might not bring back a victory over the kings. They are underestimating Gideon's ability to bring back a win over the two kings.

Gideon's rejoinders to the two cities are words of judgment. For Succoth's underestimation of his ability to defeat the kings, there will be tearing of flesh with thorns and briars—painful to be sure. For Penuel there will be the destruction of a tower—one that apparently will fall on people or kill the people contained therein. Harsh judgments are reserved for those underestimating the power of this future conqueror.

Still in pursuit of the two kings, Gideon takes advantage of the sense of security of the kings' troops. Their defenses are not on high alert for an attack by Gideon; they too are underestimating him and his three hundred men. Gideon will come by an unexpected route to overtake the armies. He will capture the kings, and the underestimating army will be thrown into a panic when they see the might of Gideon as victor.

Jesus's return will come with judgment for those who have underestimated his ability to defeat the kings of the earth. Jesus's future war against the kings of the earth will remove the false sense of security against his judgment that many hold.

Many now live as if the power structures of this present world are the final authorities in the universe. What the authorities on Wall Street, in Hollywood, or on Capitol Hill establish as truth or morality, many accept as gospel and live their lives accordingly. Rather than defy the masses and messages of this age, we accept their versions of living and success as the only pictures to which our lives might conform. Moreover, few of us are willing to speak defiant justice against the unjust actions of governments around the world, including our own.

Acceptance of these unrighteous rules as gospel and refusal to acknowledge their wickedness reveals, in effect, that we think their rule is final. But the final rule of the earth belongs to Jesus, just as he presently rules from heaven. Just as he one day will defeat all kings who rage against his rule, so now he has authority over every world leader—all of whose hearts he can turn and kingdoms he can exalt or humble.

When Jesus does return in glory, Scripture reveals that the kings of this earth will bow to him. They will not have any false sense of security. He will war against them and shatter them. The combined militaries of this world will be like green plastic toy army soldiers to him. He will dash them to pieces like pottery, consuming them with flaming fire, destroying them with blasts of fury from his spoken word (Ps 2:9; 2 Thess 1:8; 2:8; Heb 12:29; Rev 17:14).

Sixth-century BC Chinese philosopher and founder of Taoism, Lao Tzu, famously said, "There is no greater danger than underestimating your opponent." Those who oppose Christ make this most dangerous mistake. Rejecting Christ is not a matter of religious or philosophical choice. It is an issue of underestimating who he is as the divine Son and what he will do upon his return to be established as King of kings.

Wrong Estimation Receives Proportional Vengeance
JUDGES 8:13-21

The Christian Standard Bible indicates Gideon "returned from the battle by the Ascent of Heres" (v. 13). Although the CSB translation does not reflect the ascent of the route "east of Nobah and Jogbehah" in 8:11, one still discerns the typological ascent-descent motif with the descent down the "Ascent of Heres." Upon his descent to Succoth, now with Zebah and Zalmunna in his hands, he captures a young man of Succoth and interrogates him so that he might not underestimate the number of persons he will judge; he will have an accurate count—an accurate assessment—unlike his enemies.

Appearing as the victorious warrior, he brings the words of his detractors back on their heads. I imagine the leaders of Succoth are shocked at the success of Gideon's three hundred over Zebah and Zalmunna's fifteen thousand. Whether their underestimation was reasonable (based on the sizes of the armies) is of no consequence: they receive the promised discipline for refusing to help Gideon en route to victory, underestimating his power to defeat the kings.[28] The judgment goes to the elders, which seems to make the judgment proportionate to the crime. The men who spoke previously seem to have been the elders of the city. They now receive the penalty due their impertinence. Worse is the judgment for Penuel, maybe reflective of a more forceful rejection of Gideon. Their tower is leveled as promised, but the men of their town meet death rather than only the ripping of

---

[28] Andrew Bowling suggests that the discipline meant they were flogged with briars and thorns—a punishment that certainly would have fulfilled the promised tearing of their skin ("Judges," 167). Daniel Block similarly says that Gideon employed switches for punishment (*Judges, Ruth*, 293).

their skin and the life of shame to follow. Underestimating Gideon cost them their lives.[29]

Now that he has given proof of his capture of Zebah and Zalmunna to Succoth, Gideon can commence with the judgment of these Midianite enemies. His question "What kind of men did you kill at Tabor?" allows the kings to answer with words that reveal they knew the greatness of their victims; they knew they were killing royalty when they saw these men—men like Gideon himself. What they did not know fully is that they were killing Gideon's own relatives. For not sparing the brothers of Gideon, they will receive an appropriate judgment.

Gideon, however, will overestimate the strength of his son to kill the kings. Zebah and Zalmmuna's taunting reply will set up a scenario in which Gideon must not rely on a child to do what it takes the strength of a man to do. The two kings now have an accurate estimation of Gideon's power, but it is too late for them to benefit from it. Gideon puts to death the two kings and then takes small spoils in comparison to the number of brothers whose death he avenged.

In terms of typology, our backwards-looking perspective from the NT sees the writer of Judges pointing toward Jesus's return as victorious King. Just as Gideon accomplishes an initial victory, ascends to bring about complete victory, descends as victorious son of a king, and then metes out his enemies' judgment proportionate to their words against him, so will Jesus—victorious on the cross, ascended to glorious rule, returning to be crowned Lord of lords—*bring judgment in death proportionate to his enemies' words against him.* Just as Gideon did not leave judgment of the kings to the hand of his child, so Jesus will not leave the judgment of the nations' hostilities against his will to the judging hands of his children.

In the NT, several dimensions of future judgment are manifest. Believers will judge the world and the angels, but the angels will unleash judgment against the earth for the Son of God (Matt 13:39,49-50; 16:27; 24:31; 1 Cor 6:2-3). All judgment belongs to the Son of God, but the parable of the tenants warns us that the vineyard owner will destroy the faithless stewards who killed the landowner's son (Mark 12:9; John 5:22).

---

[29] Gideon's actions against men from Israel seem unreasonable—something that should be reserved for the nations; he is doing what is right in his own eyes. However, the writer is showing that by underestimating him the men receive judgment that normally would be reserved for an enemy nation.

The Father will make Jesus's enemies a footstool on which Jesus can rest his feet (Heb 10:13; see also Eph 1:22 and Heb 2:8).

All believers will stand and give an account of our works to Christ, yet all persons will give an account of their lives to God (Rom 14:10-12; 2 Cor 5:10; Heb 4:13; 13:17; 1 Pet 4:5; Jude 15; Rev 1:7). While Christ will allow the church to shine by the authority granted to her in Christ, it will not make us Christ. The Son of God and the Father will be the final arbiters of judgment for all crimes committed against them. They will dole out what their enemies deserve.

Final Estimation Glorifies the Father and Rewards the Undeserving
JUDGES 8:22-35

This episode will end on two rather precarious and sad notes. Gideon's request for a portion of the spoil after his victory gives the rule of Jabesh to the Lord and subdues Midian. But that same request results in ensnaring the people in whoredom over his ephod, even as the land finds forty years of rest. Gideon is going to make a right estimation of himself before God and understand that the Lord is the one who rules over his people.[30] This seems to stand in contrast to the relativism the Judges writer notes when Israel is without a king.

Gideon ascribes rule to the Lord. Nevertheless, the request for the people's earrings underestimates both how the people will judge the rulership of the Lord and the victory of Gideon and how easily the people can become ensnared by idolatry. As they worship Gideon's ephod, the people are attributing victory to the medium of Gideon's words rather than to the prophetic words of victory and the Lord himself. Living among the nations rather than destroying them contributes to their belief that the victory over Midian is not the direct result of the intervention of the Lord alone. The land has rest from attacks from Midian and war for two full generations. Yet in that same period they have no rest from idolatry because the victorious warrior underestimates the power of sin in the lives of the people.

---

[30] Gideon will not be perfect or consistent in his estimation, for he will name his son "My Father Is King." Nevertheless, he will ascribe rule to the Lord in the story below.

In the second postlude to Gideon's leadership, the events surrounding Gideon's good-old-age death yields a particular son—Abimelech—among the seventy sons born to him. Within these same events one witnesses Israel's lack of faithfulness both to God and to the house of Gideon for Gideon's doing good on Israel's behalf.

Rightly, Gideon lives in his own home as an ordinary servant who was used of the Lord. He does not assume the role of leader but lets the Lord lead the people through Gideon's presence as a judge. Wrongly doing what is right in his own eyes, Gideon takes many wives and has sons by them, and he also has a son by a concubine. One could see how the people could remain ensnared in sin by having leaders with the relative morality of Gideon. Rightly, however, the people still have him buried honorably.

Wrongly, the people immediately commence in evil upon the death of this judge as they did upon the deaths of all the judges in this book. They will worship the Canaanite gods of Baal. They will not worship the Lord who provided their victories. Being without love for God, they will show no love toward the household of the one who defeated Midian in war. The memory of the good he did for Israel is short-lived.

The aftermath of Jesus's final victory over his enemies will stand in stark contrast to the final victory of Gideon. The typology of the story manifests itself in a negative example that allows one to see what is true about Christ. Like Gideon, Jesus will yield the final rule of God's people to God the Father. Paul writes in 1 Corinthians 15,

> *Then comes the end, when he hands over the kingdom to God the Father, when he abolishes all rule and all authority and power. For he must reign until he puts all his enemies under his feet. The last enemy to be abolished is death. For God has put everything under his feet. Now when it says "everything" is put under him, it is obvious that he who puts everything under him is the exception. When everything is subject to Christ, then the Son himself will also be subject to the one who subjected everything to him, so that God may be all in all.* (1 Cor 15:24-28)

Jesus will be honored as King and Lord of all. Yet he is the Son of God the Father. He lives to bring glory to the Father (see John 17:2,4).[31] He will acknowledge the final rule of the Father.

---

[31] The Father is the one who gives authority to the Son to do his works (John 5:19,20,22,26,27,30).

While doing so, Jesus will not need to receive spoils from his own; he will give to his own, and his gifts will lead to greater worship of the Father rather than any hint of worship of any idol of man.

Jesus will have one bride, not seventy, and certainly no concubine. Jesus will not have a son, for he is the Son, and we are sons in him. Jesus's people—Israel in particular, his biological family—have been forgotten throughout history and have forgotten their God (except the many thousands of Messianic Jews who are a present, faithful remnant of Israel). Part of the grace of God in Christ toward us is that Jesus's reward will go to people who are not always faithful to him.

Reflect and Discuss

1. Define *typology* and give an analogy that will explain how typological stories function.
2. What causes Ephraim's consternation? What seems to justify their dispute with Gideon?
3. What is the importance to this story of having a right account of history?
4. Based on Gideon's responses to the Ephraimites throughout the story, how does he view his role in Israel's victories? How should this inform how we view the role of our spiritual leaders in our churches?
5. How do the Midianites underestimate Gideon in this story? What do they miss or lose by their underestimations?
6. In practical terms, where have you underestimated the power of Christ to secure a needed blessing for you? What was the result?
7. Why are we tempted to doubt a God who already has shown himself victorious in times too numerous to count?
8. What would have been the right way for Israel to respond to the Lord for the victories achieved through Gideon?
9. Why did Gideon make an ephod? What might he have been thinking? When have you made a similar mistake that might have misled others into sin, even if you did so unknowingly?
10. What would have been a right way for Israel to have responded to Gideon's family?

Promoting Character-Qualified Leadership

JUDGES 9

Main Idea: We must pick leaders based on character and not on close relationships in order to avoid reaping destruction on the leader and the church.

I.   **Revisit Credentials When You See Reckless Actions (9:1-6).**
    A.   Request to family to rule (9:1-3)
    B.   Reckless slaughter of rivals (9:4-5c)
    C.   Escape of the youngest brother (9:5d)
    D.   Exaltation without recompense (9:6)

II. **Listen to Integrity Challenges Even from Young Voices (9:7-21).**
    A.   Exhortation to listen (9:7)
    B.   Fable of the bramble (9:8-15)
    C.   Evaluation of integrity (9:16-20)
    D.   Flight to Beer (9:21)

III. **Weigh Evil Consequences over Prolonged Tenure (9:22-25).**

IV. **See Through Boastful Claims to Actual Conquests (9:26-41).**
    A.   Shechem's affirmation of Gaal (9:26-27)
    B.   Zebul's anger with Gaal (9:30-34)
    C.   Abimelech's ambushing of Gaal (9:35-41)

V.   **Prevent Victories from Becoming Vulnerabilities, Even Where God Is Vindicating (9:42-57).**
    A.   Advantage and victory in the field (9:42-45)
    B.   Advantage and victory at the Tower of Shechem (9:46-49)
    C.   Advantage but defeat at the Tower of Thebez (9:50-57)

In November 1960, John F. Kennedy won election to become the President of the United States. When he named his potential cabinet appointees, among them was a familiar name: he nominated his brother Robert F. Kennedy as attorney general.

Modern sensibilities might recoil immediately at the thought of having one's brother in such a high-ranking position: "Isn't that nepotism?" "Doesn't even the US military prohibit one's relative from being in one's chain of command?" "What if there were a need for one of them to point out an unwise, erroneous, or unethical decision by the other; could the AG prosecute his brother, and could the president fire his brother AG?" An even more significant suspicion for us today would be, "Did he pick him just on the basis of a familial relationship?" On both the right and left sides of the political aisle, the American public has had misgivings with family members having too great roles in the administration of a president. We have seen troubles from Travelgate to probes into suspected Russian collusion.[32]

But Bobby Kennedy was not the little brother exalted with only his blood relationship as the basis of selection. Prior to becoming AG, Robert Kennedy graduated from Harvard University and University of Virginia School of Law after having served in the US Navy. He served as a lawyer for the Department of Justice and chief counsel of the committee that investigated the trade union led by Jimmy Hoffa. He was recognized for having a good legal mind and the backbone to tackle tough justice issues. Rather than being given a brotherly gift, Robert Kennedy demonstrated the selection was a valid one by meeting the qualifications for the role to which he was appointed. The key roles Robert Kennedy played in the Civil Rights legislation of the 1960s gave witness to his qualification.

Like the caution we feel when a president places a near relative in a high place in the administration, churches should exercise caution when promoting leaders based on familial relationships. While one's brother, sister, father, mother, son, or daughter might be eager to fill a role, and promoting such a person could assume a good leader's leadership portfolio is transferable via blood or marriage, Scripture demands that we consider much more in choosing a leader of God's people. Scripture demands more because the picking of any unqualified leader has detrimental ramifications for both the leader and God's people. It therefore is God who calls us to promote character-qualified

---

[32] "Travelgate" refers to a 1993 scandal involving the firing of career White House travel office personnel in which Hillary Clinton, wife of then President Bill Clinton, came to the fore as a key person in the firings. See Heidi M. Przybyla, "Clinton Controversies: A Brief History," *USA Today*, September 6, 2016, https://www.usatoday.com/story/news/politics/onpolitics/2016/09/06/clinton-controversies-brief-history/89652638, accessed December 7, 2020. On the potential for President Donald Trump's son being charged for a crime related to Russian interference in the 2016 election, see Maggie Haberman and Michael S. Schmidt, "Trump Has Discussed with Advisors Pardons for His 3 Eldest Children and Giuliani," *New York Times*, December 1, 2020, https://www.nytimescom/2020/12/01/us/politics/rudy-giuliani-pardon.html, accessed December 7, 2020.

leadership. Here are the means by which that is accomplished and the consequences that such qualification intends to avoid.

Revisit Credentials When You See Reckless Actions
JUDGES 9:1-6

Request to Family to Rule (9:1-3)

After the death of Gideon—who also went by "Jerubbaal"—Gideon's son Abimelech tries to weasel his way into becoming king. He has seventy brothers who could rival him for king, but he will go quickly to his widowed mother's relatives and use them to accomplish his agenda. Positioning himself as the heir apparent, maybe even drawing the sympathy vote in the aftermath of the death of his father, he uses the ancient equivalent of the saying, "Blood is thicker than water," to have the family campaign for him all over Shechem.

Reckless Slaughter of Rivals (9:4-5c)

Looking only at the biological relationship, the relatives promote Abimelech among the leadership of Shechem, and the relatives embrace the support of one of their own. Being Baal worshipers, they draw money from one of the temples dedicated to and memorializing a covenant they made with Baal, and they give the money to Abimelech for him to do as he pleases. Seemingly, Baal will approve of his money going for both the hiring of rabble-rousers who have even less scruples than Abimelech and for the cold-blooded slaughter of his seventy brothers. Quite gruesome is the picture of the new-to-ruling Abimelech, dragging in one brother after another, heartlessly ignoring the bloodied stone before him and any screams from his brothers, and slaughtering each one like a sacrificial beast to the false god. In contrast to a contrite leader, who might have thought to offer a sacrifice for his own sins before the God of Israel, Abimelech announces his rule with fearful callousness of epic proportions.

Escape of the Youngest Brother (9:5d)

During the horrific turn of events in Shechem and Jerubbaal's house, one still sees the invisible hand of the Almighty at work. The youngest of Abimelech's brothers remains alive, having hidden himself in the chaos of the fratricide. In his killing spree, Abimelech probably is too frenzied to notice that his count of murdered rivals is off by one person. The escape of Jotham reveals greater carelessness by Abimelech—a carelessness the Lord will use to accomplish his good purposes.

Exaltation without Recompense (9:6)

Consistent with Israel's behavior throughout the book of Judges, the people of Shechem ignore completely the moral decadence of Abimelech's rise to leadership. Whereas they should hold him accountable for complete indifference toward the Lord's commandment and stipulations against murder, they ignore the character of the one they elect to rule, thereby becoming complicit in each one of the unjust deaths. The slaughter of the brothers should have been the impetus for a recall and removal from office. Instead, the leaders of Shechem carry the blood of Abimelech's brothers on their hands.

It takes great courage for an organization to admit to a mistake when significant character flaws surface in a newly selected leader. It takes even greater courage to act graciously but expeditiously to remove such a leader.

From the outside, I once witnessed a church acknowledge two moral failures in the life of a new leader. Instead of pursuing the kind but swift removal of the leader, they retained the leader even after the second failing became publicly known.

I also witnessed a Christian organization admit to making an error in selecting a leader because of the leader's swift change of the vision of the organization. The organization acted to remove the leader—even though there was not a moral failure—and issued a public statement explaining their decision.

In revisiting both institutions' decisions toward the tenure of their leaders, it seems that the difference between the actions rested on the leaders' willingness to humbly admit failure on their part. Rather than trying to save the faces of those who recruited, vetted, and approved the chosen leader, they looked at the danger of keeping the flawed leader and let the threat of harm to the organization outweigh the insults they would receive for forcing their institution to go through another selection process. In the years to follow, the actions of the leader who should also have been deposed have proven the error of the first institution and the wisdom of the second. Shechem should have revisited the credentials once they saw the reckless actions.

Listen to Integrity Challenges Even from Young Voices
JUDGES 9:7-21

The escaped Jotham will call attention to the evil of Abimelech even though Shechem's leaders have not. Jotham's cry to the leaders of Shechem from the top of Mount Gerizim challenges all the citizens of Shechem to evaluate whether their reception of Abimelech is in good faith or will lead to their obliteration.

Exhortation to Listen (9:7)

Calling from Mount Gerizim provides Jotham both the venue for all to hear and a place of safety for further escape. One can imagine this young voice challenging those who were older and approving of Abimelech, and the people at first take to smiling at the young man standing so high above them. But his choice of heights combined with "and may God listen to you" gives his exhortation a tone of seriousness that demands the attention of the citizens.

Fable of the Bramble (9:8-15)

Jotham provides a parable to manifest the failure of the leaders of Shechem to be discerning about their endorsement of one who has revealed himself to be a monstrous figure. In the parable, the trees have a regent vacancy. To fill the vacancy, they first go to the best of trees to court them to come rule all the trees. But neither the olive nor fig trees are willing to leave their positions of honor, success, and prosperity to assume reign of the trees. They see leaving their positions as demotions.

Leaving the best trees, they go to the vine. Like the best trees, the vine's product pleases both the divine and the human, and the vine yields great fruit from his work. Therefore, the vine also rejects the offer to rule, since it would be a demotion.

Having exhausted their exceptional candidates, the trees go to the bramble. Unlike the outstanding tree and vine candidates, the bramble comes with no portfolio of pleasing anyone in the heavens or on the earth. He has no beneficial fruit to offer as a representation of what the trees might experience under his rule. There is no conversation of the move to kingship amounting to a demotion.

Instead, the bramble, recognizing the incredible condescension on the part of the trees, elicits a good-faith agreement with the trees. The offer to make a wild shrub king over the taller and leaf-bearing trees is so unusual, the bramble needs assurance that the offer to follow his rule is genuine. All the bramble can offer is shade, which is not as good as the shade trees can offer because the shrub is so close to the ground. Therefore, the bramble concludes he will give his shade for a genuine proposal, but he offers a curse if the offer is not genuine: *the bramble will bring fire to destroy the majestic cedars of Lebanon.*

Evaluation of Integrity (9:16-20)

True to the genre of *parable,* the story intends to point to the historical realities surrounding the audience. In the words of the bramble to the trees, Jotham invites Shechem to evaluate "if [they] have acted faithfully and honestly" both in the exaltation of Abimelech to kingship and in their response to the slaughter of the sons of Jerubbaal. The evaluation needs to be comprehensive, comparing the works of Jerubbaal to rescue Shechem with Abimelech's killing of Jerubbaal's sons, his bramble-like status as the offspring of a slave, and the "because he is [our] brother" election platform. If they find they have done right, there should be rejoicing in their election of Abimelech. However, if they evaluate and find that they have done wrong, like the bramble, Jotham offers a curse: *may Abimelech and the citizens of the two territories each devour the other with fire.* That is, may they destroy each other—Abimelech because of the slaughter and the citizens for failure to hold the ruler accountable for his crime.

    Implicit in Jotham's exhortation is an accusation of a lack of discernment on the part of the people of Shechem and Beth-millo. They cannot see that they have resigned themselves to the poorest possible choice for leadership. Like the bramble bush, Abimelech can offer nothing of value that makes him worthy of being established as ruler. They are signing their own destruction by their inaction toward his injustices.

Flight to Beer (9:21)

After challenging the people to rethink their choice of ruler and to remove him, it is not wise for Jotham to wait for their response. Quickly, he flees to Beer to escape Abimelech, who has shown himself eager to rid the world of any competition to his rule from a relative.

    Of course, Jotham is right on all counts. Abimelech lacks the character to lead, the people of Shechem and Beth-millo have acted in foolishness, the citizens should evaluate their actions, they have not properly rewarded the house of Jerubbaal for his leadership on their behalf, and if they do not act, they face certain destruction through Abimelech. But Jotham is younger than Abimelech, his mother's relatives, and Abimelech's peers. It would be easy to dismiss his voice as jealous words coming from a cowardly brother using Mount Gerizim to exalt himself rather than standing to take on Abimelech and/ or the citizens of Shechem. Being younger puts Jotham at a natural disadvantage.

The writer of Judges is making an important point for us: *this younger brother can see what those older than he do not see—at least in this one instance.* While we associate wisdom with the aged and immaturity with the young, such associations are not absolute. A younger person can act with wisdom greater than older persons, and some older persons are immature and undiscerning when it comes to matters of righteousness and godliness. Making an evaluation of Jotham's words based on his age relative to Abimelech's would be just as superficial as exalting Abimelech solely on the basis of bloodline.

Sometimes young people—because they lack the guile and power-thirsty motives of older adults—are better detectors of bad character than adults. What we are willing to dismiss en route to accomplishing agendas, they are willing to highlight because we have taught them to distinguish between right and wrong. They are willing to say they heard a leader use sub-Christian language, make inappropriate gestures, participate in questionable activities, and exit from places Christian leaders should not have been found. Yes, we must be careful if they make accusations, just as we would exercise caution if an adult made an accusation against someone's character. But we must not write off their concerns about questionable leadership simply because they are young.

Weigh Evil Consequences over Prolonged Tenure
JUDGES 9:22-25

Three years pass under the rule of Abimelech. In the third year, the Lord acts to bring about the cursing of which he spoke through Jotham. As one "most holy, most wise, most free, most absolute [who is] working all things according to the counsel of His own immutable and most righteous will, for His own glory" (*1689 Confession*) and as one "infinite, eternal, and unchangeable in His being, wisdom, power, holiness, justice, goodness and truth" (Keach, *1677 Baptist Catechism*), the Lord determines to use evil to accomplish his purposes. The eternally good God, who cannot look on evil or tempt others with evil, can and does use evil spiritual forces to accomplish his purposes in judgment.

The treacherous dealings of the men of Shechem with Abimelech—due to the evil spirit God sent between them—brings recompense to Abimelech and the leaders of Shechem. Abimelech must face cosmic justice for the slaughter of his seventy brothers. The leaders must face the Judge for their complicity in strengthening Abimelech to kill by giving him rule over his brothers and all Shechem. The Lord uses the evil spirit to spur evil men to be in conflict with one another and to lead them toward the judgment due their evil ways.

During Abimelech's time in office, there is no safety for people traveling to and from Shechem. The absence of safety due to the thievery of the men of Shechem reflects on the rule of Abimelech. The proliferation of evil reveals more weaknesses in his leadership ability and greater character flaws as he hears of the men's dealings and seemingly does nothing. The text is silent about Abimelech's doing anything to confront evil under his rule because, being both unqualified to lead and evil himself, he cannot respond to the evil of others. Characterization of his rule as evil should indicate to the people of Shechem that the time for the end of this rule has come.

Providentially, the Lord creates an evil signpost to point to the source of evil among a people. Little odd items, like people being robbed on the mountaintops at will, should cause the people to ask, "What is happening among us? Why isn't the king doing anything about the evil in his kingdom?"

See Through Boastful Claims to Actual Conquests
JUDGES 9:26-41

Shechem's Affirmation of Gaal (9:26-27)

While the men of Shechem are playing sport with the possessions of travelers through Shechem, Gaal manages to appear on the scene with his relatives with no place of origin mentioned. Still having no thought of making judgment of character, and being at odds with Abimelech, the people of Shechem take the confidence once directed toward Abimelech and now direct it toward this stranger. With a festival to their god, they celebrate Gaal and revile the rule of Abimelech, their king.

During the celebration, Gaal makes a verbal challenge to Abimelech's rule. He fills the challenge with phraseology of identity, contrasting and comparing lineage and associations: *Abimelech the son of Jerubbaal versus Hamor the father of the progenitor of the people of Shechem; Zebul—who must not be from Shechem—being a close associate of Abimelech*. Gaal uses the same strategy Abimelech used to come to power, offering the people one of their own to lead them. With boastful words, Gaal offers the removal of the king they have come to hate and challenges Abimelech to bring his army to fight for the right to the throne.

Zebul's Anger with Gaal (9:30-34)

Zebul, who seems to have vice-rule of Shechem under King Abimelech, becomes angered by the words of Gaal. He sends messengers to bait Abimelech to lay an ambush for Gaal secretly. Zebul's strategy is evident: *send a warning with a sense of urgency, and send a plan that offers a path to victory*. Zebul tells Abimelech that he must act tonight and that he can ambush the unsuspecting Gaal with a surprise attack. Certainly not wanting to lose his rule or his life, Abimelech stations four companies of troops to attack Gaal in the morning. The stage is set to see whether Gaal has the might to back his words of challenge.

Abimelech's Ambushing of Gaal (9:35-41)

Somehow Gaal and Zebul wind up in the gate of the city together in the morning. When Gaal comes to the gate, his presence must be the appointed sign or opportune time for Abimelech's men to attack. With the attack commencing, Zebul speaks deceptive words to make Gaal mistake the ambush for shadows of the mountains. That delay in time to prepare for battle should not make a difference if Gaal really has the ability to overcome Abimelech. With sarcasm, the vengeful Zebul scoffs at the boasting of Gaal as he finally affirms the reality of an attack against Gaal.

Gaal does engage Abimelech with fighting men from among the people of Shechem. With many casualties in his wake, Gaal flees the pursing Abimelech. But Zebul drives the weakened clan of Gaal out of Shechem—the way the people of Shechem should have driven out Abimelech. The fighting and loss show Gaal's challenge to have been empty words of boasting from a man who might have had too much wine at his own festival. He could not do that of which he boasted. The

people—many now dead—did not have evidence that he had the qualifications to lead.

Many of us can think of professional sports personalities who
boasted of their strength before a formidable foe. One thinks of all
Muhammad Ali's trash talk, Gary Payton's boast of his ability to check
Michael Jordan, or Adrian Peterson saying that he is the Michael Jordan
of football. Boasting like that is just a tactic to psych out an opponent or
a means of boosting one's self-confidence. There is a difference, however, when an Ali taunts an opponent by saying, "He's too ugly to be
world champion," and the boasting of the likes of Payton and Peterson:
Ali always proved that he had within him the might he claimed with his words.

When looking for leaders of God's people, what a person claims
about his or her own ability is not enough to make a person a leader.
Leading God's people is, in fact, leading people who are at war—at war
with supernatural enemy forces for the establishment of God's rule on
the earth. Those who lead must be able to bring about victories for God's
people in the work of the ministry. Their track records should have evidence of leading God's people successfully. They should be more than
people of mere talk.

Prevent Victories from Becoming Vulnerabilities, Even Where God Is Vindicating
JUDGES 9:42-57

In these final three scenes, Abimelech will attempt to take advantage of
people's vulnerable positions in order to gain victories over them. He
still seems to be going after those from Shechem who supported Gaal
in the attempt to overthrow his rule. He finally shows real leadership
abilities, although it is only motivated by a threat to his own rule and
life rather than being fueled by a love of God or his people. He does
not seek a rule of righteousness but only leads where he can murder
the opposition, consistent with the character he has displayed since his
ascent to the throne.

Advantage and Victory in the Field (9:42-45)

When Abimelech hears the people are outside the city walls, he divides
his people into three companies, reminiscent of the four-unit attack on
Gaal. Shechem's position in the field leaves them vulnerable, offering a

great chance for victory for Abimelech. Abimelech fights a full day and conquers the people of Shechem. In order to put an exclamation point on his win, he sows the city with salt in order to place a curse on it.[33]

Advantage and Victory at the Tower of Shechem (9:46-49)

Abimelech then hears of the gathering of the leaders of the Tower of Shechem in one place. This tower is dedicated to the god "El," a common generic name for a Canaanite deity, often interchangeable for "Baal." The people look to El to save them from Abimelech.

Abimelech again seeks to take advantage of people who are vulnerable because they only have one means of escape from a tower. Abimelech calls the people following him to Mount Zalmon to imitate his example with haste to burn down the stronghold, bringing the deaths of a thousand people. He thus gains a second actual victory, including what would be perceived to be a victory over El.

Advantage but Defeat at the Tower of Thebez (9:50-57)

Abimelech then attempts to capture Thebez fully by drawing near the tower to burn it with fire. Seemingly following the means of success at the Tower of Shechem, Abimelech uses the same method to attack those making themselves vulnerable in another tower.

However, Abimelech's two huge victories leave him vulnerable to death by a woman's millstone. What therefore appeared to be paths to certain victories left Abimelech himself vulnerable to defeat. Not wanting the dishonor of being defeated by a woman, he has his armor-bearer deal the coup de grâce.[34] In truth, though, he was stopped in his tracks by a woman when he did not discern his vulnerability before the people of the tower.

---

[33] Trent Butler suggests that sowing salt is an act of cursing: "He blatantly shows his enmity toward the city by sowing salt on it" (*Judges*, 248). Butler references F. C. Fensham, "Salt as Curse in the Old Testament and the Ancient Near East," *BA* 25 (1962) 48–50. Daniel Block also writes, "Since salt renders a land infertile, by spreading salt on a city a conqueror may have sought to guarantee that it would never rise again. But more likely is the suggestion that this was a ritual act invoking an irrevocable curse on the site" (*Judges, Ruth*, 330).

[34] The dishonor of a defeat of a male warrior by a woman was visited earlier in the story of Deborah and Barak (4:6-9; 5:24-27).

Abimelech's defeat yields two results in the story, such that fighting ceases and the Lord provides recompense. First, the followers of Abimelech stop fighting when they see he has died. Apparently, they were only fighting Abimelech's war, not one they saw as necessary for survival. Abimelech's war was an attempt to cleanse away his enemies, not a battle to maintain the lives of anyone in Shechem. Therefore, when he dies, his personal agenda dies with him.

Second, the Lord brings recompense to both Abimelech and the people of Shechem according to the curse uttered by Jotham. Fire certainly comes out from Abimelech, both figuratively and literally. Figuratively, he is responsible for the robberies and deaths of many in Shechem (9:25,40,43-45). Literally, Abimelech's killings included those he burned with fire (9:49).

Similarly, the people of Shechem devour Abimelech with fire, figuratively. His people are attacked and robbed, he meets a challenge from Gaal that will force him to live at Arumah, and he dies a dishonorable death at the hands of a woman. The Lord accomplishes justice for the deaths of the seventy brothers against both Abimelech and his passive accomplices—the people of Shechem. But the sovereign working of God is not cause to ignore the flaws in character and judgment that leave a leader like Abimelech open to defeat.

Application

In a society in which professions often are passed from fathers to sons, occasionally one meets a pastor who positions his son to succeed him. If the church adores its pastor and/or judges him to be successful at leading, the granting of the pastorate to a son can come without challenge, especially if the son proceeds to get formal biblical and theological training and shows himself to be a decent communicator.

However, the success of a father does not guarantee the success of a son. Neither does the success of a mother guarantee the success of a daughter. Because one's father was a faithful deacon does not mean the offspring will be a faithful deacon, minister, teacher, musician, administrator, team leader, project manager, trustee, steward, banker, or business owner. Each person's qualifications need careful examination.

Yet those examining must use discernment and humility, for even qualified leaders face spiritual warfare that can appear to be disasters. Wise persons among us must distinguish between the warfare defeats by qualified leaders who faced intense spiritual conflict and exercised wisdom as opposed to those who had a string of defeats because their character left them vulnerable to disasters.

Judges 9 intends for the reader to understand that an implication of the gospel is that it matters to the Lord that people of God-fearing character lead his people. While one might think this is obvious and goes without saying, the practice of many to give little examination to future leadership in the body of Christ belies this notion.

A church absent of a pastor for a few years will pressure a search committee to expedite its search and be less picky about its candidates. A church needing a music director will complain about the delay in putting forth a candidate as it perceives the liveliness of its corporate worship services waning. The complaints intend to press the pastor, elders, and/or search committee into hiring whatever candidate seems to provide great musical leadership, even if this means shortening the process of doing proper background checks. Such truncated examinations give rise to Abimelechs in congregations. Jesus died and rose again for a church he is beautifying with his love and presence. His body—his bride—needs leaders whose character is consistent with Jesus's goal for his people. It needs leadership that is seeking to take on the character of Christ, being willing to suffer for the people for their joy and good and for the glory of God the Father.

Reflect and Discuss

1. Based on your reading of Judges 9, why might term limits be good in churches for nonvocational leaders like elders, deacons, and trustees?

2. Do you have the courage to speak lovingly, graciously, and courageously with a leader privately about flaws in his/her character for the sake of the good of the local assembly and the leader himself/ herself? What will it take for you to become a person of Christian courage?

3. When have you experienced a search committee or hiring committee failing to do its due diligence on a candidate, and what was the outcome?

4. In a local congregation, how do we keep from simply putting forward the most likable people, or people we think will accomplish

our agendas to remain conservative, keep from supporting certain initiatives, and keep the pastor in check to do what we wish?

5. Based on the people's initial responses to Abimelech, why is it important for church members to understand the meaning of the gospel and its implications for leadership?

6. How can you participate in your congregation's intentional development of the *character* of pre-leaders, not just *skills* to organize, cast vision, and rule?

7. If you had been a leader in Beth-millo, what steps could you have taken to reverse the course of action once the seventy brothers had been slaughtered?

8. How do you view the voices of younger believers on matters of ministry and policy in your church?

9. What is the point of the parable of the bramble?

10. How is the "fire" of the parable of the bramble fulfilled in this story?

Hope for a Deteriorating Society

JUDGES 10

Main Idea: Israel's deterioration into rampant idolatry and slavery to Ammon finds hope in their repentance and their recognition of the absence of a deliverer among them.

I.   **They Slid Away from the Savior (10:1-5).**
II. **They Provoked the Lord to Anger (10:6-9).**
III. **They Repented from Forsaking Their Deliverer (10:10-16).**
IV. **They Looked Outside of Themselves for a Warrior (10:17-18).**

In Judges 10, we are heading south dreadfully. Israel has done more than falling off the horse. We will witness the beginning of the wholesale deterioration of society. Consider verse 6:

> Then the Israelites again did what was evil in the sight of the LORD. They worshiped the Baals and the Ashtoreths, the gods of Aram, Sidon, and Moab, and the gods of the Ammonites and the Philistines. They abandoned the LORD and did not worship him.

Israel goes downward from the Lord, crashing all vestiges of a holy and righteous society before the Lord with their actions. One has to wonder if there is any hope for this deteriorating society.

How in the world did Israel come to this place? Let's retrace their steps in Judges 10 to see how we can find hope amid the deterioration that happened in ancient Israel and is happening within our own contemporary culture.

They Slid Away from the Savior
JUDGES 10:1-5

The chapter starts off well enough. Tola and Jair arise in sequence after Abimelech and provide twenty-three and twenty-two years of successive peace, respectively. That's a total of forty-five years of peace. Even the expected relapse after the death of Tola is absent from the story.

Seemingly, forty-five years of following the Lord is not enough prosperity, peace, freedom, and joy for Israel to commit themselves to another forty-five years of obedience. Instead, they run after many gods instead of the Lord. That fact alone reveals that some things were defective in Israel.

First, *no one is removing the Canaanites through the* cherem *principle*—the command to destroy completely the nations and their gods so that they do not become snares to Israel (Exod 22:20; Deut 7:1-7; 20:17). They really could have used some courageous members within their assembly to draw sharp lines between right and wrong.

Second, *no one is following the Shema*—the call to hear the law of the Lord and teach their children to follow it (Deut 6:4-9). The generations of the Israelites after the generation that received Deuteronomy have not learned to follow the Lord who delivered them from Egypt, neither have they embraced the first two commandments, nor have they learned from the Pentateuch's record of the history of Israel's successes and failures.

Third, *the priesthood must be corrupt or nonfunctioning.* The priests do not intercede to call for daily sin offerings and the annual Day of Atonement—rites within the law that would have revealed Israel's idolatry as sin. Neither are they reminding the people of the entirety of the law (Deut 31:9-13). Israel would have done well to have spiritual leaders who could guide their spiritual health.

So Jair of Gilead dies, and the people of Israel return to doing what is right in each individual's eyes. Relativism is the rule of the day.

They Provoked the Lord to Anger
JUDGES 10:6-9

This list of false gods to which Israel turned for hope, life, peace, comfort, healing, and safety is long. Although only Baal and the Ashtoreths are named, the plurality of gods served from each nation indicates that a minimum of twelve false gods was in play, each vying for a place at the table of worship. Although the Lord delivers Israel from oppression in each region of Israel and the promised land, time and again they return to idols, in effect taking the Lord's faithfulness for granted.

We cannot fathom what it means to God for us to forsake him for other lovers. In Scripture, to commit idolatry is to commit adultery against our heavenly Lover (Jer 3:1-14,20; 5:7; Ezek 23:36-37; Hos 2:2-13;

9:1)! As one of my former professors was known for saying, "Every sin tortures God." His statement does not mean the immutable and impassible God is affected in his character by something external. Instead, it means that sin deeply offends and affronts the Holy God.

Here is God, faithful to us before we take life's first breath and then past death throughout all eternity. He drops plagues on Egypt, passes over Israel's sins, provides manna from heaven for food and water from rock for drink, routs kings and many armies en route to and in the land of Canaan, and then repeatedly acts in mercy toward Israel's cries in spite of the challenges to Moses, the failure of the spies, and their ongoing return to idolatry. Now Israel turns to other gods in trust, giving the credit and honor to them that is due to the Lord, when God never once has wronged them or let them down.

If I were the Lord, I would be more than a little hurt by my wife or my child acting this way.[35] The rebellion of our children pains us who are rebellious children of God ourselves. Adultery of a spouse pains us even more than having rebellious children, even though we have not been completely faithful to God; we are adulterous before him. Therefore, rebellious adultery before a perfect Spouse and Parent must cause a depth of pain, anguish, and rejection for which we have no true feelings or words to describe. If one of us were the Lord, Israel might have had to wander around the desert for more than forty years!

So when the text says the anger of the Lord was kindled against Israel, understand why his emotions and righteous character are stirred in this manner. Almost the entirety of Israel comes under the devastating power of Ammonites and Philistines for eighteen years—for the entire length of childhood for one generation (to put it into perspective). Israel was "greatly oppressed," says the final editor of Judges.

It is not so easy for the contemporary pastor to speak of God's people—the church—angering God. It is difficult to keep happy guests coming or to make calls for more giving if you talk about such things too much. Instead, we are allowed to think of ourselves as generally pleasing the Lord at all times. But the book of Judges intends for us to understand that we—God's people—sometimes serve other gods.

---

[35] In Isa 54:5, Israel is the "wife" of the Lord. Many texts carry this idea implicitly, like Isa 50:1, which assumes Israel, the "mother," has a certificate of divorce from the Lord—a certificate given to a wife. See also Jer 3:8; Ezek 16:32-34; Hos 2:2.

In order to glimpse how modern idolatry works, it might be good to consider the visible outcomes of our idolatries, as exemplified in some of the perennial frustrating, questionable, difficult, or disheartening experiences we have as believers when we try so hard to fight against them.

For example, there is *the consistent reality of believers' lack in sharing their faith.* This could be a sign that we have made a god of the fear of people, and it has ensnared us into silence.

Or there is *the concern over marital commitment* to whatever degree, even though marriage is "holy . . . an honorable estate . . . beatified and honored by Christ's presence at the wedding of Cana in Galilee," as we say at Christian weddings. Maybe this reveals that personal happiness, immorality, and bitterness have risen to godlike status.

There also is *the struggle of believers in each generation to release children to answer a calling to ministry immediately after high school.* In every generation the church in America struggles to allow children to go to a Bible college for education, to major in Bible or ministry training, to answer a call to missions, or to accept a call to ministry among the marginalized. "What will you do with such a degree?" we ask. Answer: *Serve the Lord in the hopes of making disciples among 6.5 billion lost people.* We have a shortage of Great Commission workers that is far greater than the shortage of middle-skilled workers, nurses, police officers, and public school teachers. Yet our reticence toward yielding our children for ministry and missions might reveal worship of prosperity and safety. (Do not think I am throwing stones here, for I myself am not trying to line-jump for the ministry assignment to the South Side of Chicago. At the time of the writing of this chapter, I have been in a process of confessing my own fears and wrestling through my own idols before the Lord.)

The god of *unredeemed time wasted in cyberspace* takes away from developing community, meditating on Scripture, and deepening in prayer, and it often adds to pride, arrogance, and conflict in our social media posts. And, of course, there is the obvious *god of pornography* that demeans women, fuels sex trafficking and prostitution both locally and globally, and keeps teens, men, and women bound in sin, guilt, and shame for many years—some even for a lifetime.

The Lord cannot be pleased with these other lovers! We dare not kindle his discipline against us. While we have been saved from eternal wrath by the blood of his Son, as Romans 5:9 says, what of Romans 13:4-5 that says of the government to believers, "Be afraid . . . [he is]

an avenger who carries out God's wrath on the wrongdoer" (ESV), and what of the admonition to holiness in Ephesians 5:6 that tells believers that there are sins from which we should refrain because they bring God's wrath on the [unbelieving] sons of disobedience? In their society's deterioration, Israel provoked God to *anger*.

They Repented from Forsaking Their Deliverer
JUDGES 10:10-16

After eighteen years of total misery, the Lord finally has Israel's attention. In grace, they are awakened to see that the Lord is the answer to their dilemma. So they will turn to him as they have done in the past. Their turning is a turning of *repentance*—away from their sin and idolatry and to the Lord—in three discernable and paradigmatic actions:

First, *they confess their sins*, being specific and truthful about the error of their ways. They say what the narrator has said about them: "We have abandoned our God," which is said in verses 6 and 10. The Lord affirms it in verse 13.

Second, *they humble themselves before God*. The Lord speaks words of judgment to them, recounting both his record of faithfulness and their sins, and then saying he will save them no longer, leaving them in the hands of their false gods that cannot save! Israel, recognizing the now even greater desperation of their oppression, says, "We have sinned. Deal with us as you see fit; only rescue us today!" *God, do whatever! Make us your slaves, strip us of our clothing, smash our houses, bring the drought or disease you promised for our disobedience—whatever seems good to you; we will not object. Just save us!* This is like the cry of a wayward child returning home to say, "Dad, Mom, I am sorry. I have seen the error of my hotheaded, foul-mouthed, selfish, immoral, harmful, and self-destructive ways, and I will get whatever help you say I need to get, and I will obey whatever rules you make. Only please take me back in off the streets, please!"

Third, *they obey*. The obedience demonstrates what has taken place in their hearts and minds. Their confession and words of humility are not lip service. There is a change of heart behind their words. They get rid of their foreign gods and serve the Lord. They do not spout words and maintain the same actions or confess while keeping their idols in a chest behind their house in case they feel a need to grab them again. They "put away" the foreign gods in obedience to the first two commandments. Their confession, humility before God, and obedience demonstrate *repentance.*

God's people as a whole must come to a place of surrender like Israel's. We need confession, humility, and obedience over things— from ungodly forms of church splits, to cover-up of sexual abuse by staff members, to lack of ministry to the needs of seniors on one hand, to feelings of entitlement and the right to be served on the part of seniors on the other. When Israel confesses, humbles herself, and continues in obedience, the Lord's heart, full of mercy, breaks over the wife and child he loves. Beautifully written, verse 16 says he became "weary" or impatient (lit. "his soul was short") over the misery of Israel. It is as if the Lord said, "I can't bear to watch them suffer my wrath any longer!" Our Lord loves us and is merciful in heart toward us.

They Looked Outside of Themselves for a Warrior
JUDGES 10:17-18

Apparently, the Ammonites are not yet ready to let Israel return to serving the Lord rather than the gods of Ammon and the other nations. This, again, is what I mean by "Canaanization" and "cultural war": Ammon does not want Israel to serve the one true God. Serving eleven other gods is fine, but serving the Lord is not. Not to mention, the ethical implications of Israel's repentance means Israel no longer will follow the ways of the nations. That is too much for the Ammonites, and they are willing to go to war with Israel to put them back in their place.

Thus, Israel prepares for war. But there is only one problem: they need someone to lead them to war. So the leaders in Gilead, most recently led by the last judge Jair (v. 4), and most recently oppressed by the Ammonites while living in the land of the Amorites (v. 8), devise a solution: if someone will lead them to fight the Ammonites, that one will become head over all the inhabitants of Gilead.

Just as the book of Judges looks for a *judge* who will bring people to the land and a *king* who will lead the people to do what is right in God's eyes, they now look for a *warrior* who will be the head over God's people.

In God's plan of redemption, Jesus is that divine Warrior who fights for his people. He is stronger than horses and chariots, and he has the forces of nature and angels at his disposal. He calls the shots as the victor in war. He battles the dark forces of this world. He is the head of his church. As William Gurnall writes,

> The strength of the general in other hosts lies in his troops. He flies, as a great commander once said to his soldiers, upon their wings; if their feathers be clipped, their power broken, he is lost; but in the army of saints, the strength of every saint, yea, of the whole host of saints, lies in the Lord of hosts. God can overcome his enemies without their hands, but they cannot so much as defend themselves without his arm. (*The Christian in Complete Armour*)

Close

One of the most memorable scenes from the *Lord of the Rings* trilogy finds the wizard Gandalf standing in the middle of the Bridge of Khazad-dûm, refusing to allow the Balrog, demon of Udûn, to cross the bridge. "You shall not pass!" exclaims Gandalf.

Seeing the scene in the movies is one thing. But reading Tolkein's prose is quite another. Here it is:

> The Balrog reached the bridge. Gandalf stood in the middle of the span, leaning on the staff in his left hand, but in his other hand Glamdring gleamed, cold and white. His enemy halted again, facing him, and the shadow about it reached out like two vast wings. It raised the whip, and the thongs whined and cracked. Fire came from its nostrils. But Gandalf stood firm.
>
> "You cannot pass," he said. The orcs stood still, and a dead silence fell. "I am a servant of the Secret Fire, wielder of the flame of Anor. You cannot pass. The dark fire will not avail you, flame of Udûn. Go back to the Shadow! You cannot pass."
>
> The Balrog made no answer. The fire in it seemed to die, but the darkness grew. It stepped forward slowly onto the bridge, and suddenly it drew itself up to a great height, and its wings were spread from wall to wall; but still Gandalf could be seen, glimmering in the gloom; he seemed small, and altogether alone: grey and bent, like a wizened tree before the onset of a storm.

From out of the shadow a red sword leaped flaming.
Glamdring glittered white in answer.
There was a ringing clash and a stab of white fire. The
Balrog fell back and its sword flew up in molten fragments.
The wizard swayed on the bridge, stepped back a pace, and
then again stood still.
"You cannot pass!" he said.
With a bound the Balrog leaped full upon the bridge. Its
whip whirled and hissed.
"He cannot stand alone!" cried Aragorn suddenly and ran
back along the bridge. "*Elendil!*" he shouted. "I am with you,
Gandalf!"
"Gondor!" cried Boromir and leaped after him.
At that moment Gandalf lifted his staff, and crying aloud
he smote the bridge before him. The staff broke asunder and
fell from his hand. A blinding sheet of white flame sprang up.
The bridge cracked. Right at the Balrog's feet it broke, and
the stone upon which it stood crashed into the gulf, while the
rest remained, poised, quivering like a tongue of rock thrust
out into emptiness.
With a terrible cry the Balrog fell forward, and its shadow
plunged down and vanished. But even as it fell it swung its
whip, and the thongs lashed and curled about the wizard's
knees, dragging him to the brink. He staggered and fell,
grasped vainly at the stone, and slid into the abyss. "Fly, you
fools!" he cried, and was gone. (*The Fellowship of the Ring*, 322)

Tolkein was right. The Shire and all Middle Earth could be saved
only one way: *Gandalf had to face the demon and plunge into darkness alone.*
No one else could go with him. No one else could win that war.
And no one but Jesus alone could go into battle against the forces
that would stand against our salvation and against redemption of fallen
society. Jesus *alone* suffers under Pontius Pilate; Jesus *alone* dies for our
sin in our place.

Firm through the fiercest drought and storm. . . .
For every sin on Him was laid; . . .
From life's first cry to final breath
Jesus commands my destiny. (Getty and Townend, "In Christ
    Alone," © copyright 2002 Thankyou Music [PRS])

Jesus rises again the third day and alone sits at the right hand of God the Father Almighty. Jesus, our *divine Warrior*, is the hope of the repentant Israel—the head of God's people whom the Gileadites seek. He is the only hope for a deteriorating society. *May we each have greater trust in him.*

Reflect and Discuss

1. How has Israel deteriorated when one arrives at this chapter?
2. After having forty-five years of peace, what might the return to evil say about the character of Israel those forty-five years?
3. What does the return to evil after forty-five years of peace say about the relative strength of any of Israel's judges?
4. How does Jesus display each of his roles as Judge, King, and Warrior for his people?
5. How would practicing the instructions of the Shema have saved Israel from this episode?
6. What responsibility of the priests could have prevented this episode in Israel?
7. Why is releasing our children and grandchildren to do ministry, especially foreign missions work, a perennial problem for believers? What worldly ideas contribute to our hesitancy to allow our offspring to pursue a calling to serve the Lord vocationally?
8. How does this chapter reveal the tender heart of the Lord toward sinners?
9. What actions seem to be involved in true repentance?
10. When have you seen Jesus act on your behalf as the divine Warrior?

Words and the Warrior King, Part 1

JUDGES 11:1-28

Main Idea: The *words* surrounding Jephthah's might as warrior clarify his headship of Israel en route to victory, and he experiences sorrow in the binding words of his vow to sacrifice his daughter to the Lord, while yet allowing his enemies' own words to bring their defeat upon his return.

I. **Even if the Words of Some Reject the Warrior, the Unworthy Will Accept Him as Their Warrior (11:1-3).**
II. **Some Who Previously Rejected the Warrior Will Change When Trouble Shows Their Need for the Warrior (11:4-11).**
III. **The Conflict Some Have with the Warrior Needs a History Lesson about God's People and the Warrior (11:12-28).**

Of the titles that come to mind when we think of who Jesus Christ is to us, *Lord, Savior, Messiah, High Priest,* and *Redeemer* are familiar. "Jesus is *Lord*" is the historical confession separating followers of Christ from those who find Caesar, money, or self to be lord. That Jesus is our *Savior* rings out every Christmas season because most stage renditions of the angels announcing the birth of Christ to the shepherds include, "For unto you is born this day in the city of David a Savior, which is Christ the Lord" (Luke 2:11 KJV). The animation of Linus saying that line in *A Charlie Brown Christmas* probably was playing in your head as you read the words.

It also might be commonplace for one to think of Jesus as one's *King.* The Reformation creeds and confessions that identify Christ as "prophet, priest, and king in his humiliation and exaltation" portray the *king* concept before us. A host of songs join the king chorus, such as Matt Redmond's "King Jesus," the spiritual "Ride on, King Jesus," Jeremy Camps's "King Jesus," Vickie Winans's "Long as I Got King Jesus," and Joseph Vogels's "Victory Chant," known by its alternative title, "Hail Jesus," because of the first lines of this kingly melody:

Hail Jesus! You're my King!
Your life frees me to sing.
I will praise You all my days.
Perfect in all Your ways.

Hail Jesus! You're my Lord!
I will obey Your Word.
I want to see Your kingdom come.
Not my will but Yours be done. (Vogels, "Victory Chant," ©
      Copyright 1988 Universal Music – Brentwood Benson
      Publ. [ASCAP])

Like the other songs with kingly terms for Jesus, this song helps us revisit the idea of Jesus as King so that we are at home thinking of Jesus as our King as much as we think of him as our sovereign Lord and Savior.

Far fewer people, however, might think of Jesus as our *Warrior* or our *Warrior*-King. The concept of Jesus as a divine Warrior permeates the Scriptures, but few songs use "Warrior" or "Warrior-King" to describe the man from Galilee. At the end time we will recognize Jesus as King of kings and Lord of lords. But will we recognize him as Warrior of warriors or as Warrior-King *par excellence?*

Identifying Jesus as Warrior-King is just one part of this quest. The other part is to see from Scripture that the words we use to speak about Jesus affirm his place as divine Warrior and King or condemn our rejection of him. The story of Jephthah weaves together the ideas of divine Warrior and our words about him, encouraging and exhorting the followers of the King to think of our own words about Jesus in light of what we know God's Word says about Jesus.

Two things are important to note about this passage before embarking on a study of the divine Warrior. First, due to its length—fifty-four verses—I will examine the passage in two parts: 11:1-28 and 11:29–12:15. The one idea of the passage will be evident in both expositions.

Second, this is a typological story. A character or characters or events in the story intend to *prefigure* Christ and some aspect of his identity and work. As a *prefigure*, it looks forward to a correspondence in the *figure*. One identifies the prefigure and the correspondence by reading the OT in light of what the NT teaches about Christ. The NT is not reinterpreting the OT figure to be Christ but recognizes the correspondences based on the person of Christ and his completed work.

In this story, Jephthah prefigures Christ as a warrior on behalf of his people.[36] However, Jephthah is only an earthly warrior. The words sur-

---

[36] In saying, "Jephthah prefigures Christ as a warrior," I am not portraying Jephthah as a positive character. He is a tragic hero. However, I am saying that this is one passage

rounding Jephthah's might as warrior clarify his headship of Israel en route to victory. These same words surrounding Jephthah's role as warrior work to reveal the significance of the words said about the divine Warrior, giving us a powerful OT portrayal of the truths of Christ we dearly hold.

Even if the Words of Some Reject the Warrior, the Unworthy Will Accept Him as Their Warrior

JUDGES 11:1-3

Jephthah's identity as the son of a prostitute brings rejection from his Gileadite brothers but reception as a mighty warrior from worthless men of Tob. The story establishes Jephthah as a valiant warrior from its beginning. The priority placed on this identity indicates the reader should view Jephthah as a mighty warrior regardless of whatever follows. It would be similar to being introduced to a petite, slender young woman serving tables at a fancy awards gala with the words, "She holds a seventh degree blackbelt in hapkido." Whatever events transpired that evening, you would view that table servant as a powerful martial artist, even if she dropped a tray of food on the guest of honor!

Jephthah, however, is born from his father's exploits with a prostitute. Without the initial description, Jephthah would be just another illegitimate son in the story of redemption. But this prostitute's son has established himself as a mighty warrior, and that is how the reader must think of Jephthah.

Jephthah is not his father's only son. Through marriage, Gilead has other sons—Jephthah's stepbrothers. To them, the mighty warrior simply is the child of another woman living among them. As a son, he would be entitled to an equal share of their inheritance. But the brothers want a larger share of the pie, and they justify driving out

---

that demonstrates that an imperfect and sinful *literary* character can contribute to a *theologically* true and positive message. One should not confuse who Jephthah is *literarily* in the Judges story (i.e., a relativistic-thinking judge who is the son of a prostitute) with the theological truth about Christ and his work in redemption. In the book of Jonah, God uses Jonah's bad actions to communicate what is true about Israel's sinful nationalism. Many other places use the literarily bad to communicate what is true. It would be philosophical and not theological to say that the Lord would never use a literary antagonist or flawed protagonist to portray theological truth. I am not saying Jephthah is a positive character in Judges or that the entirety of his actions portrays the righteous actions of Christ. I am saying that in this narrative, literarily, Jephthah's actions as warrior foreshadow the work of the divine Warrior.

Jephthah on the basis of his immoral lineage. With strong words they will reject Jephthah's might as warrior due to their problems with his birth origin.

Nevertheless, there were worthless men who could see the might of this warrior who had to flee from his own home. They find their identity with Jephthah, joining themselves to him and going on raids with him (v. 3). The rejection of the warrior by his brothers leads to his reception by lawless people.

Much like Jesus's allegorizing of the chief priests and Pharisees in the parable of the wicked tenants, the brothers tip their hand on their real motive for rejecting the warrior: *they want the full inheritance to themselves* (Matt 12:33-46). But they will cloak their motives behind misgivings with his birth, just as the ancient Jewish leaders found misgivings with Jesus's birth (John 8:41; 9:29).

Consistent with the prefiguring of Jesus, Jephthah's rejection by his own people will provide an opportunity for those who do not keep the law to follow him (see passages like Matt 22:9-10; John 1:9-12; 10:16). Although Jewish leaders use the questionable birth of Jesus as a guise for Israel to reject the Messiah, some peer past all objections to see Jesus for the mighty Warrior that he is. One thinks of the man blind from birth who placed faith in Christ despite the Jewish leaders' confusion of Jesus's origins (John 9:29) and of the sinful woman from the city whose sins Jesus forgave despite Simon the Pharisee's questioning of Jesus's status as a prophet (Luke 7:36-50). These two sinners saw the true identity of the one who provided victory over sin for them, and they placed faith in him despite the rejection by their Jewish brothers.

Some Who Previously Rejected the Warrior Will Change When Trouble Shows Their Need for the Warrior
JUDGES 11:4-11

A day comes when a foe too big for Israel sits on Gilead's doorstep. Israel does not have the military leadership necessary to fight the Ammonites. Apparently, someone brings up *Jephthah* as the man for the job. Can you imagine that discussion?

> "You mean that son of a prostitute? He doesn't qualify to be our leader!"

"But if we are being honest, we all know he is a mighty
warrior. The only reason we banished him is to make sure
those recruits over there had a larger inheritance."

"But if we call him, we would be admitting we were wrong
for banishing him."

"Who cares about that now? We need someone to lead us
against Ammon!"

Realizing they have a chance of survival and victory with Jephthah
leading them, the warrior search committee issues a call through the
elders of Israel. The emissaries sent to Jephthah do not hide their
motives for seeking him: "Come, be our commander, and let's fight the
Ammonites." They are only coming to him for his skill, not because they
feel a need to apologize for casting him away or that they find worth in
him beyond his birth circumstances—circumstances beyond his control.

Jephthah, however, forces them to remember their past actions and
to acknowledge their utilitarian approach to him. They are only turning
to him now because of their trouble with Ammon. If they were not too
weak to deliver themselves, he still would be to them only the son of a
prostitute. When they affirm their true motives, Jephthah gains more than
what they first stated explicitly: they want him—the one they cast away—to
be their leader (literally, "head"). In promise to Jephthah for returning to
be their warrior, they will follow Jephthah as their leader and commander
of their troops. All commit themselves by words of oath, which Jephthah
repeats to them in a binding oath before the Lord at Mizpah.

Throughout Scripture, many figures play a type of Jesus's being
rejected at his first attempt to be a leader for Israel, only to be accepted
at a second attempt. Joseph was rejected and left to die by his brothers
when he announced the future rule revealed in his dream, but when they
met him in Egypt, they accepted him as the one to save them from the
famine (Acts 7:9-13). Moses was rejected as leader when he attempted
to rescue his Hebrew brothers the first time. When he returned from
exile, he was received as leader so Israel might leave the oppression of
Egypt (Acts 7:23-29,35-36). Similar could be said of David's rejection as
king then reception at his return from exile or of Job's rejection by his
friends but acceptance when they needed his intercession. Great would
such a list of figures be!

Jephthah is rejected by his brothers and exiled. But when they need
him to lead them, they receive him as their leader, head, deliverer, and

warrior. Their trouble with Ammon brings them to a place in which their rejection must yield to his mighty skill as warrior. Redemptive history shows the same will be true of Israel when they welcome the one whom they have pierced (Zech 12:9-10) and say, "Blessed is he who comes in the name of the LORD!" (Ps 118:26 ESV; see also Matt 21:9; 23:39; Mark 11:9; Luke 13:35; 19:38).

Occasionally an unbeliever will ask, "Why does it seem that people start to believe in God when they are in trouble? Doesn't that show that confessions are only for the weak or that in a foxhole anyone will profess Christ out of fear of death?" One appropriate answer to this question would be that such a conclusion is true in one sense: *until we see that sin and death are enemies too powerful for us to overcome on our own, we will not see the need for Christ.* Only when one needs Christ to go to war against an enemy too great for us do we call on the one we have rejected and ask him to be the leader and head over our lives. As long as we can live life somewhat successfully without help from others, we will rest on our own self-sufficiency. We do not even pause to ask if human self-sufficiency is enough to please God and gain life after death.

Jesus is the only one who has gone to war against death and won! He is the Warrior we need on our side to defeat the power of sin and death. He is the one who will provide life for us as the resurrected Victor and King.

The Conflict Some Have with the Warrior Needs a History Lesson about God's People and the Warrior
JUDGES 11:12-28

Upon becoming head of Israel, Jephthah wisely sends a diplomatic envoy to discern why the king of the Ammonites suddenly wants to attack Israel. He learns that the king of Ammon has an old beef about land that he believes Israel wrongly took from Ammon when Israel left Egypt. However, Jephthah will give the king a history lesson about Israel's possession of the land that will correct the erroneous understanding that had led the king of Ammon to try to take some of Israel's inheritance by war. The warrior-king of Israel will have four points of explanation for the king of Ammon.

First, *Israel remained at Kadesh rather than passing through Edom or Moab* (vv. 14-17). When the king of Edom brought his troops against Israel, Israel backed down on traversing Edom. When Balak then summoned

Balaam, Balaam might have blessed Israel, but Israel did not travel through Moab.

Second, *the Lord dispossessed Sihon and the Amorites and their lands* (vv. 18-23). Avoiding Moab, Israel sent word to Sihon the King of the Amorites to request permission to pass through their lands. Sihon brought out his people against Israel to make war to keep them from the land. Sihon provoked the conflict, but the Lord provided the military victory for Israel. Twice the writer says, "The LORD God of Israel" brought victory over Sihon and the Amorites (vv. 21,23). The Lord gave the Amorite territory—including that belonging to Ammon—to Israel. Since the Lord dispossessed the Amorites, Jephthah concludes, it would be wise for the king of the Ammonites not to challenge Israel and her Lord.

Third, *Ammon does not have what it takes to possess the land the Lord has given Israel to possess* (vv. 24-27). Building on the history of the Lord giving Ammon's lands to Israel, Jephthah lays out the bare, cold, hard facts of Ammon's weakness. Even if they put forth their greatest efforts, they cannot possess the land for three reasons: (1) Their god, Chemosh, has not been powerful enough to get the land for them. Even if he was a real god (which he was not), he obviously was no match for the Lord God of Israel who secured the land for his people. (2) Sihon is not as strong as Balak, king of Moab, and Balak was no match for Israel. This almost sounds like a taunt to say, "Sit down, little boy. You're not ready for an adult fight." (3) Ammon had three hundred years to take the land but did not. The implication seems to be that they did not take it then because they could not, and neither can they now because they are not powerful enough as a people.

Fourth, *Ammon is sinning against the Lord by making war with the Lord's people* (v. 27). When Jephthah calls for the judgment of God, he is certain he is in the right and Ammon is in the wrong. Through the Lord's judgment of their actions, their sinfulness will be confirmed.

Yet even the finely crafted, historically accurate, well-reasoned four-point sermon is unconvincing to the king of Ammon. The king rejects the truth about Israel's history of dealings with Ammon and thus is saying he will not back down from trying to take the land by war.

The church has blights in her history like the Inquisition, support of the trans-Atlantic slave trade, and hatred of the Jewish people through both silence during the Holocaust and perennial anti-Semitism. Things like this and many others sometimes cause people to hate the church and reject the message of Christ. However, the foibles of the church are only one part of its story. The true history records Christ making his church prevail over the gates of hell and giving society many things to make present life better. The Lord provides good in society through the hand of the church throughout the entirety of the church's history. Many have tried to rid the world of the church, but the Lord causes her to stand in a dark world.

However, even if we can paint a true picture of what the church has done in history, that does not mean people will receive Christ or find the church to be a place of God's presence. Like the king of Ammon, many consider the truth of the divine Warrior's historical work on the cross and in the tomb something they can reject in favor of their own truths. Their conflict appears to be with the church; ultimately, however, their conflict is with Christ.

Application

First, as representatives of Christ, we need to distinguish "cultural war" language from "spiritual war" language. That is, we do face a war in the unseen realm. However, that does not mean everything we do not like in this life, or every political position with which we disagree, is a sign of a war against the church. If we get spiritual warfare and cultural warfare confused, we will deny the gospel and possibly preach "culture" in its place.

Certainly, there are places where the two wars overlap. So this means we have to be even more discerning and careful with our language. For example, we might disagree with the culture on the establishment of mixed-gender use or genderless restrooms. But we do not do so because our "yuck" factor is the same as some secularists'. Instead, we stand for the sake of protecting those who would be vulnerable to assault when both genders share such settings because we love our neighbor. We stand too because the protection of the innocence of our children flows from that same love of neighbor and biblical wisdom directing our children's lives toward purity. We would be right to view biological-gender distinctions based on the created order. But it would be unwise for us to enter the genderless bathroom debate on this basis, for we can hold to the biological-gender truth regardless of the sign on a bathroom. Entering the debate for the former reasons keeps the war spiritual rather than cultural. The latter reason for debate attempts to preserve a cultural artifact we do not need to hold to stand with Christ in a spiritual war.

Second, we should be willing to concede the mistakes the church has made in history. This is being honest and truthful toward those we hope will receive the message of Christ. Admitting truth does not automatically denigrate the church and does not denigrate her message. Instead, it affirms us as people of truth who, in humility, can admit that we have not always done what is right in the sight of our Lord. To deny or hide the truths of our failures is, in effect, to preach a lie—to preach that we have perfectly followed Christ. The world can see through such deception and will reject Christ based on Christ's representatives' failure to be a people of truth.

Reflect and Discuss

1. With what titles of Christ in the NT are you most familiar, and what do those titles mean for your walk with him?
2. What is a song about Christ being "King" that you hold dearly and can sing as a reminder of his role as King in your life?
3. If Christ is King, what does that indicate about his church, and how would you support your conclusion with Scripture?
4. What passages come to mind for you when you think of Christ as Warrior, and what does his role as Warrior mean for your witness in the world?
5. What does the present writer mean when referring to this passage as "a typological story"?
6. How does Jephthah's role as a warrior on behalf of Israel differ from Christ's role as divine Warrior on behalf of his people?
7. What does this story suggest about people's motives in either accepting or rejecting Christ as their divine Warrior?
8. What does Christ's work as King do for Israel with respect to both the promises of the OT and the law of Moses?
9. What does Christ's work as King do for the church with respect both to our sins and to persecution for his name?
10. Since Christ is divine Warrior on our behalf, what attitude and effort should characterize our proclamation of the gospel to the lost and our daily witness to hostile unbelievers in our midst?

Words and the Warrior King, Part 2

JUDGES 11:29–12:15

Main Idea: The *words* surrounding Jephthah's might as warrior clarify his headship of Israel en route to victory, and he experiences sorrow in the binding words of his vow to sacrifice his daughter to the Lord while yet allowing his enemies' own words to bring their defeat upon his return.

I. The Victory Secured by the Warrior Comes with Binding Words about the Sacrifice of the Warrior (11:29-33).
II. The Sorrow While Celebrating the Warrior Should Meet with Sober-Mindedness about the Vow of the Warrior (11:34-39).
III. The Threats of Those Excluded from the Victory of the Warrior Meet Final Defeat with Their Own Words under the Rule of the Warrior (12:1-7).
IV. The Legacy of the Warrior Leaves Powerful yet Flawed People in Leadership after the Warrior (12:8-15).

In the last chapter we considered the story of the rejected warrior and leader, Jephthah, as a typological story. It is written in a way to point toward Jesus, the divine Warrior-King. Jephthah (the type) and Jesus (the antitype) have at least three points of correspondence in the first three movements of the story.

First, as Jephthah was rejected to keep him from sharing in the inheritance of his brothers because of his unacceptable birth status, so Jesus was rejected by his own in Israel when he came to provide their promised inheritance, also due to a question about his birth status—whether he was the virgin-born Son of God. But both men still managed to have followers who seemingly did not stumble over their birth histories.

Second, just as the leaders of Gilead sought Jephthah to be their leader and commander and received him as their head when they needed a warrior against a great enemy, so too, during the end times, Israel will seek their Messiah to deliver them from their foes and receive the one whom they previously pierced as their Head, Warrior,

Deliverer, and King upon his return. The first-time-rejected-second-time-accepted theme runs throughout Scripture with many portraying a type of Jesus. Stephen picks up on this idea in Scripture as he preaches to the Jewish leaders who crucified Jesus, showing them from history that they treated every one of the prophets with the same two-step acceptance process.

Third, the king of the Ammonites needs the warrior to correct him on the history of Israel's prosperity in relation to their lands. Similarly, those proclaiming Jesus as Warrior-King need to paint a correct picture of the church's successes and failures so that skeptics might not bring hatred upon Jesus because of their misunderstanding about the church.

The three points of correspondence do not yet complete the story of Jephthah or of the typology the story intends to portray. Four additional points of correspondence fill out a more complete picture about the warrior, giving us a rich theology of Christ as divine Warrior. Using our Augustinian lenses for reading the OT and NT, we will be able to discern the completed revelation of the Jephthah story in the work of Christ to wage war on behalf of his people as King. We shall see with the Westminster Shorter Catechism, "As a king, Christ brings us under His power, rules and defends us, and restrains and conquers all His and all our enemies" (Keely and Rollinson, *Westminster*, Question 26).

The Victory Secured by the Warrior Comes with Binding Words about the Sacrifice of the Warrior
JUDGES 11:29-33

The arrival of the Spirit of the Lord on Jephthah harks back to the victories of Shamgar and Gideon (3:10; 6:34). The reader should anticipate a victory for Jephthah, as the Lord has clothed him with special empowerment to accomplish the task on behalf of the Lord. The presence of the Spirit shows the Lord's definite appointment of Jephthah to this work.

After passing through regions to get to the cities of Ammon, Jephthah opens his mouth to make a vow. He will give binding words to the Lord to secure a victory against Ammon. The words are unnecessary, however, because the presence of the Spirit already shows the Lord's will to prosper Jephthah in his fight. Thus, the vow is rash, made in the relativistic veins of Israel's decision-making throughout the period of the judges. In Jephthah's own eyes a vow is needed to move the Lord to defeat Ammon. In truth, the Lord already has signaled victory for Jephthah by clothing him with the Spirit.[37]

The words of the vow have a range that allows for Jephthah to mean "whoever is first" or "whatever is first." Jephthah probably is thinking an animal will come out first, but he makes his vow without considering that a person could come out first. His words bind him to make a sacrificial death so that he might secure victory from the Lord for Israel over her enemy. He will defeat twenty cities en route to victory, wiping them out. He will subdue the Ammonites entirely.

The typology of this section points toward the sacrifice of the Son of God to bring about the victory of salvation for God's people. From all eternity, the Father, Son, and Spirit have decreed the victory of the Son in salvation. In the OT, Psalms 2 and 110 both speak words reflective of the eternal decree:

> *I will declare the Lord's decree.*
> *He said to me, "You are my Son;*
> *today I have become your Father.*
> *Ask of me,*
> *and I will make the nations your inheritance*
> *and the ends of the earth your possession." (Ps 2:7-8)*

> *This is the declaration of the Lord*
> *to my Lord:*
> *"Sit at my right hand*
> *until I make your enemies your footstool."*
> *The Lord will extend your mighty scepter from Zion.*
> *Rule over your surrounding enemies. (Ps 110:1-2)*

In both Psalm 2 and Psalm 110, the Father has spoken of the victory over the nations of the earth and over the enemies of God *prior to* the incarnation of the Son of God. The "decree" and declaration seem to suggest the statements are proclaimed from eternity past.

The NT also speaks to the sure victory of Christ *prior to* his advent:

---

[37] "Once again God reached out in mercy and empowered this self-made leader for his own (Yahweh's) agenda. Whether or not Jephthah was aware of his divine empowerment is not clear, but the Spirit seems to have prompted him to tour the Transjordanian regions to recruit troops for the coming battle" (Block, *Judges, Ruth*, 365).

Though he was delivered up according to God's determined plan and foreknowledge, you used lawless people to nail him to a cross and kill him. God raised him up, ending the pains of death, because it was not possible for him to be held by death. (Acts 2:23-24)

For, in fact, in this city both Herod and Pontius Pilate, with the Gentiles and the people of Israel, assembled together against your holy servant Jesus, whom you anointed, to do whatever your hand and your will had predestined to take place. (Acts 4:27-28)

The apostles repeatedly acknowledge the eternal decree of Christ's victory. No enemy—not even death—shall defeat Christ or thwart his victorious rule for Israel and the church over their enemies.

Unlike Jephthah, Jesus does not make any rash vows, for he is sure of his victory. Yet we are certain the members of the Trinity agreed on the death of Christ. This would mean Christ *agreed* to provide redemption through a substitutionary sacrifice. In love, his words of agreement in eternity past bound him to the Trinity to provide redemption to us.

The Sorrow While Celebrating the Warrior Should Meet with Sober-Mindedness about the Vow of the Warrior
JUDGES 11:34-39

What should now be the happiest moment in our story becomes the saddest. Just when we think we can celebrate the victory of the rejected son, we are confronted with the consequences of the error of his choices. Just when we look forward to a family rejoicing together in Dad's accomplishments, we come to find that the accomplishments come with an unfortunate price tag.

In attempting to manipulate a victory the presence of the Spirit had already promised him, Jephthah vows that the first thing coming out the door of his home would be sacrificed to the Lord. Upon arriving home, his daughter comes to meet him, ready to party with him over the celebration. Like Miriam after crossing the Red Sea, Jephthah's daughter comes with tambourines and dancing to show great fanfare to her victorious father. She is the first thing out of Jephthah's door. She is now the substance of his vow.

Even more unfortunately for Jephthah, the daughter he must sacrifice is his only child. Besides this daughter, he has no other from his loins, no other to cherish like this one or to sacrifice. This daughter alone will fulfill the vows.

Knowing his vow of sacrifice and that this daughter now must be the one to fulfill it, Jephthah comes to the greatest point of despair. You can see his overwhelming despair in the tearing of his clothes.[38] You can hear his agonizing grief over the coming sacrifice of his daughter in his exclamatory words: "No!" One can imagine the primordial scream of disbelief with the loudest of shrieks. Surely Jephthah now sees what his words have done. He feels the weight of his words in light of the truth that now attends the victory.

"Not my daughter!" he cries. The relationship comes to the fore of the thought of the sacrificial offering that must be made. The love for his daughter is as great as the need to fulfill the promise. To this end he is "devastated" and "low." Yet he will fulfill the unfortunate vow.

The response of the daughter, however, is sobering. First, rather than turn on her father and ask, "How could you do something so stupid?" or say, "No, I will not let you kill me for the sake of a victory for Israel," she tells Jephthah to do as he has vowed. She will not try to escape; she will not castigate him. Instead, she links the words back to the victory accomplished, exhorting her father to be faithful to his word even as the Lord was faithful to provide victory.[39]

Second, she only asks that she can mourn that she will die without sexual fulfillment in marriage. She knows that her father must keep his vow.[40] However, she also knows that what appears to be her primary earthly hope as a young girl—that she would marry—is now impossible.

---

[38] Trent Butler agrees: "He immediately acts out his grief symbolically by tearing his clothes" (*Judges*, 290).

[39] Daniel Block's observation on the words of the daughter in 11:36-37 is significant: "This comment is remarkable for two reasons. First, through the speech of this young girl the narrator offers a theological interpretation of the battle. The use of the verb *nāqam*, 'to execute vengeance, just punishment,' answers to Jephthah's declaration in v. 27, 'Let the LORD, the Judge, decide this dispute this day between the Israelites and the Ammonites.' Yahweh had indeed rendered judgment, which is expressed in the outcome of the battle. Second, the young girl courageously and dutifully charged her father to do to her what he had vowed" (*Judges, Ruth*, 373).

[40] "The daughter knows that vows made are vows paid, for as Hamilton states, 'Scripture makes no provision for withdrawing or annulling a vow made to God'" (Butler, *Judges*, 291). Butler cites Victor Hamilton, *Handbook on the Historical Books: Joshua, Judges, Ruth, Samuel, Kings, Chronicles, Ezra, Nehemiah, Esther* (Grand Rapids: Baker Academic, 2008), 145.

Her hope is not for a nonmarital sexual union, for that she could have
had in spades during the period of the judges by acting like a prostitute.
Instead, the exaltation of marriage shines through the period of the
judges. The young lady wishes for marital fulfillment—a hope she will
have to experience in the world to come.

For two months she and her friends mourn her virginity—a period
that must have been as painful for Jephthah as for his virgin daughter.
In losing her life she would never be married in this life and would leave
behind friends and family. In losing her life, Jephthah would be left
without a child or a line to follow him.

Some question whether Jephthah killed his daughter in order to
fulfill his vow or fulfilled it by some other means. How could he have
done such a thing? How could the Lord have approved or allowed this
murderous offering? Yet, without the modern objections to child sacrifice, one immediately could understand how one in the period of the
judges would have followed through with killing his own child. If doing
what is right in one's own eyes was the order of the day, Jephthah could
have sacrificed his daughter without giving thought to the law of God.
As Andrew Bowling writes,

> It is axiomatic that God prohibited human sacrifice.
> However, it is conceivable that a man living in Jephthah's
> age, "revering" God in his own half-savage way, could commit
> such an atrocious act, erroneously considering it an act of
> reverence. This kind of ignorant tragedy would no more
> reflect on God's character than would any other of the many
> atrocities committed erroneously but sincerely by God's
> people. Jephthah's sacrifice would be a reflection on his
> primitive comprehension of Yahwism, not on Yahweh himself.
> ("Judges," 170)

After the completion of the vow, the women in Israel commemo-
rate the death of the daughter by recounting her sacrifice. There would
be an annual four-day festival to remember the sacrifice the daughter
made for the victory of Israel over her enemies.

In considering the typology of Christ in this episode, one gains
insight into both the Father and the Son. While the sacrifice of the Son
was pleasing in God's sight and brings praise and thanksgiving from
those the Son saves (Isa 53:10; 2 Cor 9:15; Eph 1:3-5; 1 Pet 1:3-8), the act
still took a great emotional toll on the Father. The Father is not callous,

only concerned about the fact of salvation. When Scripture speaks of the death of Christ, it frames it as the working of the Father toward his only begotten child (John 3:16). Unlike Abraham, whose only child was spared from certain death, the Father follows through with giving his only Son as an act of love.[41]

The Threats of Those Excluded from the Victory of the Warrior Meet Final Defeat with Their Own Words under the Rule of the Warrior
JUDGES 12:1-7

The aftermath of Jephthah's victory does not end with the sacrificial death of his daughter. Like Gideon, Jephthah will encounter the jealous, hotheaded Ephraimites who feel that they were excluded from participating in the victory (cf. 8:1-4). However, unlike the Gideon episode, the men of Ephraim come prepared to burn down Jephthah's home with Jephthah inside. They are completely ungrateful for the victory over Ammon and insensitive to the sacrifice of Jephthah's only child and the grief surrounding it, and they bring to the scene a level of anger for which the situation does not call. They are prepared to go to war against Jephthah for securing the victory for Israel without their help.

Apparently, however, Jephthah did call for the men of Ephraim to join him in battle, but they refused the offer. Now that victory is past, they come acting as if they really wanted a piece of the action. Their earlier rejection of joining Jephthah makes their complaint suspect; perhaps they feared losing their lives, were unsure of victory, were not willing to submit to Jephthah's rule, or a combination of all three. Their appearance now seems to want to take advantage of Jephthah when he should be celebrating and/or is most unsuspecting of, and unprepared for, another immediate battle. In any case, with their threats they set themselves against the warrior whom the Lord has used to bring victory in Israel.

Like his words to the king of Ammon, Jephthah tells the Ephraimites the true history of the call to war, again proclaiming the Lord as the true

---

[41] "In fact, with the expression *yĕḥîdâ*, 'only child,' the narrator intentionally links this account with the account of Abraham's sacrifice of Isaac as a whole burnt offering in Genesis 22, where Isaac is identified as Abraham's son, his *yāḥîd*, 'only child'" (Block, *Judges, Ruth*, 371).

victor in Israel's conflicts with her enemies (see 11:21,23). This places the men of Ephraim in the position of enemies of the Lord with their threat of war. Jephthah is right to question their reasons for coming to fight him.

Jephthah engages the men of Gilead against Ephraim. Although not disclosed previously in the passage, the Ephraimites issued taunting words in the past about Gilead. The words suggest that the Gileadites, like their leader formerly, are only refugees dependent on Ephraim and Manasseh (see Block, *Judges, Ruth*, 383, and Butler, *Judges*, 295). Again, their words about the people of God are directed against the warrior for God's people. Yet defeated Ephraim must flee like refugees. But they cannot return home, for Gilead captures all the crossing spots over the Jordan that would allow Ephraim to escape.

Knowing also that the dialects of Gilead and Ephraim differ, the Gileadites devise a test to identify Ephraimites attempting to pose as non-Ephraimites as they cross the fords. "Shibboleth" and "Sibboleth" differ by one letter in the Hebrew, as in the English. The Ephraimites would fail at pronouncing the Hebrew letter *shin* with the "sh" sound, instead speaking the "s" sound of the Hebrew letter *samech*. While not directed at the warrior Jephthah, the words that flow from the Ephraimites conflict with Jephthah's decision to go to war without waiting for the Ephraimites to join him. The Ephraimites' own words—the words of threat and the failed pronunciation—both work to bring about their own deaths.

Words matter. What we say about Jesus matters. Words of scoffing, denigration, disparagement, and rejection toward Jesus do not go without notice before the Almighty. Jesus said, "I tell you that on the day of judgment people will have to account for every careless word they speak. For by your words you will be acquitted, and by your words you will be condemned" (Matt 12:36-37). Repeatedly the NT indicates that the judgment of God will examine all our acts, including all our words. In Athens Paul told the agnostic audience, "[God] has set a day when he is going to judge the world in righteousness by the man he has appointed. He has provided proof of this to everyone by raising him from the dead" (Acts 17:31).

Not one person who speaks evil of Jesus will not find himself squirming in fear before the judgment of God. With perfect accounting of every word, he will examine every life, every second, every motive, every intent, and every action, and he will render judgment accordingly. Every item displeasing to him will further condemn the mouth that dismissed Jesus or spoke ill of him. With fire he will destroy those who have hated him and denied his existence with their words. The only hope one has is faith in the all-victorious Warrior, Jesus.

The Legacy of the Warrior Leaves Powerful yet Flawed People in Leadership after the Warrior
JUDGES 12:8-15

Like all the judges in Israel before and after him, Jephthah goes the way of all the earth. After his six years of rule, three judges with minor stories will follow: Ibzan, Elon, and Abdon. Their judgeships show length of rule and power provision for their posterity before they each die. Their judgeships also reveal the flaws in their character—their relativistic mindsets. Their stories too point to the hope of a final flawless Judge who will bring final rest to his people.

The stories of the three judges rightly go with the story of Jephthah. In the plan of the book of Judges, the major judge stories—the longer stories—control the narrative's flow. The minor stories round out the picture of the judges and bring the number of judges to twelve so that the reader thinks of the twelve tribes being represented by the activities of the judges. These three minor stories do not stand alone. They act as closure to the Jephthah story before we enter the longest story of a judge—Samson in Judges 13–16.

Since he was from Bethlehem, one might think Ibzan would be a righteous judge. However, he has thirty sons and daughters, suggesting he has multiple wives and concubines. If he had only one wife with whom he was faithful to produce thirty offspring, it would have presented such an anomaly to the period of the judges it is difficult to imagine that the writer would not have stated it clearly! Instead, Ibzan's flawed morality is evident in the giving of his children to spouses outside the covenant people of God. For Ibzan, whom his children married was a relative matter rather than a matter of obedience to the law of God.[42] Ibzan does what is right in his own eyes for seven years of rule rather than destroying the peoples of the nations.

---

[42] Deuteronomy 7:3-4 forbids the Israelites to give their children in marriage to people outside of Israel. See also Exod 34:14-16; Josh 23:12-13; 1 Kgs 11:2.

We only know of the place of origin, place of death and burial, and length of rule of Elon. The Zebulinite led Israel for ten years. Being sandwiched between Ibzan and Abdon, we can guess that he also is flawed with a relativistic worldview, even though no details are given.

Abdon appears to have been an older man when he came to rule, having lived long enough to have thirty grandsons. The stating of his rule with forty sons and thirty grandsons leaves out any mention of wives, concubines, daughters, and granddaughters. However, it does mention the seventy beasts Abdon provided for his sons and grandsons to ride, which was in violation of the command to the kings of Israel to refrain from multiplying horses.[43]

Although the location of Pirathon is unknown, the writer mentions the location three times,[44] placing it within the boundaries of the Amalekites inhabited by the Ephraimites. Abdon's home is among the people who sought to fight against Gideon and Jephthah, and he remained in a land of one of the peoples of the nations rather than destroying that nation. Abdon, too, uses a relativistic worldview to make his decisions like those around him. To him, the law does not bind him to be faithful in marriage, refrain from multiplying horses, or destroy the surrounding nations. With the conclusion of his eight years of rule, Israel has spent twenty-five years living under the leadership of men who do what is right in their own eyes, after having lived under the rule of the warrior Jephthah for six years.

In the history of redemption, upon his departure from earth to return to his former glory, Christ appointed the church to proclaim the message of his death and resurrection. The church, the body of Christ, is the visible representation of Christ through those who followed him. Since his ascension, believers have been left after him to be the mysterious yet visible expression of his rule on earth.

---

[43] Deuteronomy 17:16. While judges were not kings per se, Abimelech served in that role as judge (Judg 9:6,16), and Jephthah, in effect, played the role of king as the head and leader of Israel (cf. 11:9,11). The refrain concerning the absence of a king in Israel in 17:6; 18:1; 19:1; and 21:25 recognizes that the monarchy had not begun in Israel. The original recipients of the book who lived during the period of Israel's divided kingdom might have viewed the role of Jephthah as equivalent to that of their kings. The number of donkeys would have brought to mind the prohibition against multiplying horses in Deut 17.

[44] In v. 15 "when he died" is literally "when Abdon son of Hillel the Pirathonite died."

Unfortunately, however, like Ibzon, Elon, and Abdon, we follow the divine Warrior as flawed people—even we who lead churches. We do not keep his standards perfectly—not in our marriages and family life or in contentment with his provision or in our witness to the people of the nations. The work of the divine Warrior through us is grace. When Christ, the divine Warrior-King and Judge returns, then all who follow him will have the law of God written on their hearts, and we will follow him as people without flaw—without spot or wrinkle, holy and blameless.

Reflect and Discuss

1. By way of review, in your own words, explain the concept of *typology* with respect to the Scriptures.
2. Jephthah was the military commander who conquered the Ammonites on behalf of Israel. Christ is the King who conquered sin on behalf of those who would believe in him. Was Jephthah a type of Christ? How so?
3. According to the Westminster Shorter Catechism (WSC), what are Christ's works toward us in his role as King?
4. What aspects of the WSC's kingly Christ do you see in the story of Jephthah?
5. According to both the OT and the NT, how does the eternal decree of God relate to the death of Christ?
6. What option did Jephthah have other than to sacrifice his daughter?
7. In what sense is Jephthah's daughter also a type of Christ?
8. When has a well-meaning but rash promise or vow placed you in a difficult predicament?
9. What does Ephraim's delay to Jephthah's call to arms indicate about Ephraim?
10. When we find our church leaders are flawed people, what should be our responses to their words and acts of leadership?

A Journey of Hope for Barren People

JUDGES 13

Main Idea: To bring an immature husband and barren wife to worship God together, allow him to learn the identity of Jesus gradually, as part of God's plan to deliver his people.

I.   **Our Hope Is Tied to Deliverance of God's People (13:1).**
II. **Our Hope Rests in Full Obedience to What We Know about the Son (13:2-14).**
    A.   The angel of the Lord and the barren woman (13:2-7)
    B.   The angel of the Lord and the barren man (13:8-14)
III. **Our Hope Should Produce Worship as We See the Divine Identity of the Son (13:15-20).**
    A.   Manoah's detaining the angel (13:15-16)
    B.   Manoah's honoring the angel (13:17-18)
    C.   Manoah's and his wife's worshiping the angel (13:19-20)
IV. **Our Hope Gives Perspective on Death as We Watch the Son's Work as Savior (13:21-25).**
    A.   Perspective of Fear (13:21-22)
    B.   Perspective of Reason (13:23)
    C.   Perspective of Progress (13:24-25)

Watching a friend walk through barrenness is painful for all involved. Few things ache as much as the longing for a child when pregnancy is difficult or absent. Although my wife and I never walked through total barrenness, we do remember the hurt inside we felt when we knew the child inside my wife had an in-utero defect that was not going to allow the child to survive thirty minutes of life outside the womb. We know the dream deferred when several young moms in one's own Sunday school class are holding babies born within proximity of our stillbirth. Every giggle or cry from one of those children magnifies the emptiness in the couple's lap. The birthday celebrations the next couple of years for those one- and two-year-olds trigger returns to the voids where there should be a child. For the one who is completely barren, the depth of hurt is greater than for those holding at least one child.

Different from the suffering women experience by the inability to become pregnant is the suffering a woman experiences when married to a spiritually immature husband. The presence of a wife in a pew without her husband is a visible reminder of this crushing reality. In the most intimate relationship, the hope of joy of living by the power of the Spirit together is absent. Watching the maturing, God-fearing husband of one's sister or girlfriend stirs the emptiness of the more mature wife—an emptiness akin to barrenness of the childless women.

A great thing about knowing God the Creator personally is that there is hope for the barren, wounded, bitter, and grieving woman and for the frustrated, angry, unequally yoked, and despairing wife. There is hope for their significant others who travel with them through their season of darkness. It is the same hope shared by a troubled church and ancient Israel as they journey with the Lord in their dealing with the peoples of the world.

On the journey for Manoah's wife to overcome her bitterness, for Manoah to share her understanding and worship the Lord, and for Israel to be delivered from the oppressive hand of the Philistines, one reads of four things about the hope we have in the Lord to overcome the emptiness. These four things each point to the Son of God as the real hope of believers.

Our Hope Is Tied to Deliverance of God's People
JUDGES 13:1

Judges 13:1 is the seventh time in Judges we read a form of the words, "The Israelites again did what was evil in the Lord's sight" (other mentions are in Judg 2:11; 3:7,12; 4:1; 6:1; and 10:6). After the first mention in 2:11, the refrain often introduces numerical years of a judgment of oppression for their evil—such as eight years under Cushan-rishathaim or eighteen under Eglon (3:8,14). Many mentions of the phrase also provide numerical years of peace the land experiences under the previous judge, such as forty years each under Othniel and Deborah (3:11; 5:31). The end of the reign of one or more judges comes within proximity of the insertion of the phrase (3:11; 10:2,5).

In the whole of the book of Judges, the occurrence of the phrase in 13:1 parallels the refrain, "Everyone did whatever seemed right to him" (17:6; 21:25). The choice for relativism rather than complete obedience leads to evil rather than any general moral goodness. After this last occurrence of Israel's relapse into evil, the writer will portray the magnitude of the results of rampant relativism in Judges 17–21, leaving the reader to think, "The people of Israel again did what was evil in the sight of the Lord."

The oppression Israel faces in 13:1 will last forty years, being the longest stint of oppression for their corporate abandonment of the Lord. With the mentioning of forty years, one should think of Israel's years of wandering in the wilderness for the rebellion at Kadesh-barnea as God's people feared entering the promised land. As in the forty years of wandering, two generations of Israel grow up under judgment rather than prosperity; they grow up as slaves under the Philistines for this return to evil. Some of God's people spent the majority, if not the entirety, of their adult lives in cruel bondage. Several decades passed before there was any sign of a military warrior to come release them. The last period of peace was but a distant memory to many; it was unknown to those who were toddlers at the start of the oppression or born once the forty years began.

Yet with every turn of the refrain of Israel's reindulgence in evil, one hopes for deliverance. The writer raises this hope in this passage by introducing the bondage of Israel before any mention of the barrenness of Manoah's wife and the future birth of a son. This passage first concerns the hope that God will deliver his people from four decades of Philistine oppression. Israel is barren of judges and peace in her land in 13:1. Only in providing hope for Israel's barrenness will the Lord make provision to resolve Manoah's wife's barrenness and to open Manoah's eyes so he can see God and worship him in fear.

Every believer's life is one part of what the Lord is doing to both strengthen his church and provide the message of salvation to people in bondage to sin. Not one believer lives life for herself or himself only. Each believer is a member of the holy nation called to proclaim the praises of God (1 Pet 2:9).

This means that every aspect of our lives is part of what the Lord is doing to provide salvation to the world through the church's witness to the gospel. This includes all marital activity and all single-life activity; all aspects of having, raising, and releasing children; and all aspects of one's occupation and leisure pursuits. It also includes all our sufferings and failings, including barren parts of our lives.

The Lord hears our prayers regarding the voids we face. His offers of hope are wrapped in his promises to deliver his church. We would do well, therefore, to offer our emptiness as a means for him to rescue people to himself. For some this will result in the birth, adoption, or foster care of one or more children. For others this will mean a life of barrenness in which the Lord provides joy, hope, and fellowship through surrendered service to him in forms other than biological, adoptive, fostering, or surrogate parenthood. For some it will mean seeing an unbelieving spouse cry out for salvation or an immature spouse maturing in the Lord; for others it will mean being wed to one whose commitment to Christ is questionable or absent or not being wed at all but finding joy, hope, and peace as a member of the bride of Christ in a form other than a thriving earthly marriage. For every believer, our hope is that Christ our Savior will deliver us from this world to his everlasting kingdom.

Our Hope Rests in Full Obedience to What We Know about the Son
JUDGES 13:2-14

With the writer hinting that whatever follows is part of the Lord's plan to deliver his people from oppression, the reader now has perspective for the story of Manoah and his wife. The passage will identify Manoah by name and mention him first, inviting the reader to focus on his activities in the passage. Yet the movement of the story equally depends on the unnamed wife's interactions with the angel of the Lord.

The Angel of the Lord and the Barren Woman (13:2-7)

The angel of the Lord will appear and reveal a coming end to Manoah's wife's childlessness. Three times one reads, "You will conceive and give birth to a son," and twice one reads, "The boy will be a Nazirite to God from birth." With certainty the barrenness of Manoah and his wife is coming to an end.

However, just as this is no ordinary conception but one with angelic pronouncement, this will be no ordinary life, as the angel warns Manoah's wife and then the wife repeats to Manoah. While carrying the child within her, the wife must refrain from drinking wine or beer and from eating anything unclean (vv. 4,7). The angel also tells Manoah's wife that the boy's hair must never be cut (v. 5). This last prohibition the wife fails to repeat to Manoah, and the angel of the Lord does not speak to Manoah directly.[45] Yet it is an important stipulation because the boy will be a Nazirite in the Lord's presence from birth. He will deliver Israel from their Philistine oppression.

This boy is the first (and only) Nazirite specified in Scripture, so the reader's expectation for the child should be high. The Nazirite stipulations in Numbers 6 indicate that the Nazirite vows were normally voluntary, and any man or woman could commit to them. The Nazirite—meaning "separated one"—could not drink anything alcoholic or eat anything produced from the grapevine. The Nazirite could not have a haircut or touch anything dead or unclean. So the standards for this boy are high and chosen for him before he is conceived. Considering Numbers 6, the angel seems to inform the wife of Manoah that this son is separated to God uniquely for the Lord to use to accomplish a mighty task.

The Angel of the Lord and the Barren Man (13:8-14)

Manoah is not present when the angel speaks to his wife; his initial knowledge of the birth and calling of the boy come secondhand from his wife, and she neglects to mention the prohibition related to shaving the boy's hair. So Manoah will ask the Lord for the angel to return to give instructions for raising this child. What Manoah has heard is not sufficient for him, possibly because he did not hear the instructions directly or because he does not think such instructions are enough to make the boy into a deliverer of Israel.

The Lord does hear Manoah's prayer and resends the angel of the Lord. Yet Manoah is not present when the angel again speaks to the wife. Manoah's wife will have to alert him to the return of the angel, and he will have to follow her to the place of meeting. The encounter will fill in Manoah's lack of knowledge about the angel but will not give any additional revelation about the boy. What seems to be important for Manoah is increasing his understanding of the angel.

From his wife, Manoah has information about the visitor who pronounced the birth of the child. But what he knows is not from a personal

---

[45] The prohibition against cutting the boy's hair is part of Manoah's responsibility because it would have been covered under, "Your wife needs to do everything I told her. . . . Your wife must do everything I have commanded her" (vv. 13-14). Even though the angel did not speak the words about no razor coming upon the boy's hair directly to Manoah, the angel made Manoah a steward of the words to his wife.

encounter with the angel. That knowledge is minimal: (1) The angel is a "man of God" and not "the angel of God" at this point; (2) he looks like an angel of God in his appearance—an appearance that is indeed awesome but not necessarily *divine*; (3) his place of origin is unknown, so it is not certain that he is from heaven; (4) he did not offer his name to the wife, so his name is unknown, leaving him with a possible earthly identity. Manoah has no reason to suspect that his wife has met with God, and he has no knowledge of the identity of the entity who will speak to him.

The only information Manoah will initially receive about the angel of the Lord is affirmation that the one who speaks to him is the one—the "man of God"—who spoke to his wife. The only information the angel gives Manoah about the boy is that Manoah's wife must obey the instructions the angel gave to her previously. This seems to mean that the knowledge Manoah has about the boy is sufficient to raise him into a deliverer.

Manoah was a husband whose wife had knowledge about the coming birth of a son and some knowledge about the angel who spoke. Manoah only had such knowledge via his wife, and his knowledge was incomplete. But the angel's reiterating of instructions rather than adding instructions means that the little information Manoah had on the son was enough to give him hope.

Unfortunately, many men in spiritual situations like Manoah's are intimidated away from the church by fear of what they do not know about God, Scripture, and/or Christ. They want to know what their mature Christian wives know, but the husbands have lesser knowledge for whatever reason. However, the goal is not to be a man who is not outdone by a woman. That is a competition of nonsense that we carry over from sports, education, the workforce, and secular relationship ideas—one that suggests a man is weak if his knowledge and abilities are less than that of a woman or that a man will not be respected if he is not as knowledgeable as his wife. Such ideas thrust power and control to the pinnacle of their worldviews rather than establishing the glory of Christ at the zenith of their worldviews. They want men to be in power, not grow in the knowledge of Christ.

All the Lord requires of us is that whatever knowledge we have of his Son, we do all that is in accordance with that knowledge. This puts a stewardship on us to grow in our knowledge of Christ. But it also frees us from needing to have a master class knowledge of God, the Scriptures, and Christ before we can have hope in Christ. Manoah gradually comes to know more about the angel of the Lord and only needs to be obedient to what is already known about the son to be born—the same knowledge his wife has and gave to him, no more and no less. There is no shame in learning slowly.

Our Hope Should Produce Worship as We See the Divine Identity of the Son
JUDGES 13:15-20

Everything in this next scene concerns Manoah's rapidly increasing knowledge of the angel of the Lord until he comes to full knowledge of the angel's identity. As he grows, his barrenness of knowing God fully dissipates and results in Manoah's becoming a worshiper.

Manoah's Detaining the Angel (13:15-16)

Manoah still lacks knowledge of the full identity of his visitor. Apparently thinking this is a man of God only, Manoah offers common hospitality and requests to detain the guest as he would any other person. For the reader, however, there are echoes to both Abraham's and Gideon's preparations of a young goat or young calf for the visit of the angel of the Lord (Gen 18:5-8; Judg 6:19). The preparation of the offering for the Lord anticipates the revelation Gideon experienced. The one who has come is not an eater of food. As the writer comments, Manoah is unaware that his dialogue is with the angel of the Lord.

Manoah's Honoring the Angel (13:17-18)

Apparently, the angel's words on offering the food to the Lord rather than for the angel to eat finally raises Manoah's curiosity enough for him to seek the visitor's identity. He needs the guest's name so that he may give him credit when the child is born and his words prove to be true. Manoah is not bashful about not knowing the name of the visitor. Any possible shame in knowing less than his wife has disappeared. In his innocent asking, Manoah will gain more revelation about the angel and his name.

Manoah asks the angel's name, fully expecting an answer from one he thinks is a superlative human being. But the angel adds more to his identity by withholding his name. Where one asks a question like Moses's question at the theophany of the burning bush, one receives an answer like the one from Jacob's night visitor. The name of Manoah's guest is greater than human—"beyond understanding." But Manoah does not seem to bring Jacob's encounter to mind; he remains in the dark about the divine character of the one he questions.

Manoah's and His Wife's Worshiping the Angel (13:19-20)

Having no clear answer about the name, Manoah obeys the angel and prepares to offer the goat with a grain offering. Manoah soon will be able to connect the name that is beyond understanding to the one who does miraculous things.

As he makes this offering, for the first time in the story Manoah and his wife will be together for the revelation from the angel. Manoah will not be barren of the knowledge of the angel's identity when his wife receives it; this time they will share their moment of revelation together. Both are watching what happens next.

The angel shoots up toward heaven through the flame, doing a miracle that is beyond human, beyond understanding. He reveals his identity as the divine angel of the Lord without saying to Manoah and his wife, "I am the angel of the Lord." Gradually, as Manoah and his wife watch, they are able to conclude for themselves the true name of the one they thought was simply a man of God. This is the preincarnate second member of the triune God. The married couple awaiting a child and the deliverance of Israel together now know their hopes rest in the words of God himself to them. Together they will bow in worship before the messenger who has revealed himself, giving them certainty of the child for which they hope.

In February 2021, a fierce winter storm blanketed much of the state of Texas, causing much flooding, lack of heat and water for many residents, and loss to the power grid. During that storm, Ted Cruz, US senator from Texas, took his family to Cancun on vacation while much of the state suffered. The uproar that happened in response to Cruz's trip possibly has ruined his chances of becoming president of the United States (Peoples and Bleiberg, "Obviously a Mistake").

In June of that same year, the US witnessed hundreds of immigrants coming to the US via the US-Mexico border. The crossings, especially as they concerned children coming to the US without their parents, created a crisis along the border. During this crisis, US Vice President Kamala Harris made a trip to Guatemala to work with Guatemala to slow migration from that country to the US.

Shortly after her trip, in an interview with NBC News anchor Lester Holt, the news journalist highlighted the vice president's lack of a visit to the US-Mexican border (Morin, "VP Kamala Harris Pushes Back"). The vice president visited the border a few weeks later, but the damage of her previous absence followed her. For both the vice president and the senator, absence during a time of need did not sit well with their constituency—the people they were called to serve.

Manoah's wife might have had cause to feel angst toward Manoah. When a messenger came to announce the end of her great barrenness, twice he was absent. When he does show up, he questions the angel's identity with respect to the first appearance to his wife, offers him food he refuses, and further inquires into the messenger's name even though the messenger has not been forthcoming in offering it. How embarrassing, if not also rude! If Manoah just had been present when his wife was hearing the Lord's words from the messenger, this line of inquiry would have been unnecessary. Surely Manoah's absence could have been the cause for his wife's loss of respect.

However, when the messenger finally makes known his identity as the divine angel of the Lord—the prebodily Son of God—all that Manoah has not done in the past is unimportant. What is important is that both he and his wife fall facedown and worship the Lord. I suspect Manoah's wife was glad to have him by her side worshiping the angel.

No one fully understands all of who Jesus is at any one point. One believer might be more mature in understanding and practice in one aspect of the knowledge of God's will, and another believer may have more maturity in a different area. Whether one has been walking with Christ for ten years or forty years, the foibles due to the immaturity and spiritual absence of a spouse are not a priority when the spouse finally begins to worship Christ. What is important is that both bow together before Christ in grace, as the Lord is the one making the Son known more fully to each of us.

Our Hope Gives Perspective on Death as We Watch the Son's Work as Savior
JUDGES 13:21-25

Perspective of Fear (13:21-22)

The angel of the Lord vanishes into the flame, having reached the end of his need to appear to Manoah and his wife. Manoah reasons from the things the angel said and did that this was no ordinary man of God; this was the angel of the Lord. The angel allows Manoah to see that he had been standing in the presence of God, questioning God's identity and offering God hospitality! Manoah had just stood face-to-face with God.

When Manoah considers the full revelation of the angel, he concludes that he and his wife will die because they have seen the face of God. Manoah shows familiarity with many Scriptures that teach that humans cannot see the face of God and live. People lack the capacity to bear receiving the full glory of infinite holiness within our finite beings. Sin would be obliterated in the presence of the holy God. Moreover, the sinner is worthy of death before God the Judge. As finite beings are thoroughly full of sin, standing in the presence of God in one's earthly, fallen humanity would mean certain death. Manoah is correct to conclude that death would be the appropriate outcome of standing in the presence of God face-to-face, especially after not recognizing him immediately and bowing down at once.

Perspective of Reason (13:23)

However, it is evident in this passage that Manoah's wife has a greater understanding of God and his ways than Manoah. She is the one to whom the angel originally speaks, who reiterates the commands of the angel, who does not question the identity of the angel, who brings Manoah to the angelic visitor, bows in worship with Manoah, and who now reasons to a different conclusion based on experiences with the angel.

The acceptance of the goat and grain offerings means the couple is accepted before God. Seeing the angel going up into the flame would have been unnecessary if they would not live to tell about it. The revelation about the son to be born means that Manoah and his wife will live to see their son deliver Israel. These truths add up to manifest the grace of God toward Manoah and his wife in the unmasking of the angel's identity. They are not going to die; they have hope of living because of the angel's words.

Perspective of Progress (13:24-25)

The hope of Manoah and his wife to have a son comes to reality as "the woman gave birth to a son and named him Samson." The words anticipate the words revealed to Isaiah that later are fulfilled in the birth of Jesus: "The virgin will conceive, have a son, and name him Immanuel" (Isa 7:14).

The child will grow with God's blessings, just as one later sees that "Jesus increased in wisdom and stature, and in favor with God and with people" (Luke 2:52). The blessing of the Lord on Samson is consistent with the hope of a judge whom the Lord will use to rescue Israel from oppression.

The Spirit of the Lord who empowered Othniel, Gideon, and Jephthah begins to work in Samson to move him into the calling to destroy the Philistines. The presence of the Spirit of the Lord anticipates victories like those had by the three previous specially empowered warriors. The reader is watching the work of the Lord in the promised son, looking forward to the freedom of God's people.

Waiting often is the most difficult part of hope. Along the time line of the accomplishment of God's purposes and answers to prayers, some days can feel as if the Lord were not listening and that a bad situation is hopeless. However, no one else in Israel was present when the angel spoke, nor can anyone else connect the blessing and growth in Samson to the future deliverance of Israel. But the deliverance is certain even though the nation does not see the unique working of God in Samson as he grows like any other blessed Israelite son.

Neither do God's people now see all the Lord is doing to reconcile the world to himself and to bring final salvation to many. In our difficulties and disappointments, we tend to look at the situation that oppresses rather than the promises of deliverance in Christ. But our hope is in the Son who is full of the Spirit of the Lord. He will deliver God's barren people.

Review and Discuss

1. Describe your experience of walking through the pain of infertility, stillbirth, miscarriage, or death of a young child personally or with a friend's loss. (Discuss with great sensitivity if in a group setting.)
2. Describe your experience of walking through the difficulty of marriage to an unbeliever, of an immature spouse, or of watching a parent, sibling, or friend do so.
3. What role does hope play in maturing as a Christian and growing in our love of the Lord and of our neighbor?
4. Consider a present concern or struggle in your life. What would it mean for you to view this concern as part of the Lord's good plan for redeeming others to himself? What would you feel about your

concern if it meant the salvation of a handful of people and/or the growth of fellow members of your local assembly?

5. Why might it have been so easy for Israel to return to sin after the death of a judge, knowing that each previous choice to do so led to years of oppression?

6. What does the namelessness of Manoah's wife do for the tone of the passage as you are reading?

7. What might be the significance of the writer's losing the prohibition of cutting the boy's hair as the passage develops?

8. What contributes to the phenomenon of wives being present in public worship in greater numbers than men? What could congregations do to serve such families with the hope of seeing husband and wife worshiping together?

9. What are some ways your local church could better serve families grieving infertility?

10. Read Numbers 6 in full. What would Samson have experienced in childhood and teen life as a Nazirite? What might growing up as a Nazirite have contributed to the character one later sees in Samson?

Aged Wisdom for Contemporary Challenges

JUDGES 14

Main Idea: The failure to seek wisdom of aged saints for our contemporary challenges invites troubles that can only be resolved by grace.

I. The Aged Should Point Us Back to the Covenant of God (14:1-4).
II. The Aged Should Point Us toward the Law of God (14:5-9).
III. The Aged Can Direct Us with Wisdom from God (14:10-17).
IV. The Aged Show Us the Way of the Grace of God (14:19-20).

I think one universal wish people have is to know the future. We wish we could see what is coming around the corner tomorrow, next week, next month, and next year, or even what is headed our way in a decade. Of course, we can do some things like forecast weather—unless you live in proximity to Lake Michigan. We can tell what markets will do, get the Triple Crown winner right, and predict which three people will tie up the church business meeting with absolutely unnecessary questions. But even things like that involve some use of trends and measurements.

What I mean is something different. I mean starting with *nada* and then being able to say, "Got it!" We wish for such power because knowledge of the future would give us the ability to do things like make the right investments, know which risks to take, choose the best paths or directions, or avoid making mistakes—definitely the really costly ones.

While there is no actual way to do more than estimate or forecast, there is one good way we can tell the future. If we perceive "telling the future" as being in this spot now and trying to make the decision or decisions that will put us in the best spot tonight, tomorrow, next week, or twenty years from now, there is a way to do that. "I wish I knew then what I know now" can go from idea to production, even skipping R&D, and we can be in that down-the-road spot *now*—especially with respect to surviving and thriving within our cultural encroachment, oppression, and even war if we will do one thing Samson failed to do. We must seek the wisdom of those who are older so they can tell us—from their future vantage point of being twenty or more years ahead of us in life—what decision they would have made in our shoes twenty or more years of life ago. Chapter 14 allows us to explore some *whys* and *hows* of gaining aged wisdom for contemporary challenges.

The Aged Should Point Us Back to the Covenant of God
JUDGES 14:1-4

Samson goes to Timnah and sees a girl who is just everything and much more in his sight. He runs back home excited with emotion to demand that his parents get her hand in marriage. There is only one problem: she is not from Israel, and Mom and Dad want to know why Samson can't just marry that nice girl next door who always plays the role of one of the midwives in the Passover play and whose father is an Aaronic priest. Why, Samson, why do you have to get a girl who is from the "uncircumcised Philistines"?

The word *uncircumcised* points Samson and us back to Genesis 17 and the Abrahamic covenant. That is what the aged should do: they should point us back to the covenant of God. Samson's parents are saying to him that as an Israelite he is related to the Lord and the Philistines are not. Circumcision is a sign of Israel's unique relationship with the Lord, as given to Abraham and his offspring. It set apart Israel from the people of the nations as holy and peculiar, loved by God as his own (Deut 7:2). That relationship must color even your marital choice. In fact, we Israelites are not supposed to give our sons away to the women of noncovenant nations but instead are to destroy those peoples.

But Samson, singing the main chorus of the book of Judges—"I will do what is right in my own eyes"—demands that his parents get this girl because "she's the right one for me." He rejects their gentle prodding of wisdom and ignores the covenant that intended his blessing.

When Martin Luther, father of the Protestant Reformation, faced temptation, he would shout out, "I am a baptized man!" Luther realized that the sign of baptism marked him as distinct, and he could point to that rite as a means for motivating the right decision.

Grayer-haired members of our congregations should do something similar for us—at least those grayer-haired members who are mature in Christ, and older parents in particular—based on this passage. In all our decision-making, the mature older saints should remind us that our relationship with Christ matters in all decisions. It is not that being a Christian draws a line in the sand for our dating, marriage, and business partnership practices only. Those who are older can say to us in every area of life, "Now let me tell you how I would make that decision as a believer."

Even when the wisdom of the aged is scorned, the sovereignty of God still is at work. For unknown to the covenant-wise parents is God's plan to destroy the Philistines through Samson. Sovereignty means the Lord's will is accomplished. But as the Samson story shows, it does not mean that poor decisions made under the sovereignty of God will be without hardship to us.

The Aged Should Point Us toward the Law of God
JUDGES 14:5-9

Samson and his parents head to Timnah to fetch this heathen gal and land themselves in the vineyards of Timnah. Now these seem to be large vineyards, and the parents must have been in them at some great distance from Samson because a lion attacks Samson and they do not even hear it.

Samson, however, with the power of the Spirit of the Lord on him, grabs the lion and rips him apart the way one would dismember a young lamb in preparation for a meal. (That's some spectacular filling of the Spirit!) But he keeps the attack hidden from his parents, and they head into Timnah and talk with the woman about marrying Samson. Apparently, Samson did not stain his clothes or break a sweat in process, for he acts like nothing ever happened and gets away with it.

The writer does not speak of the return trip home but only of the trip back again, for Samson passes the body of the dead lion in the vineyard of Timnah. Inside this carcass, amid the decay, some bees make their home and by now have a hive big enough to produce a sizable amount of honey—enough for Samson to grab some, eat along the route, and share with his parents. But again, Samson does not disclose to his parents that the honey comes from a dead carcass. If he had, his aged parents might have pointed him toward the law of God.

From Judges 13 we know that Samson was a Nazirite. He had a special designation, anointing, and calling.[46] He could not eat or drink anything from the grapevine—not even *in utero* (v. 4; see also Num 6:3-4). He could

---

[46] See Num 6:1-21 for the stipulations and prohibitions for those designated as Nazirites.

not cut his hair, said the angel of the Lord to his parents (v. 5; see also Num 6:5). The full stipulations of the Nazirite vow in Numbers 6 add this:

> He must not go near a dead body during the time he consecrates himself to the LORD. He is not to defile himself for his father or mother, or his brother or sister, when they die, while the mark of consecration to his God is on his head. He is holy to the LORD during the time of consecration. (Num 6:6-8)

Had he told his parents about the death of the lion, they could have said to him, "Son, you cannot touch dead things because the law of God says so. Whatever you do, son, do not go back and touch that lion or any other dead thing! Son, next time a lion is coming to attack you, please, simply swat the lion away or put it in a sleep hold." If Samson had looked into the law of God after speaking to his parents, he could have repented from breaking the law. He also would have refrained from making his parents complicit in his trespasses.

When my children were young, they watched a children's TV show called *The Proud Family*. The main character, Mr. Proud, an inventor, would often take risks that led to accidents or bodily harm. However, before he would make such decisions, a person hearing or seeing what he was about to do would say, "Remember what happened the last time, Mr. Proud." Inevitably the proud inventor would not listen to the warning and would soon injure himself or make a mess with great embarrassment.

Stocked with both years of living *and* the discernment that comes with having the mind of Christ, aged believers should stand in our lives to say to us, "May I tell you what happened the last time someone tried to defraud business partners rather than gathering wealth by honest labor?" (see Prov 13:11), or "Let me tell you what happened the last time—the last thousand times!—someone treated their family with a lack of graciousness in all things" (see Eph 6:4). They should play a role in our lives that allows them to say to us, "Don't be proud. Do what the Word of God tells us to do."

The Aged Can Direct Us with Wisdom from God
JUDGES 14:10-17

Now having the bride in hand, Samson and his dad go to prepare the wedding reception. Samson is imitating the Philistines' young men's ceremonies. It seems they are offering thirty attendants to be like groomsmen for Samson. So Samson, apparently proud of his defeat of the lion and still thinking of it, poses a riddle with a wager to the Philistine cohort. At stake are thirty linen garments and thirty sets of men's clothes. It is an expensive wager and a difficult riddle that they have one week to resolve. But they cannot do so within the first three days of the feast.

Not wanting to lose the bet and give Samson clothing at their own expense, the men threaten Samson's wife's life. They do not even say they will extract the price of the garments from the wife and her father. Instead, being uncircumcised Philistines who do not have the righteous law of God in mind, they threaten her and her father with death by *fire*. This forces the girl to beg and press Samson for the riddle's answer.

After a few days of her weeping, Samson gives in. How interesting it is that he tells her he has not yet told his father and mother the riddle. Samson should have told his mother and father the riddle, for had he done so, they could have directed him with wisdom from God. Samson's parents could have told him that he should not have asked the riddle and that he should have known that those without the Israelite law would have come after his wife and father-in-law to hurt him. If he had told his parents, they could have said to him, "Boy, that riddle is dumb! What is the answer? Go right away and get out of that wager or tell the Philistines the answer!"

As the reader knows, Samson cannot tell Dad and Mom the riddle because he would have to admit touching the lion's carcass. His compromise is turning into an endless cycle of wrongs. As my wife consistently warned our children in their younger years, "You know something is wrong if you have to hide it from your parents."

Instead, the Philistines' threat forces Samson to tell the riddle to the Philistine girl, who tells it to the Philistine companions. Then, on the seventh day before the sun goes down—just in the nick of time— the Philistines approach Samson with the answer to the riddle, probably speaking with victorious, mocking smiles and wagging tongues: "Samson, some sweet honey came out of a lion you killed. *Na-na na-na boo-boo.*" We can imagine the thirty men sitting back with their arms folded, some of them high fiving one another and dancing around Samson like an instigating sibling.

Why did they wag their tongues at a man they now know can rip a *lion* to pieces? What did they expect to happen next, especially since they pressed his wife to get the answer and should suspect that he knows as much? They get a harsh answer back: "If you hadn't plowed with my young cow, you wouldn't know my riddle now!" (Another word for "young cow" is *heifer*. Since verse 3 we have been wanting to say with Samson's parents, "Why do you want one of those Philistine *heifers*?") You have to love the bovine imagery of Samson! *You stole my calfless cow to plow your field because you and your cow could not get it done on your own, and now you come bragging about getting the work in your field done at the expense of my cow? What good is she to me now? Oh, no! You're going to pay for that!*

The Aged Show Us the Way of the Grace of God
14:19-20

The Spirit of the Lord comes upon Samson. He kills thirty men in Ashkelon, the largest Philistine city, to get the thirty outfits for the men. He acts contrary to the law of God even while filled with the Spirit of God as he goes about his rampage. Then, still angry over losing the bet and the plowing of his heifer, he goes back to his father's house, for in the house of the aged, he will find the grace of God. What do I mean?

Samson assumes that even in murder, anger, foolishness, breaking the Nazirite vow, and making his parents complicit in such, his father will take him back. Is he deserving of the free return and shelter? No. Should his parents provide shelter for this lawbreaker at the threat that the Philistines now will seek revenge for the lives of the thirty? No. Should he be able to come back without apology or admittance of wrongdoing? No. How then does he go back? *By grace: his father shows him grace.* Having destroyed his marriage and taken the lives of thirty Philistines, Samson needs grace.

The aged show us the way of grace. It is fascinating how those who have lived long are able to find a way to administer more and more grace into a situation where we who are younger largely see a need for law. As grandparents you see this, offering your child a way to deal with their own children far more graciously than you would have dealt with your own children when they were younger. Is this only a factor of being able to have the grandchildren for a short period and then return them to their parents? No, I do not believe any mature, believing grandparent is that flippant or sophomoric. Instead, I think that having parented, grandparents of a certain age have the twenty-year or more perspective that makes them say to themselves, "I've seen this before, in my own children. I remember how I handled this twenty or thirty years ago. Now that I have lived longer, walked with the Lord much longer, and have years of reflection, I would handle this situation with much more grace" (in whatever form that grace takes).

Older pastors do something similar in giving advice to younger pastors, as do older administrators and teachers to new teachers and young administrators, and as do managers and entrepreneurs near retirement toward those just getting off the ground in their professional careers. The seasoned believer shows the younger one how to exercise grace toward angry customers, troubling students, dissatisfied parents of students, and difficult employees. They do so in the hopes that the younger believers will be even better at their tasks than those now older were from the onset of parenting, teaching, managing, coaching, investing, learning, and growing into adulthood.

Samson's heifer episode reminds us that the way of grace is the way of Christ. Are we deserving of the free return to the Father and of shelter under his mercy? No. Should God provide for us who have broken his law and who have enemies who want to destroy us? No. Should we be able to come back with simple repentance toward our wrongdoing? No, because repentance cannot pay the penalty for the laws that have been broken. How then does one go back to God? By grace: the Father gives us grace through his Son, Jesus Christ, our Lord.

Christ is the one who looks at our faults, mishaps, and mistakes and says he will not return to us justice in measure for measure. Instead of making us earn our way to righteousness, which we could not do, he gives us his righteousness freely. He then takes the penalty due our sins on himself. The Scripture calls this working of Christ *grace*—the gift of eternal life given freely to us but at great cost to Jesus.

Application

Here are some things we each might do to gain aged wisdom:

Adults should learn to seek older, mature saints for wisdom on decisions. This includes decisions on home buying, changing jobs, investing, resolving conflicts, managing life in general, addressing marital problems, and of course, raising children. Mature saints exist for the purpose of passing on wisdom, especially in places where the Word of God does not give specifics on your situation.

Children should learn to develop the habit of asking their parents for wisdom and then doing what they say. Please reject the lies of the world that teach you to reject your parents—lies that our friends promote when they question our parents' rules or suggest that our parents are only being traditional or old-fashioned and that they are out of date, out of touch, and out of style with what is right. That is, only what is right in your friends' eyes.

The Lord gives parents to guide children. If you did not need guidance, you would have been born into the world with adult reasoning skills and the knowledge and wisdom to go with it. But you were born into the world not even knowing how to get food or clothes. You were thrown into dependency on your parents so you would learn to trust them to guide you.

My children know that although I have a string of accomplishments, much learning, and have lived more than a half century of life, when I need to make a decision that can be life altering, I pick up the phone and call my father—an older, wiser, God-fearing saint. "Dad, what do you think about this?" I give him all the information I have available and tell him I will pray and wait for him to respond. I need to know what the future says about the decision I am about to make. So I wait for the future to call me back and tell me what happened the last time someone attempted to do what I am about to do.

As adults and servants in our churches, we all need to be readers of church history. We need to hear from our spiritual parents how to face the Philistines of our own day, for they have faced them in the past. That is part of the point of reading history and church history: to learn from the successes and mistakes of those of an older generation as the church engages culture. History tells us about the Crusades, the Inquisition, engagement with Copernicus and Galileo, slavery, the Salem witch trials, the prosperity gospel movement, the church's response to the revolutions of the sixties and the Vietnam War, and much more. It also tells us about Luther's Ninety-Five Theses, Calvin's Geneva Reform, the way the Black church in the US fueled the Civil Rights Movement's nonviolent tendencies, Schaefer's L'Abri, the Lausanne Movement, and the 1995 SBC Apology for Racism. Reflection on all these and more historical points are filled with wisdom for us to use in thinking about how to look at contemporary challenges. The aged saints have left bread crumbs for us until we make it home to be with them and our Lord Jesus.

Reflect and Discuss

1. When a child or friend is as adamant about a foolish decision as Samson is about being with a Philistine girl, what should our response be?
2. What is one decision you need to make for which you wish you could see into the future for the wisdom needed to decide rightly?
3. Name a time when you appealed to someone older for wisdom and their wisdom saved you from making a bad decision. What would have happened if you had done what was right in your own eyes?
4. When have you received grace from an older believer when you thought you were going to receive words of law—of judgment?
5. Why is it so difficult for young parents to demonstrate the grace grandparents often demonstrate toward their grandchildren?
6. If you are younger than fifty years old, ask your parents and/ or other older, mature believers what some decisions are they wish they had made differently when they were under fifty years old and why.
7. How can the most mature, older believers begin to build *gracious,* parent-like relationships with teens and young adults?
8. Why do many young children of believers and/or believing young children view their parents as enemies rather than as sources of wisdom? Why do some believing adult children view their parents similarly?
9. What events and decisions in church history might be informative to help your local assembly make decisions facing it right now?
10. How do we become people who love to demonstrate grace toward others like the grace God demonstrates toward us at all times through Christ?

A Strong Plan for Manhandling Frustration

JUDGES 15

Main Idea: A man's attempts at handling frustrating things in the power of his human strength rather than in the power of the indwelling Spirit comes with costs to himself, his family, and the church, despite great victories over some of his frustrations by the power of God and temporary times of peace in his life.[47]

I. Satisfy Your Unfulfilled Burning in Marriage with Creativity rather than Burning Your Family (15:1-6).
II. Secure Justice for Your Family with God-Honoring Resources rather than Forcing Your Friends to Bring Justice on You (15:7-17).
III. Silence Ridicule of Your Enemies in Prayer rather than Robbing God of His Glory (15:17-19).
IV. Separate Your Personal Success from Your Frustrations so that You See Your Need for God (15:20).

M any now have forgotten how hard it seemed to be for musical artist Chris Brown to endure his 2011 interview with *Good Morning America*'s Robyn Roberts. On the day he launched a new album, Roberts asked him questions surrounding the legal fallout of his assault of singing star Rihanna. Brown, who was scheduled to perform two concerts on the news show, stormed off after performing one song, threw a chair into the window of his dressing room, confronted a segment producer, and chose not to perform a second concert.[48]

---

[47] I derive the application statement above based on the meaning of the passage: *Samson's attempts at handling frustrating events in the power of his human strength comes with costs to himself, his wife and her family, and Judah, despite great victories over the Philistines by the power of God and rule in Israel for twenty years.*

[48] "Chris Brown's Outburst," *ABC News*, March 23, 2011, https://abcnews.go .com/Nightline/video/chris-browns-outburst-13199230; "Chris Brown Storms Off Set of 'Good Morning America'," *ABC News*, March 22, 2011, https://abcnews.go.com /Entertainment/chris-brown-storms-off-set-good-morning-america/story?id=13193040; "Despite Tantrum, Chris Brown Invited Back on 'GMA'," *Washington Post*, March 23, 2011, https://www.washingtonpost.com/lifestyle/style/the-tv-column-despite-tantrum-chris -brown-invited-back-on-gma/2011/03/23/AB9Lz8KB_story.html; Lisa de Mores, "Chris Brown Apologizes . . . Kinda," *Washington Post*, March 24, 2011, https://www.washingtonpost

What a way to handle frustration!

Frustrations—we all have them. There are things we want out of life that we just cannot get fulfilled:

- You just want a good school for your child to attend, but the current teacher is not working toward your child's success.
- You only want a little respect in your house, but it seems like the more you hope for it with patience, the further away it seems to be.
- You want to pursue your dreams, but you have people in your life who are like dead weight—who can't see that your dreams would mean blessings for them also.
- You just want to secure some justice, but the lady with the scales will not tip them in your favor.

When you face frustrations, the great temptation can be to handle it in the power of the old nature, to get what you want by any means—by threat, by despondency, by cheating, by taking matters into your own hands and not waiting for the people with authority to act, or by any other means that will allow you to vent your frustrations. We forget, however, that there are costs to handling our personal frustrations Chris Brown-style. Yet, by turning around the negative example of Samson, one can see that there always is a God-honoring way of dealing with the most frustrating people and problems in our lives. From Samson one can discern *a strong plan for manhandling frustrations*.

Satisfy Your Unfulfilled Burning in Marriage with Creativity rather than Burning Your Family
JUDGES 15:1-6

Samson is that powerful judge—that military leader in Israel—best known for an episode with a girl named Delilah. But long before he met Delilah, he was a man in trouble with his passions, as discussed in previous chapters:

.com/blogs/tv-column/post/chris-brown-apologizeskinda/2011/03/24/ABwsxeOB
_blog.html; idem, "Chris Brown Storms Off 'Good Morning America' after Rihanna Question," *Washington Post*, March 22, 2011, https://www.washingtonpost.com/blogs /tv-column/post/chris-brown-storms-off-good-morning-america-after-rihanna-question /2011/03/22/ABupFHDB_blog.html.

- He was an Israelite under the law but wanted a wife from the Philistines.
- He was a Nazirite from birth but would eat honey from a beehive in a carcass when he was hungry.
- When the Philistines squeezed the answer to a riddle out of his wife by threatening to burn her and her father's house down, he killed thirty men in another town to give their clothes as payment to those who solved the riddle. Then he left his wife without a consummated marriage and went back to his father's house.

He is a man out of control, quick to give in to his earthly passions, even though the narrative often depicts him securing victories by the Spirit of God.

When this scene begins, Samson has calmed down enough to figure out that he would like to consummate his marriage (v. 1; cf. 16:1). He is in the doghouse, so he knows if something is going to happen in the bedroom, he better not come to the door without an expensive, gift-wrapped goat from an upscale store in his hand. However, when he arrives at the door of his father-law's house, he is stopped before he can get a foot in the door. Dad, based on Samson's previous actions and thinking Samson was finished with his relationship with his wife, gave his daughter to Samson's best man and offers the beautiful younger sister to please Samson instead.

Now Samson is *frustrated*; he is *sexually* frustrated. His plan was to have his fill of his wife, but the show has been stopped because of his own previous outburst. He will deal with his pent-up burning desires— his inability to consummate his marriage—creatively by tying together three hundred foxes in pairs by the tails with torches and setting them loose in the wheat fields and orchards of the Philistines. He will think he is justified in striking at the heart of their economy and religious belief system because they were the ones who put the squeeze on his wife.

The result of Samson's antics is that the Philistines come back and burn down the home of his wife and father-in-law just like they originally threatened. But he easily could have avoided this *and* had his sexual pleasure fulfilled if he had just taken the younger, beautiful daughter to be his bride, since the first marriage was annulled. Thus, from Samson we learn that one should *satisfy unfulfilled burning in marriage with creativity rather than burning your family.*

Samson's sinful desires told him to tie three hundred foxes together with torches and let them loose. The running foxes' attempts to free themselves would create zigzags through the fields, burning all the grain. How did he think of such a thing? What creativity!

But if Samson could think creatively in his frustration, he could have proposed a creative solution to his sexual problem or taken the one staring him in the face (i.e., the other daughter). If he had taken that same creative energy for tying tails and put it to good use, rather than just grabbing a goat off the shelf, he could have come to the younger daughter's house with fox coats, fox shawls, fox hats, fox rugs, fox-bone jewelry, and fox comforters, too! He could have handed Dad a wealth of fox meat for the winter. That younger bride would have been so impressed that he would not have had to worry about being frustrated in the bedroom for quite a while. He also would not have provoked the ire of the Philistines toward his father-in-law.

It is painful to watch men burn their families because of frustrations in the bedroom. For example, a wife becomes cold because of stress with her work or children, and the husband responds by staying in his den at night to surf websites fit only for demons' viewing. Or a wife makes a complaint about being unfulfilled, and instead of figuring out how to serve her, he looks for intimacy with a different woman who won't complain.

But these things burn families—they *harm* families. They leave a dad who can't tell his son how to control his passions. They destroy a family through divorce; they bring continuous yelling and fighting. They create insecure and despondent children who become distrustful of authority figures. (Maybe your dad is or was like this, showing his need to yield his passions to the power of Christ.)

It would be better for a frustrated man to take an unplanned family vacation just for vacation's sake. Tell your boss you are going to use some leave and tell your wife it is just for her (or, wives, just for him). It would be better to find a marriage conference, have the room stocked with some gifts upon arrival, and even skip a few formal conference sessions for private marital sessions in one's room. It would be better to show up at the wife's office for lunch and increase the number of conversation times during the day until the wife has talked out her concerns, worry, and stress, and to wait on the Lord to change her heart. Satisfy unfulfilled burning *within* your marriage, and *if you are not married, do not listen to, watch, or participate in activities that will make you burn sexually, because you are supposed to honor God in your body.*

Secure Justice for Your Family with God-Honoring Resources rather than Forcing Your Friends to Bring Justice on You
JUDGES 15:7-17

Samson is not to be outdone by any Philistine. No one will tell him whom to marry. No one will get away with burning his family. He now wants *justice*, but in the form of *revenge* rather than due process. He has to get them back for what they have done to his people. So he strikes down many of their men, leaving them in a mangle of legs wrapped in one another like ancient wrestling. Then he retreats to the cleft of a rock at Etam. This temporarily and wrongly satisfies his frustration to set things right for his wife's and father-in-law's deaths.

As the rulers over Israel, the Philistines have had enough of this Israelite's rebellion. First their fields were burned, and now their warriors have been humiliated. They are going to deal with Samson once and for all. So they raid Lehi in Judah and encamp around Judah for war, forcing Judah to collect the great strong man out of the cleft in their region.

Taking three thousand men—because they would need at least that many to tackle Samson—Judah intends to hand him over to the Philistines. But note Samson's words that reveal his heart and frustration: "I have done to them what they did to me."

Samson has stooped to the level of his enemies, and justifiably so in his own mind. Yet the men of Judah must bind him or bring the wrath of the Philistines on themselves. Samson's response to what happened to his family, rather than satisfying him, has gotten him into more trouble. Samson's pains teach us to *secure justice for your family with God-honoring resources rather than forcing your friends to bring justice on you.*

By his actions, *Samson asked for this.* He saw injustice toward his family, but his response was just as unjust.[49] He is about to get what he deserves. Yet he retains enough of his wits to negotiate with Judah to keep them from killing him (v. 13). When he comes to the Philistines, and with

---

[49] Granted, (1) the Israelites were commanded to destroy the nations of Canaan, and (2) the Lord intends to use Samson to destroy the Philistines; nevertheless, Samson's actions reveal an angry, vengeful heart and capriciousness. Samson is not just intending to destroy those unwilling to make peace, nor is he bringing judgment only upon those responsible for the deaths of his former wife and father-in-law, nor is he leading Israel to be freed from the Philistine oppression as did other judges. Samson is out of control, acting from personal, unrighteous passions.

their war cry they think they have victory in hand, the Holy Spirit looses him from his bonds. He takes the jawbone of a dead donkey and has his way of revenge on one thousand of the Philistines, getting his justice for himself in a sense greater than the previous act of vengeance.

One of the frustrating things we face in the fallen world is injustices toward our families. At those times, much like Samson, often we are not willing to use God-honoring resources to obtain justice, for righteous means of accomplishing justice seem to be processes that are too slow or too weak for our liking. But Samson's story should make us reconsider unwise responses to injustices toward our families:

- Do not slug a coach for yanking your child—the star player (in your eyes)—off the court or field because your child is not getting the playing time or encouragement you think your child should get. Your friends will have to tell you that you are in the wrong for doing this.
- Don't read the riot act at school when you are fed up with a teacher's or the administration's treatment of your children. If the school calls the police on you, do not expect sympathy from fellow believers when you are in trouble because you sought your own solution to the problem. Attacking the school is not justice. Your Christian friends have to support what is just.
- Whatever you do, if your spouse's boss is guilty of mistreatment, don't go to work with your spouse the following day or call the boss on the phone!
- If someone has injured a member of your family or stolen from you, do not pull your car in front of their house in order to threaten them. Let the process of law do its work.

In September 2007, O. J. Simpson entered a room of the Palace-Station hotel-casino with three other men and at gunpoint stole sports memorabilia. When police questioned him, he denied using a gun but admitted to stealing the items because he said they had been stolen from him. The Juice served nine years of a thirty-three-year sentence and remains on parole.[50] Why? Because he took care of injustice by his own means.

---

[50] "O. J. Part of 'Military-Style Invasion' of Hotel Room, Witness Says," *CNN*, Nov 8, 2007, http://edition.cnn.com/2007/US/law/11/08/simpson, accessed April 14, 2021; Paul Vercammen and Faith Karimi, "O. J. Simpson out of Nevada Prison after 9 Years,

You can use EEO and your appeal processes at work. You can ask for a meeting with teachers and principals. You can meet calmly with a coach. You can ask for a meeting with the pastor rather than repeating havoc in all the ministries or bolting for the next church after you make a mess of things at your church. Spiritual maturity includes knowing that God is the judge of the whole earth, and he will do right (see Gen 18:23-25; Deut 32:4; Job 8:3; 34:10). He is called a "strong tower" (Ps 61:3; Prov 18:10) because he is! He is called a "fortress" (2 Sam 22:2; Pss 18:2; 31:2-3; 46:7,11; 48:3; 59:9,16,17; 62:2,6; 91:9) because he is! He is called a "shield" (Deut 33:29; 2 Sam 22:3; Pss 3:3; 18:2,30; 84:9,11; 119:114; Prov 2:7; 30:5) because he is! The Lord can secure justice for your family. Don't make him bring his justice on you.

Silence Ridicule of Your Enemies in Prayer rather than Robbing God of His Glory
JUDGES 15:17-19

Having single-handedly defeated a thousand men, Samson is just a little bit thirsty. But apparently there is no water anywhere to be found. To a man whose passions are out of control, this means to him that he is bound to die. He *thinks* in extremes as much as he *acts* in extremes. He gives a five-hundred-dollar response to a five-cent problem. He is like Esau, who would sell his right to the larger inheritance and line of blessing for a bowl of stew: "Let me eat some of that red stuff, because I'm exhausted. . . . I'm about to die, so what good is a birthright to me?" (Gen 25:30,32). He is like the student who throws away a whole semester based on one relationship breakup.

Dying of thirst means he will fall into the hands of the Philistines when they come to clean up or avenge their dead friends. That will mean ridicule for Samson: they could chop off his head, sing songs about how he couldn't hold his jawbone any longer, and/or drag his body back to their towns as if they defeated him on their own. Frustrated about the potential to be ridiculed, Samson points a finger of blame at *God* (v. 18).

Isn't this odd? He recognizes that the Spirit of God brought him the victory (vv. 14,18). He recognizes that God rescued him and that he

Plans to Stay in Vegas," *CNN*, Oct 2, 2017, https://www.cnn.com/2017/10/01/us/oj -simpson-released-from-prison/index.html.

is a servant of the Lord, not vice versa. However, the tone of his prayer is that God owes him! There is no way God could let him get ridiculed. "How dare you, God!" is the tone. "How dare you lift me up in victory one minute and bring me to shame or ruin the next minute!"

It is a good thing we serve a merciful God. Somehow God looks past the last part of Samson's prayer—a part that should simply have been, "Let your will be done"—and he responds to the first part that glorifies God for the victory! God splits the rock, Samson drinks and is revived, and then he walks off without so much as a thank-you.

Part of what takes us out of control in our moments of frustration is weakness in prayer, and more so, prayer that is more concerned about our face and shame than about what the sovereign God is doing to glorify himself. When we think we are going to be ridiculed, we need prayers of "God, please handle this" and of "If this is the time you intend to crush your servant with your own hand, may your name be magnified."

Being more concerned about himself than what pleases God, Samson will blame God for his frustrating situation. But if Samson had a daily prayer life, giving the Lord thanks, confessing his own sins, and seeking God's power for victory, this prayer would have been one of thanks—one that would have freed him from being frustrated by a tiresome struggle and an apparent lack of provision.

The resource the believer in Jesus has at a frustrating time of life is that he or she can go to the Lord in prayer and wait for the Lord to display his power. Reformer John Calvin, speaking of our knowledge of God the Creator, said it like this:

> We must be persuaded not only that as [God] once formed the world, so he sustains it by his boundless power, governs it by his wisdom, preserves it by his goodness, in particular, rules the human race with justice and judgment, bears with them in mercy, shields them by his protection; but also that not a particle of light, or wisdom, or justice, or power, or rectitude, or genuine truth, will anywhere be found, which does not flow from him, and of which he is not the cause; in this way we must learn to expect and ask all things from him, and thankfully ascribe to him whatever we receive. (*Institutes*, I.2.1)

When you are frustrated, go to the Lord in prayer. Develop a prayer life by carving out a set time daily to sit in quietness before him, taking your concerns, confessions, and thanksgiving to him. Those who have believed on Jesus can approach God like this because Jesus, in satisfying God's wrath as our substitute, gave us access to God through Christ's death. We can go behind the veil to the holy of holies into the presence of the Father because we are approaching him with the blood of Christ splattered on us. *Silence ridicule through prayer.*

Separate Your Personal Success from Your Frustrations so that You See Your Need for God
JUDGES 15:20

The narrative ends on an important note in verse 20. Samson led Israel as a military leader for twenty years. That is a reign equivalent to five successive American presidential cycles—the time of one full generation's maturation from birth into adulthood. Through him the Lord was able to deliver Israel from their Philistine oppressors.

One could think Samson is a success. In fact, he himself could think that, for in terms of what society generally identifies as success, Samson has accomplished it. He is the professional success, long-standing leader, and the last man standing. However, on the inside he is one frustrated man, and before God he is a failure. His professional success and survival mask his real need for God. God will allow Samson to live in his feigned self-success, for the Lord will not beg people to come to him for help. The Lord needs even his own followers to keep failing until they can see their own need for God. If you really want to handle life's frustrations in a Christ-honoring manner, *separate your personal success from your frustrations so you see your need for God.*

If you cannot overcome your frustrations enough to handle them righteously, your issue is not people doing things actively to frustrate you. Frustrating people come and go. Your issue is what you will do in response to the frustrating acts of others, or what you do or do not have the ability to do. Either you can overcome your frustrations by God's power, like the US Marines improvise, adapt, and overcome challenges to a mission, or you can become more and more frustrated. Either you deal honestly with the fact that you are not pleased with what is going on in your life, or you allow a few financial, social, and professional successes to mask your symptoms and provide temporary and fleeting satisfaction. You can keep banging your head against the wall, clutching your fists, fighting the people who love you most, and blaming everyone rather than taking blame, *or you can learn to walk with Jesus, for Jesus knows all about frustrations.*

Having come to his own people and not being received by them (John 1:11), having come to Jerusalem to try to gather them as a hen gathers her chicks (Matt 23:37), and having stretched out his arms all day long to a stiff-necked and rebellious people (Rom 10:21), our Lord Jesus knows much about handling disappointment, injustice, rebellious family members, and all sorts of frustrations! He nailed our frustrations and the mishandling of them to the cross and left them buried in the grave. He gives power by his Spirit to overcome our frustrations in a way that will not burn our families, bring justice back on us, rob God of his glory, or mask our need for God.

When you face situations like Samson and get up to your neck in frustrations, manhandle your frustrations by taking them to the one man who can handle them! *Be stronger than Samson by taking your frustrations to Jesus.*

Reflect and Discuss

1. What decisions did Samson make in Judges 14 that led to his own creation of his frustrations in Judges 15? What could he have done differently in Judges 14 in order to prevent the first frustrating items in Judges 15?
2. How does Judges 15 reflect the thrust that characterizes Judges—of each person establishing a personal, relative morality?
3. What would have been a wiser response to the Philistines' burning of his former wife and father-in-law?
4. Discuss a time when you handled a frustrating incident within your home impulsively, uncaringly, or unwisely. What were the results of your actions, and what should you have done differently?
5. What is the problem with Samson's saying, "I have done to them what they did to me"?
6. Discuss a time when your response to frustration had a costly impact on your Christian witness.
7. What does Samson's harboring of frustrations both before and after having the Spirit of the Lord come upon him indicate about the presence of the Holy Spirit during your failures to handle frustrating things honorably before the Lord?

8. When the Lord places his Spirit upon the frustrated Samson in this episode, what does this teach you about the Lord's fulfillment of his plans?
9. What Christian habits do you need to incorporate into your life in order to handle frustrations with more patience, grace, and dependency on the Spirit?
10. Why is it often immediately after times of personal prayer that believers yield to the temptation to mishandle frustrating people?

The Fatality of Strength without Wisdom

JUDGES 16

Main Idea: At the times of the Philistines' attempts to destroy Samson through opportunities afforded by his affections toward the Philistine prostitute and Delilah, his humbling and the exaltation of his strength rest on his wisdom toward the source of his strength in the presence of the uncircumcised.

I.   Escaping a Fatality Is about Grace More than Wisdom or Strength (16:1-3).
II. Falling toward Fatality Only Needs the Push of Your Lust with Strong Seduction (16:4-22).
III. Being a Fatality Does Not Have to Be a Total Tragedy for One Who Seeks the Savior (16:23-31).

Believers probably do not think enough about the significance of having an enemy and being in a spiritual war. Some believers might not want to be thought of as people who put too much stock in enchanted things when the practical experience is ever before us. Others may not want to give too much credit to the enemy when it concerns our trials and sufferings.

Wisely, a pastor once said to me concerning spiritual warfare, "When I think of being in a war, I think of someone on the other side trying to kill me." Our enemy is coming at us with all intent to kill us and destroy us in every way possible until we are dead.

Yet he doesn't have to work hard on some of us to destroy us. Instead, he simply waits for us to yield to the temptations with which we knowingly or unknowingly flirt. We deliver ourselves into the enemy's clutches when we are not wise in the use of our spiritual strengths when facing lustful temptations.

The horrid events of Samson's final story direct the reader's attention to the fatality that befalls a strong man who learns too late that he should use his strength with wisdom. Glibly and without discernment, Samson shows his strength only after failing to use it to turn from his lustful patterns. His choices will cost him everything. His story stands like a neon sign to deter us from becoming spiritual fatalities by being foolish toward the strength given to us and the temptations that lie before us.

Escaping a Fatality Is about Grace More than Wisdom or Strength

JUDGES 16:1-3

In this episode, one meets Samson in Gaza—right on Philistine turf. One would hope Samson is there to defeat Israel's enemy and deliver Israel from the long, oppressive arm of the Philistines. Instead, Samson is back to his exploits with a Philistine woman, having never consummated his marriage to the first one. Only this time Samson has found a prostitute. He is breaking God's laws related to Nazirite standards, engaging in prostitution, and failing to remove the Canaanites from the promised land.

While he is with this prostitute, the Philistines learn of Samson's presence in Philistine territory. They see an opportunity to kill him when his mind and heart are occupied with the sexual encounter. Even though he is a strong man, his lust has put him in a vulnerable position in which his enemy can rid the earth of him. Samson is not being wise as he fulfills his lusts on Philistine soils. Quietly, the Philistines plan a surprise attack on him.

Based on his choices, Samson should meet death in this scene. However, he inexplicably happens to awake at midnight. In awaking, Samson grabs the doors of the gate of the city and corresponding posts and carries them from Gaza to the outskirts of Hebron. In doing so, he escapes a death trap he does not see but that had been laid by his choices toward his unbridled passions.

Samson does not outsmart the Philistines. He doesn't know they are waiting for him because they are being quiet. He knows there is a chance they are there because he is in Gaza; Samson is playing with fire and knows it. Thus, he cannot get up and say, "See, I'm still strong even though I went to Gaza on their turf and messed with one of their unclean women, against the Nazirite vow, and no one could do anything about it." Instead, he should be saying, "Forgive me, Lord, and thank you for your grace. I need to honor my Nazirite vows and the whole law." Unfortunately, the pyrrhic victory seems to contribute to dropping his guard with Delilah.

If you have fallen from God's law into lusts of any type, such as substance abuse or the many forms of immorality, including adultery, pornography, or homosexuality, it would be wrong for you to think the absence of an immediate consequence means that you have outwitted the world, your family, the church, or the judgment of God. Instead, you have experienced the patient hand of the Lord as he gives you a chance to repent before your sins catch up to you.

I think of people who loot stores in riots or flash mobs, of corporate embezzlers who think no one will see the funny numbers in the books, and of digital thieves who think they never will be found. They do not seem to understand that the Lord is watching them, that surveillance is almost everywhere, that many others have tried to get away with the same sins and crimes and were caught, and that the legal enforcers take their time to collect the data to make a case against perpetrators. You're not getting away; you are looking at delayed judgment and an opportunity to turn away from sin.

Ghislaine Noelle Marion Maxwell went into hiding shortly after the arrest of her acquaintance, Jeffery Epstein, in July 2019. With her talking only through her lawyers, attempts were made to locate her at multiple addresses and locations as far away as the US Virgin Islands. Maxwell probably thought she had outsmarted federal authorities for good before she was arrested in New Hampshire in July 2020. The FBI used a StingRay mobile phone tracking device on a phone she used to call her lawyer and family to find her location. She was not smarter than the law; she was riding on borrowed time. Escaping is about grace. Anyone living in sin should not fool herself or himself into thinking otherwise.

Falling toward Fatality Only Needs the Push of Your Lust with Strong Seduction
JUDGES 16:4-22

With his lust in overdrive, Samson goes from the unnamed prostitute to the infamous Delilah. Delilah has upstaged the prostitute in history because of her role in Samson's downfall. Unlike the prostitute, she has the benefit of financial backing to betray Samson and remain loyal to her people. But she is not necessarily craftier than the prostitute. Samson's lust for each woman is the same. He has set the stage for his own destruction.

As with the prostitute, Samson meets Delilah on Philistine turf in the valley of Sorek on the border of the tribe of Dan. He has once again had success with his lust in Philistine lands. He has no reason to suspect that anything will be different. He is blind to his lust—so blind that he continues to go outside Israel during the period of the judges, when there was plenty of immoral wisdom within Israel. The Philistines will again attempt to take advantage of Samson's lusts to ambush him.[51] They invite Delilah to "persuade," "trick" (NET), "seduce" (ESV), "lure" (NIV), "entice" (NASB), or "coax" (NRSV) Samson to reveal his source of strength, offering her great financial incentive to be deceptive.[52] Delilah immediately goes to work trying to pull from Samson the only secret that separates him from all other men and allows him to defeat all without rival.

The reader observes three rounds of Delilah peppering Samson, Samson lying about his strength, Delilah binding Samson and testing his ability to escape an ambush, Samson freeing himself, and Delilah feeling mocked by Samson. Not one of the superstitious attempts works: not fresh bowstrings, not new ropes, and not weaving his hair into the loom and pinning it. But something deadlier is at work: with each round of searching for Samson's strength, Samson moved the answer dial closer to his weakness. He goes from undried bowstrings to new ropes to a trap related to his hair. The movement demonstrates Samson's lust for Delilah, working in combination with her offer of illicit love for him, to weary him without his noticing.

The writer will show one additional round of back-and-forth between Delilah and Samson. Delilah prefaces her efforts by questioning Samson's claim to love her, by magnifying his lies, and by relentlessly coming after him for the answer. She is not asking casual questions like a tourist on a tour trolley; she is badgering him with the strength of an inquisition council, which she can do since he wants to hold on to the illicit sex she offers to him. His lust will keep him in a vulnerable position in which he will be subjected to her persistent nagging until "she

---

[51] "The Philistine leaders know what kind of man they are dealing with and plot to exploit Samson's self-indulgence" (Bowling, "Judges," 173).

[52] On the 5,500 silver coins, over a decade ago Trent Butler concluded, "Projecting that to the modern scene and taking $25 thousand as the average annual wage, the governors' total offer to Delilah would approach $15 million. This lets us see how valuable the capture of public enemy number one was for the Philistine governors and what an incentive Delilah had to betray her lover" (*Judges*, 349–50).

wore him out," says the CSB,[53] but more literally she pestered him until "he became short to death" (CSB footnote).

Samson finally gives in and reveals the only secret that keeps him a step ahead of the Philistines. In modern terms, Samson might as well have broadcast his online banking ID and passcode on social media while hoping no one would use it to liquidate his accounts. Because he has allowed his lust to put him in Delilah's grip, he is going to lose all advantage over his enemies. In this round of Delilah's seeking the source of his strength, the outcome will be different for Samson—and most costly.

Where the reader expects to see an act of national bondage in the Judges cycle, one finds Samson asleep on Delilah's lap having his hair shaved from his head. Delilah has tormented him until his strength departed from him. The inspired editor intends the reader to see these actions as Samson's binding. His lust has bound him in the lap of the woman who has challenged his statements of love for her. Rather than his lust giving him joy, happiness, and freedom, its fulfillment is deception, bondage, torment, and weakness. The writer intends the reader to see that one's relative morality gives many choices, but only has one consequence.

With her payment from the five Philistine lords in hand, Delilah sells Samson into the hands of his pursuers and apparently will have no remorse for doing so. She will enjoy what her seduction and devotion have enabled her to afford, and Samson will be collateral damage, tossed away like inedible scraps of food on a dinner plate heading down the garbage disposal. This time will be the last scream to alert Samson to a Philistine attack. She knows this is no fire drill, and it is evident to her that Samson has revealed the full contents of his heart to her. She will take his heart and smash it into fine powder with her villainy.

Samson cannot respond to an attack as he did previously. Unknown to him, his strength has departed. The Lord's presence and approval through the working of the Holy Spirit are missing. Samson has broken the Nazirite vow in a manner that seems irreparable.

---

[53] "She nagged him" is "she forced him with her words" in the Hebrew. On this, Butler writes, "One may translate v 16 to say: 'When she harassed him daily with her words, she had pestered him so much that he became sick to death (or so impatient he was ready to die)'" (*Judges*, 350).

Like the fictional characters Oedipus, who gouged out his own eyes, and Gloucester, who had his eyes gouged out by his enemies, so Samson will lose his eyes so that his enemies are the last thing he ever sees. Like Zedekiah after him, Samson will spend the rest of his life in the dark, experiencing pain far worse than any corneal abrasion. Again, effectively the author is screaming at the audience, "This is where disobedience to the covenant ends—not in a happy life comparable to the Philistines', but in agony, darkness, and imprisonment, and in the friendless, shamed, powerless grinding of a millstone in futility and humiliation." His eyes are darkened because he allowed a razor to touch his head because he gave in to his lustful temptations.

Every believer is vulnerable to temptation's destructive ways and outcomes. No believer reaches perfection in this life. Every one of us has a weakness toward sinful areas that could be a tool of the enemy's assault on us. Paul calls us both to stand in the evil warfare with alertness and to take the way of escape from every temptation (see 1 Cor 10:12-13; Eph 6:13-14). The lust could be for power, fame, or companionship, or the desire to distance oneself from loneliness, lack of respect, or the missing love of a parent. The enemy can exploit any of these lusts and all others to bring our lives to painful, enslaving ruin.

This chapter specifically emphasizes the danger of the temptation of lust for illicit sex. Samson desires what he equates with love but does not seek to honor the Lord with the commitment of marriage within God's covenant standards that would make the sexual intimacy holy and sacred. He doesn't even honor Delilah with a proposal that would make it legitimate. The longing for sex outside of one's marriage brings the most serious of consequences if one yields to this temptation (Prov 7:21-23). The gruesome descriptions of Samson experiencing torment, the loss of the favor of the Lord and his superhuman strength, self-deception toward his own abilities, binding, painful laceration of his eyes, prisoner transport to Gaza, and humbling to the labor of a slave in a mill intend to provoke fear toward sexual immorality. The writer does not portray Samson returning to work with a half-guilty smile and happy daydreams of secret rendezvous. This is not the TV and movie depiction of a man returning home in normal routine only to have a wife later find the hair of a mistress on his clothing. Samson is reduced as a person from whole to missing his eyes, from super strength to being under the power of the Philistines, from freedom to roam from Gaza to Hebron to one with a permanent address in a Gaza mill, and from fearsome warrior to mocked slave—sold into slavery like a beast of burden by his illicit lover. He made foolish choices, thinking he could summon strength to overcome the enemy's attack at a moment's notice. He found that yielding to temptation can take away all the strength from the Lord one might think he or she has.

Yet Samson, because he is the prophesied, God-decreed deliverer of Israel from the oppression of the Philistines, will soon be able to feel stubble where his head has been shaved. Samson will regain his hair, and the sovereign Lord will accomplish his purpose despite Samson's disobedience. He will judge the Philistines and rescue Israel. He will not rescue Samson, however. The consequences of choosing rebellion and sin remain.

Being a Fatality Does Not Have to Be a Total Tragedy for One Who Seeks the Savior
JUDGES 16:23-31

What we next see is the closest thing we have to a deathbed conversion for Samson in this story. Nearly three thousand Philistines are gathered to worship their god, Dagon, for his defeat of Samson. They are praising Dagon for providing the victory over their enemy: "[The Philistines] offer a great sacrifice to their god Dagon" (v. 23). "They rejoiced" (v. 23). "Our god has handed over our enemy" (v. 23). "They praised their god" (v. 24). "Our god has handed over to us our enemy" (v. 24). And all of this occurs in a "temple" (v. 26). To the Philistines, Dagon is superior to the God of Israel, for he has defeated the champion of those who pray to Israel's God.

The worship celebration quickly gives way to a show as the Philistines call for Samson to "entertain" the merry congregants (vv. 25,27). They wish to humiliate the prisoner, mocking the former champion as one diminished to a performer in a circus. Why they had him stand between the pillars is unknown to us. One imagines that the vast majority of the gleeful throng can see the would-be entertainer if he stands there.

Even when his humiliation increases as he is led by a young man rather than fearsome warriors, the sightless champion keeps his wits about him. He asks his guide to position him where he can touch the post so he will have a place to lean like a weary traveler or exhausted soldier. Samson, sensing his strength has returned with his hair, has plans other than resting a weakened body on a pillar.

Samson will utter his last cries to the "Lord GOD" (or "sovereign LORD")—Adonai YHWH.[54] His prayer asks the Lord to remember him—to take note of him or act on his behalf (Block, *Judges, Ruth*, 467). He cries out again to God, for God to strengthen him only once more. Although Samson's motivation is to gain vengeance on the Philistines in one act for taking his two eyes, his cry witnesses trust in the Lord.[55] He requests to die just as he selfishly seeks vengeance on his enemies. His choices will be fatal for both the Philistines and himself.

Yet, when Samson leans the strength of his weight against the pillars, it is tragic only for the Philistines. The author honors Samson with his last words about Samson. First, Samson's greatest victory occurs as he dies to judge the Philistines. He dies as a warrior mightier than he was

---

[54] Butler notes, "It is only when Samson reaches the end of his rope and slams up against his dependence on God that he comes to some realization of his need for God" (Butler, *Judges*, 353). Butler cites Dennis T. Olson, "The Book of Judges: Introduction, Commentary and Reflections," in *New Interpreter's Bible* (Nashville: Abingdon Press, 1998), 861.

[55] Block writes, "Samson's requests are totally self-centered. In his plea for God to remember and strengthen him, he seems totally oblivious to the national emergency and unconcerned about the divine agenda he was raised up to fulfill. . . . Unfortunately the account offers no hint of corresponding concern for spiritual perception/sensibilities. Again the reader is struck by a total lack of concern for the divine agenda or the fate of Samson's people. . . . In looking back at the prayer as a whole, the reader must be struck by its egocentricity. . . . There is no thought for the nation he is supposed to be delivering, let alone for Yahweh whose name/reputation has been denigrated by this turn of events. Yahweh is the one who needs vindication. He is unconcerned that the victory song to the Philistines' god is a taunt against and a challenge to Yahweh. But Samson does not seem to care what is happening to Yahweh's reputation, even when the one on whose shoulders God has placed his trust languishes in prison, the victim of his own failures and, seemingly, Dagon's superiority" (Block, *Judges, Ruth*, 467–68).

Similarly, Butler says, "Samson's motive is not religious. He does not ask God to help him fulfill a forgotten mission of deliverance. His motive is still selfish revenge" (Butler, *Judges*, 353).

However, I disagree with their assessment. Samson is an immature follower of the Lord who walks within the ethos of his nation's relativism. His motivation is self-centered, but his trust is in the Lord rather than in himself. Previously, he responded to the hypothetical and real attacks of the Philistines in his own strength, as the two first-person verbs in 16:20 reveal: "*I will escape* as I did before and *shake myself free*." Now humbled, even though he senses the return of his strength, he recognizes his need for the help of the Lord who departed from him when Samson allowed his head to be shorn. This would be consistent with the Hebrews' writer placing Samson among those who lived by faith and died in faith. I would agree with the comments by Bowling: "It is to Samson's credit that, in an act of faith (Heb 11:32), he turns to God for help. It is not to his credit that his desire in turning to God is for personal vengeance rather than God's glory" (Bowling, "Judges," 174).

in life with both of his eyes. Inherent in speaking of Samson killing the Philistines is the fulfillment of his role as the deliverer of Israel (13:5).

Second, he gains an honorable burial by the tribe of Dan and his family members. They do not leave him in dishonor among the Philistine dead The carry him back from Philistine lands and the fallen house of Dagon to be buried with Manoah his father. As Manoah lived as one who had bowed before the Lord in worship, Samson now is buried with him as one who served the Lord.

Third, Samson's judgeship was one of the longest recorded rules in Israel. For those twenty years, the Philistines were no match for Israel. Israel's warrior kept them safe and delivered them from oppression. The writer wishes the reader to remember Samson as a tragic hero who called on the Lord once he had been humbled. The inspired author will not close the chapter focusing on Samson's sin and judgment.

Application

Samson's story invites the reader to ponder deeply the thoughts, feelings, and habits (or disciplines) one should incorporate into one's life to avoid falling fatally to the consequences of yielding to our lusts, especially the lust of fulfilling illicit sexual desire. Every believer would do well to remember the aphorism attributed to nineteenth-century Scottish Reformer Samuel Smiles:

> Sow a thought, and you reap an act;
> sow an act, and you reap a habit;
> sow a habit, and you reap a character;
> sow a character, and you reap a destiny.

Samson's fall to Delilah's deceit began back with his initial disregard for the law of God in asking for a wife from the Philistines. Doing what was right in his own eyes, he became the person characterized in the first thought that approved of going outside of the covenant standards to obtain a wife. Eventually that led to his comfort with Delilah, the gouging of his eyes, and his death. One can stop thoughts that diminish obedience and the consequences of disobedience with these suggested alternative thoughts and actions:

First, *we need to be concerned about honoring the Lord's name in all things.* Samson is not concerned about the Lord's witness before the Philistines. Our first and last thoughts each day should be, "So, whether you eat or drink, or whatever you do, do everything for the glory of God" (1 Cor 10:31). In all decisions and without anxiety, we should ask ourselves questions like these: "Will doing this make the Lord look majestic in the eyes of others? Will this bring honor to Christ when people hear his name? Would God himself applaud me for what I am about to say or do?" If the answer is no to any of these questions, we should turn our thoughts and actions to that which will make the Lord's greatness praiseworthy in the eyes of all.

Second, *we must remember we are not above spiritual warfare*. At all times believers participate in a spiritual war in invisible realms. If we forget that we are at war, we will be vulnerable to an attack by the evil one in which he exploits our unchecked lusts for the sake of destroying us. The reality of warfare should not cause us anxiety but rather vigilance and alertness. The words to Wormwood from Screwtape in C. S. Lewis's book named for the veteran demon are important for us:

> When the humans disbelieve in our existence we lose all the pleasing results of direct terrorism and we make no magicians. On the other hand, when they believe in us, we cannot make them materialists and sceptics. At least, not yet. (*Screwtape Letters*, 13)

To keep from becoming materialists (in the broadest sense), says Lewis, we must be cognizant of the reality of the demonic. The demons wish to take believers and everyone around them down through sin.

Third, *we need to work on self-control in all areas—including food and drink as well as speech—yielding our body and its appetites to the Lord as a sacrifice*. In Judges 13–16 Samson started losing the battle to the Philistines with the first Philistine woman and the taking of the honey from the lion's carcass. Samson shows no control when he loses the contest of the riddle and strikes down the thirty men of Ashkelon. His unruly passions come home to roost in his encounter with Delilah. Had he addressed his need for control earlier in his life, he might have developed the character of self-control needed to abstain from going to Gaza to the prostitute and setting his affections on Delilah.

Self-control is essential to the Christian life. Paul identifies it as a product of yielding to the working of the Spirit of God (Gal 5:23). He further mentions it as part of general Christian character, as does the apostle Peter (1 Cor 9:25; 1 Tim 2:9,15; 2 Tim 1:7; Titus 1:8; 2:2,5,6,12; 1 Pet 4:7; 2 Pet 1:6). Many Scriptures commend moderation in eating and drinking and forbid drunkenness (Luke 21:34; Rom 13:13; 1 Cor 6:9-10; Eph 5:18; 1 Tim 3:3,8; Titus 1:12; 1 Pet 4:3-4). The Scriptures require the believer to have control of speech and anger, to refrain from coveting, and to abstain from sexual immorality. We must submit our bodily appetites and passions to Christ. Christ does not call people to disregard control of bodily desires but to honor the God who himself does not act haphazardly, wildly, or capriciously.

We must constantly work at self-control, for the lures that tempt and ensnare us abound. We must be willing to sacrifice fulfillment of passions where they exceed the limits given by Christ. This might be cause for a regular practice of fasting. It is a call for meditation on and memorization of Scriptures related to self-control.

Fifth, *we should prioritize being in regular fellowship with God's people.* Samson should not have been in Gaza. He should have been in Dan among his tribe or among the people of Israel as a judge. Samson missed a warning flag when he passed the "Now Entering Gaza" sign, for he should have been leading Israel to destroy the Philistines. Instead, he was reveling in the bedroom of the daughter of an enemy combatant. Samson should have taken advantage of enjoying the people of God.

The Lord provides the members of the body of Christ as gifts to one another so that we might do the things that promote glorifying him and give us joy as we receive one another's goodness. He calls believers to the following practices toward one another: accept, seek good, confess sins, love, serve, honor, exalt, bear burdens, encourage, stir toward good works, pray, and show hospitality. These are formative practices that we will enjoy, including being freed from the burden and guilt of sins when we confess them rather than harbor them. These also are practices to which believers are called and can experience uniquely among fellow redeemed, Spirit-filled members of Christ's body. Our engagement with the world should not find the world our source for strength and fellowship. The bonds that build and give intimate friendship are available as part of the gospel's working among believers. In the company of believers, we will be deterred from sinful temptations.

Sixth, *we should not flirt with temptation.* As children, if we resist performing a risky dare that others in our peer group have done, we might be lured by another's challenge of "Are you chicken? Are you scared?" However, when it comes to giving in to sinful temptations, we should indeed be afraid. We should picture every passionate temptation having a sign on it that says, "Danger: High Voltage"; "Submerged and

Dangerous Hazards: Do Not Swim"; and "High Water: Do Not Drive." Flirting with temptation is not a game of chicken that anyone wins.

Seventh, *our disciplines need to include confession of weakness toward temptation and prayer for grace to honor the Lord in all things.* The only hope we have for strength to resist temptation is that the power of God will be available to us. In our own strength, we cannot stand against the enemy's schemes. Only as the Lord responds graciously to our confessions of weakness and dependency on his strength can we be successful in resisting lustful temptations. Daily we should pray, "Do not bring us into temptation, but deliver us from the evil one."

Eighth, *we need to remember that repentance is always an option before we draw our last breath.* Write this down and put it in prominent places, like a mirror you use regularly, your desk at work, or on your refrigerator: "Confession and repentance always are options." Confession and repentance remain options for the sinner. Before drawing his last breath, Samson called on the Lord as his only hope. Hope for the Lord to change us is available in this life. When we come to the next life, the choices we made in this life will have determined our destiny.

Close

Confession and repentance remain options because the Lord loves mercy. The Lord reveals himself as, "The LORD—the LORD is a compassionate and gracious God, slow to anger and abounding in faithful love and truth" (Exod 34:6; see Num 14:18; 2 Chron 30:9; Neh 9:17; Pss 86:15; 103:8; 111:4; 112:4; 116:5; 145:8; Joel 2:13; Jon 4:2). God the Father is a God of mercy (Luke 6:36; Heb 8:12; 1 Pet 1:3; 2 John 3). Christ the Son is full of mercy (Matt 9:27; 15:22; 17:15; 20:30-31; Eph 2:4; Heb 4:16).

When our lusts provide opportunity for the enemy to destroy us, we do not have to give in; we do not have to become fatalities. We have the privilege to go to Christ—the one who died and rose against to give us power to resist temptation. At his throne we will find all the mercy and help we need to honor him rather than be a tragic story before him.

Review and Discuss

1. If you were writing the story of a Nazirite son growing up to deliver Israel from the Philistines, how would the story have progressed from chapter 13 to the beginning of chapter 16? What does the

way this story progressed say about how God writes the story of redemption?

2. What might the development of Samson's story say about what the Lord is doing in our lives within the story of redemption?

3. Compare the episode of 16.1-3 to 16:4-23. What is similar between the interaction of Samson and women in these two stories?

4. Name a significant incident in which your sin should have caught up with you immediately but by grace you escaped its consequences. What did you learn from that outcome?

5. What might have motivated the Philistines to offer Delilah such a high price to entrap Samson? What does her immediate acceptance say about her view of her relationship with Samson?

6. What does Delilah's agreement to betray Samson teach believers about the unseen consequences of a relativistic morality?

7. What might have been the reasons Samson was not suspicious of a plot by Delilah and the Philistines when Delilah tested him with the words, "The Philistines are here!"?

8. What are some themes and foreshadowed items in Judges 13–15 to which Judges 16 provides closure?

9. How might one argue that Samson is the epitome of the judges?

10. What do you think Samson felt and thought when he first lost his eyes and was reduced to being a prisoner by the Philistines? What do you think the Lord intends for the reader to feel when Samson's eyes are being gouged and he is being humbled?

11. What do the efforts of Samson's enemies to defeat him in Judges 13–16 say about the schemes of the believers' enemy to destroy us?

12. Where is Christ's mercy evident in Judges 16? What might we learn about the operation of Christ's mercies in our own lives based on Samson's life?

Unjustifying Coveting, Part 1

JUDGES 17:1–18:6

Main Idea: The church's opportunities to move from covetousness to obedience should beware of seeking seemingly Christian, relativistic justification for personal advancement through evil means while yet gathering to worship Jesus until his return.[56]

I.   Offering (17:1-6)
II. Security (17:7-13)
III. Blessings (18:1-6)

Coveting is the gift that keeps on giving. Or rather, it is the sin that continues with little mention from pulpits and devotions and Bible studies. This makes sense because talking about money is difficult. How we spend our money, how we obtain our money, how we invest our money, what percentage of our money we give to philanthropic causes, how much money we have lost, how much money we give to the church, and how much money we owe are all private affairs to us. Money is between us and God, never us and the community or the church, until we have a public ethics violation, experience a legal recovery of a debt owed, or can show what our financial gifts have done for the good of humanity. Money is ours, so if we covet, it is our business just as privately as most else about our money.

Yet coveting—wishing for or desiring something you do not have— is a little different from other money-related choices, for there are direct prohibitions against coveting in Scripture. The Ten Commandments state, "Do not covet your neighbor's wife or desire your neighbor's house, his field, his male or female slave, his ox or donkey, or anything

---

[56] The historical main idea for this passage is long, reflective of the length of the passage: *Israel's—Micah's, Levite's, and Dan's—second-chance opportunities to improve their lives become shortsighted opportunities for accepting idolatrous greed masquerading for the Lord's approval of religious choices through evil justifications of their relativistic ethics the full time the house of God is in Shiloh. In each episode there is an impulse of covetousness that leads to persons advancing themselves or being concerned to do such. The greed then witnesses flimsy reasons for justifying the covetous choices. The writer indicates that this continued for the duration of the time the house of God remained in Shiloh.*

that belongs to your neighbor." The Lord tells us to work against covetousness as sin.

Moreover, coveting includes both discontentment and greed. The lack of satisfaction with what one has and the desire for something more, better, glitzier, or trendier fuels this sin. Yet we easily fall into it with all sorts of means of justifying our desires. It does not matter whether one is well-to-do or poor. You can have nothing and want more or different, or you can be like John D. Rockefeller and only have enough when you have a little more.

It is time to stop justifying covetousness, lest we become like the ancient Israelites under the judges. Exploring the ways the people of Israel justified their covetousness and the consequences that came from their choices will expose our own attempts at justifying covetousness so that we can instead honor the Lord with our desires and avoid the destruction of the judges. In doing so, we will unjustify our coveting.

There are seven justifications in Judges 17 and 18. Due to the length of this passage, we will explore the justifications in two parts: 17:1–18:6 (nineteen verses) and 18:7-31 (twenty-five verses). The two passages share one main idea.

Also, we have left the judges cycle. The remaining chapters do not mention a judge—neither major nor minor. So now we are without a king, and we are without local military deliverers. Other people in these sections (17–21) should be able to point Israel to the way of obedience. Alas, however, the writer paints a picture of a people who are beyond help or even hope of turning to the Lord. Israel's covetousness shows the first step into the point of evil with no return—with no hope of salvation from Canaanization.

Offering
JUDGES 17:1-6

Judges 17 opens with a different story—a confession of sin. Micah comes to tell his mother he stole her money—money she had cursed. This might be why he brought back the money: being a victim of the curse probably scares him. The mom issues a blessing on Micah for returning the money and dedicates the returned money to the Lord. So far, so good.

But she only issues two hundred of the eleven hundred pieces. This means she gives 18.2 percent to the Lord and keeps nine hundred pieces for herself, over 81 percent. It looks like she is superphilanthropic or sacrificial, but she is not. Then she explains the dedication: she is dedicating the money for idolatry: for the creation of two images—one carved and one metal—and an ephod, which is a priestly garment. So the reader could overlook the nine hundred pieces of silver in the mom's possession because she made an offering. Truthfully, however, the passage reveals the mother's greed and the attempt to justify it with her offering, an offering made to an idol and not truly to the Lord.

Important too is that Micah misses an opportunity to continue in repentance and to turn away from coveting completely while also helping his mom let go of her covetousness: Micah could refuse to allow the idols in his home. But seeing an opportunity for a god to be present to bless him, he accepts the idol and builds a shrine. He adds items of worship and even pulls one of his sons into the depravity of his idolatry. Now even his child will grow up thinking offering to God justifies coveting.

In our age of three-quarter-million-dollar lotteries and casinos as commonplace neighbors, followers of Christ sometimes ponder the question of the ethics of participating in gambling. Sadly, rather than having a discussion about what gambling does to our witness as believers in God Almighty, some will justify participation on the basis of the potential to give a greater offering to the Lord, e.g., "If I win $750,000, that's $75,000 I could give to the work of the Lord!" (Right; sure you would, just as casinos give to the public education in your community as was promised when the legislation approving the casino passed.[57])

Have we thought of all that we must overlook to come to this conclusion? We must overlook our own unsatisfied hearts. We also must overlook the families destroyed by gambling addiction.

Do not use offering as a cover for your real desire: you want the wealth of money from the lottery and not necessarily to give the Lord a greater offering. If you want to give the Lord a greater offering, simply

---

[57] The evidence regarding the outcomes of promised casino revenues for funding public schools varies in each state. However, as a whole, casino revenues do not benefit public schools financially for many reasons. See Lucy Dadayan, "State Revenues from Gambling: Short-Term Relief, Long-Term Disappointment," *The Blinken Report*, The Nelson A. Rockefeller Institute of Government, April 2016, https://rockinst.org/wp-content/uploads/2017/11/2016-04-12-Blinken_Report_Three-min.pdf, accessed April 2, 2021; Mimi Kirk, "For Schools, Gambling Funding Is No Jackpot," *Bloomberg City Labs*, February 21, 2017, https://www.bloomberg.com/news/articles/2017-02-21/where-casino-gambling-and-lottery-profits-really-go, accessed April 2, 2021.

make the sacrifices necessary in your discretionary budget line to give a greater offering.

Security

JUDGES 17:7-13

The narrative introduces a Levite from Bethlehem in Judah looking for a place to call his own—a place to enjoy his share of land inheritance. Levites gain inheritance differently from the other eleven tribes. They are freely allotted land in forty-eight Levitical cities within the territories of the other tribes, but that does not seem to be enough for this Levite. In his journey he lands in the house of the man who formerly coveted eleven hundred pieces of his mother's silver. Apparently, Micah's inner Midas is alive and kicking, as he is glad to welcome the sojourning Levite into his home. Micah seems to think that having one of the Lord's mediators in his home will mean material blessing for his home.

Micah, therefore, offers in-kind gifts, a position as personal advisor, and a salary to the Levite to entice him to disregard what the Mosaic law says about his duties as a minister for the nation. The Levite, himself looking for more than he has, gladly accepts this offer. What happens next shows how low Israel has fallen morally.

First, *the young man lives with Micah with the pleasure of a child born into his home.* Both Micah and the Levite should be afraid that the Lord's anger will be kindled. Instead, neither man is stressed at all over their new deal. They settle into, "Hey, Dad, how's it going?" "Fine, son. As long as you stay around, the Lord will bless me."

Second, *Micah ordains the Levite as a priest in a manner that attempts to mimic the ordination process for the Levitical priesthood but does not follow the details of the law related to the cleansing, the anointing with oil and blood, or the proper appropriation of the garments.* Micah intends for this priest to perform the service of God without the prescribed altars and the tabernacle's holy place. The one man is content to live without completing God's duties for priests because he has a place to live. The other man is content to live assuming the place of Israel and making his home assume the place of the tabernacle because he thinks he will gain material blessings from God. Both men miss their opportunities to do what is right in the eyes of the Lord—to reject their covetousness by following the law on the role of the priesthood.

Third, with certainty, *Micah expects the Lord's hand of blessing to be on him.* Apparently, he is writing the rules as to what the Lord approves and blesses. Micah is happy in self-assurance and without any regard for worshiping the Lord rightly. All that matters is that the priest seems to provide security for him.

The need for material and financial security often drives our compulsion for more. We want to know that we have enough for current needs and enough for future needs. We want to be free from any dependency on others, any sign of financial weakness, any possibility that our emergency expenses could exceed our emergency funds. *What if the primary breadwinner loses his job? What if there is a natural disaster of the "act of God" magnitude and type that maxes out my insurance? What if the rate at which we are saving is not sufficient to last my retirement and long-term healthcare needs?* All such questions make us long for a monetary certainty that excuses coveting wealth. We never have enough to feel fully secure.

The believer should not be driven by a need for providing his own security. Yes, we should be faithful stewards over all the resources the Lord provides for us. But things break and deteriorate, markets decline and inflation climbs, one's health can take a dramatic turn without notice, and it is impossible to plan for theft of one's assets or denial of claim by an insurance carrier. In all of life, the believer's assurance, protection, and victory rest in the kindness and faithfulness of Christ. It is better to be insecure about our ability to plan for all circumstances and secure about Christ's ability to keep us through all circumstances. This will address part of our desire for more wealth.

Blessings
JUDGES 18:1-6

The writer ties chapter 18 to the previous narrative by beginning with "In those days." During the time of the coveting displayed by Micah, his mother, and the Levite, moral relativism characterized the entire nation. The writer interprets the actions in chapter 17 through the lens of Israel's moral relativism. He will do the same for the remainder of this story in chapter 18.

Like the Levite, the tribe of Dan is seeking a home other than the one assigned to them by God. They were assigned land just north of Judah but failed in their duty of dispossessing the Canaanites. They have not secured a land inheritance, so the original intent to seek one seems logical. Covetousness will rear its ugly head soon enough.

Dan sends out spies to find a homeland. En route they come upon the Levite in Micah's home, having recognized his accent. In inquiring about his journey from Bethlehem to Micah's house, they do not seem concerned at all that an underaged priest is serving one individual in his home with false gods rather than waiting to properly serve the entire nation before the tabernacle of the one true God. They ask the priest to inquire of the Lord about the success of their journey, assuming that as a priest he would hear from the Lord better than they would.

The Danites are listening to the voice of the Levite. However, they are not concerned about him being a mere personal priest because they are so preoccupied with their own interests. When the Levite explains his circumstances, they immediately turn to their own concern about having a successful journey. They do not even pause to think that this priest is so out of order with regard to the Mosaic law that he cannot hear from the Lord or bless them!

The author highlights the failure of the Levite to seek the Lord for an answer. The Levite assumes blessings for the Danites, and the Danites assume the blessings without questioning how the prayerless priest could know the will of the Lord. Their assumptions allow them to overlook the obvious—that everything about this priest and his ministry is out of order. They want to have land, and they wrongly assume the Lord must want them to have land so that they will be blessed. Therefore, they will ignore the faults of the corrupt priesthood.

The assumption that the Lord wants his people to have blessing stems from a good idea: the Lord promises to bless his people and take care of their needs. But the assumption can invite a blessing-at-whatever-cost motive. That is, if blessing is absent or comes by means of delayed gratification, one might be tempted to secure it on one's own while overlooking obvious infractions against the law of God en route to the blessing.

The evidence of covetousness and greed in such thinking manifests itself in this: *few people—even believers—assume that the Lord's blessings are found in a choice to remain in a present status of less than the desired ideal or in a decision to downsize.* Why must blessing be equated with acquisition, achievement, accolade, or accomplishment? For our Lord Jesus Christ, blessing was in suffering at the hands of the chief priests, scribes, and elders of Israel, in being rejected, betrayed, condemned, handed over to the Gentiles for judgment, mocked, spat on, flogged, and killed. Blessing was in drinking the full cup of the wrath of God down to the dregs; it was in being totally submerged in the wrath of God in order to serve us (see Mark 8:31-33; 9:30-32; 10:32-34,38-40).

In doing so, Jesus had no expansion of his acceptance, no acquisition, no achievement, and no accolades. Although he was doing the will of God without sin, nothing was glorious. Jesus lost clothes and court cases, and he lost followers who temporarily deserted him. To assume that the Lord wants to bless us is good, for he is a good God who gives gifts to his children. But assuming the form is material blessing while overlooking unrighteousness is not good. Jesus did not overlook unrighteousness. He suffered for unrighteousness.

A favorite covetous-inducing pastime of many is watching HGTV. On the network one sees beautiful homes that just have not been modernized. Often the owners feel a need to move from their huge and amply furnished homes to even larger, more modern homes. Even if one lists a home for sale rather than loving to remain in it, repairs it DIY rather than move, or has their current home made over by Michael Holmes, it still is a matter of being discontented with the one and wanting something else. Even as I say this you might quickly grab the "But some houses need updating for safety, space, medical needs, or resale value" *lever* to justify coveting a new home. Save the grace we will give to those needing a medical bed, space or utility upgrades for durable home equipment, or changes to aid in the care of the differently abled, all those other reasons for a different home are some of the things that show just how accepted and pervasive coveting is among believers.

Conclusion

The Danites' encounter with the Levite only brings us to three of seven excuses God's people use to justify covetousness: *offering, security,* and *blessing.* Just as the entire narrative of the Judges increases in evil and moral darkness, so will the Danites' story. While waiting to see how the other excuses unfold, we should sing with Rhea Miller of Jesus being the one we desire the most:

> I'd rather have Jesus than silver or gold;
> I'd rather be His than have riches untold;
> I'd rather have Jesus than houses or lands.
> I'd rather be led by His nail-pierced hand.

I'd rather have Jesus than men's applause;
I'd rather be faithful to His dear cause;
I'd rather have Jesus than worldwide fame.
I'd rather be true to His holy name.

He's fairer than lilies of rarest bloom;
He's sweeter than honey from out the comb;
He's all that my hungering spirit needs.
I'd rather have Jesus and let Him lead.
    Than to be the king of a vast domain
    Or be held in sin's dread sway.
    I'd rather have Jesus than anything
    This world affords today. (Rhea F. Miller, "I'd Rather
Have Jesus")

Reflect and Discuss

1. Why is it difficult for believers to discuss personal financial matters openly with other believers?
2. What does the penchant for privacy about our money say about our motives and identities?
3. What response should Micah's mother have had to his admittance of stealing her money?
4. When the writer enters the statement about Israel's moral relativism, what does that indicate about what one reads in Judges 17:1-5?
5. What does the statement about Israel's moral relativism indicate about how the silversmith views his job and society's influence on his work?
6. Micah's mother proclaims blessing from the Lord and pays to have idols fashioned. What does this say about idolatry in the lives of the people of God?
7. Why might Micah have felt he had the freedom to invite the Levite to be his personal priest? Why might the Levite have agreed?
8. What does Micah's agreement with the priest suggest about what people will do to justify covetousness?
9. How does watching home improvement shows contribute to coveting among believers? Upon confessing such covetousness, how might believers repent from it and yet find a means of enjoying improvement shows?

10. Why is coveting an offense before God? What does our coveting say about our understanding of God?
11. Jesus did not covet. Our salvation depends on his contentment and sacrifice. What might this tell us about our sanctification and glorification?

Unjustifying Coveting, Part 2

JUDGES 18:7-31

Main Idea: The church's opportunities to move from covetousness to obedience should beware of seeking seemingly Christian, relativistic justification for personal advancement through evil means while yet gathering to worship Jesus until his return.

I. **Providence (18:7-10)**
II. **Expansion (18:11-20)**
III. **Loss (18:21-26)**
IV. **Company (18:27-31)**

In Judges 17 we explored the ways the people of Israel justified their covetousness and the consequences that came from their choices so that we could begin the process of unjustifying our own covetous desires. Our goal is to honor the Lord with our desires and avoid the destruction Israel experienced during the period of the judges.

There are seven justifications of covetousness in Judges 17 and 18. The first three are *offering, security,* and *blessing.* By *offering* we are referring to claiming our desire to acquire greater wealth is approved by God if one gives a portion of the gain to the Lord. Never mind that the portion Micah's mother gave to the Lord was small in comparison to what had been returned to her. She could have given the Lord nine hundred and kept only two hundred. Few people do such a thing, showing that the impulse behind the desire for wealth is having the wealth, not giving to the Lord.

By *security* we mean the intention to make sure we have enough funds to remain materially stable in the face of great financial challenges, including disastrous acts of God and extremely large health-care needs that are beyond what insurance pays. But the coveting is inherent in the desire's failure to trust the Lord for all our security. Security often comes in forms of "I know the Lord will provide, but we can't do nothing" or "I know the Lord takes care of us, but we can't be stupid." Even appeals to Scripture and the need to prepare for coming danger can mask covetousness. Only the Lord's grace and mercy keep us no matter what our salaries, investments, and inheritances might be. Long-term health care, legal fees, insurance denial, or cyber theft can humble anyone's financial security.

With respect to *blessing*, we can cover our covetous desires by assuming the Lord wants us to have blessings. However, we assume the blessings are an increase in material or financial wealth, not a spiritual deepening, an increase in meaningful friendships, a maturing use of our gifts, or even the grace to reduce our financial worth and downsize. The assumed definition again reveals that the goal is more wealth, not the pleasure of God. The Danites assume the Lord's blessings are spoken through the Levite, and the Levite too presumes on God without praying.

The remainder of Judges 18 exposes four additional excuses for covetousness: *providence, expansion, loss,* and *company*. Each of these ideas lurks alongside our financial decisions. The Danites' story can become our story if we are not careful to unjustify our covetous desires and learn from the evil acts of the Danites.

Providence
JUDGES 18:7-10

The Danites have commissioned five spies to search out the land of Canaan for an alternate place that they can build their inheritance. These spies have left Micah's home with words affirming the Lord's blessing to them by the mouth of a prayerless priest who is living in rebellion to God's law. That is, the Danites want to acquire inheritance, and they look to someone who will share their view on the acquisition of land rather than speaking with a faithful and holy Aaronic priest about the will of God. The Levite in question gives the Lord's blessing without even lifting his voice to God in prayer. The Danites run with the priest's human-empowered presumption of the Lord's blessings.

They carry this assumed promise of blessing with them as they spy out the land. I can imagine them whistling with delight as they continue in their search for land. The journey is a little bit lighter since they know whoever they face will fall to them. When they arrive at Laish, the Levites' words probably ring loudly in their minds.

Both the description by the narrator and the report of the Danite spies point toward the true desires of the Danites. In the narration, first, *the people are living in security*—without fear of harm coming to them in the form of war. Second, *they are "quiet and unsuspecting,"* which means they keep to themselves and, again, have no reason to think an army could be massing on their borders waiting to pounce of them.

Third, *there was no lack in the land.* Anything the Danites could need or want was plentiful in this land.

Fourth, *the land is without an oppressor.* The irony of this should not be lost on the reader. The Danites will not have to overcome a ruler in the way their judges helped the Israelites overcome their various captors. The Danites do not need to act in the role of judges—of *deliverers*—before attacking this people. The people have no lord protector.

Fifth, *they did not have an alliance with anyone to aid them in war or act as their defenders.* They live such a distance from the Sidonians that the Sidonians are of no help.

Thus, the Danite spies have come upon a completely vulnerable people whose land has everything the Danites could desire. They have the word of promised victory from the Levite. It is time to make a report of what they have discovered.

Immediately the spies call for the attack on this city! They report on the vulnerability of the city and its prosperity, adding that the land is spacious. They emphasize that the people are unsuspecting and the land lacks nothing. The combination of space, vulnerability, wealth of resources, and an encouraging word from a Levite leads the Danites to one conclusion: "God has handed [the land of Laish] over to [the Danites]." Or, in other words, the Danites concluded, *The Lord has led us to a vulnerable people who have everything we need. This is the hand of God prospering Dan; it has to be from the Lord, for it is dropped into our laps as the best opportunity. The providence of God is at work.*

Is this really the providence of God directing them to take the land of Laish? It is the hand of God in all things that brings them to Laish. But Dan has not been very discerning about the will of the Lord to this point; they are trusting an unqualified Levite to speak as a priest on behalf of God. The writer also has told us that Dan is doing what is right in their own eyes.

The law did call for the tribes of Israel to destroy the people of the nations. However, the full instructions on securing the promised land include the following words:

> When you draw near to a city to fight against it, offer terms of peace to it. And if it responds to you peaceably and it opens to you, then all the people who are found in it shall do forced labor for you and shall serve

you. But if it makes no peace with you, but makes war against you, then you shall besiege it. And when the LORD your God gives it into your hand, you shall put all its males to the sword, but the women and the little ones, the livestock, and everything else in the city, all its spoil, you shall take as plunder for yourselves. And you shall enjoy the spoil of your enemies, which the LORD your God has given you. Thus you shall do to all the cities that are very far from you, which are not cities of the nations here. (Deut 20:10-15 ESV)

Dan does not offer this quiet people any terms of peace. They treat the people of Laish as mortal enemies. Dan wants the entire inheritance for its own without having to share its resources with forced laborers. Their decimation of Laish portrays a tribe who wants it all—all the land, all its plenteous resources, and no responsibility to provide for forced laborers. They are coveting more wealth and are using the hand of God as their justification.

Expansion
JUDGES 18:11-20

Even taking a spacious land that lacks nothing will not be enough for the Danites, however. En route to conquering Laish, they land at Micah's house. The spies who had scouted the land recall the items of worship in Micah's home. Maybe they assume the idolatrous items gave a word of divination to the young Levite about the Danites' coming blessings that thus far has proven to be true. Rather than stopping to say, "Thank you," and then continuing on the journey, the spies challenge the warriors to consider whether they should pass by these items or take them for their use as a tribe.

The Danites willingly invite idolatry; they are making it easy to set up another place of worship rather than to worship at the place established by the Lord. They seem to think the items will be necessary for continued or greater blessing in the land. If they can gain even more, then they should take the objects of idol worship.

Important to the story is the repetition of "six hundred Danites . . . armed with weapons of war" in verses 11, 16, and 17. The editor wants us to see that hundreds of warriors are prepared to fight if violence is necessary to gain what Dan desires. Therefore, when Dan takes the articles of Micah's household shrine in the sight of the Levite, there is a brooding presence. But Dan does not respond to the priest's inquiry with threats; threats will come later. They respond with an opportunity—to serve the full tribe rather than the household of one.

At this point the Levite's faithfulness goes out the door. He could have let the idols go, repented from his idolatry, and appealed to Micah's house to serve the Lord. Or he could have offered to be faithful to Micah for the kindness shown and ask to stay in Micah's home while he seeks other work. But what about serving these six hundred warriors and their whole tribe? Like the Danites seeking even more than what they intended to gain in the conquest of Laish, the Levite now yields to the temptation to gain more than what he could gain in the home of one. Just imagine what a whole tribe could provide him and what significance he would have as the priest—albeit an idol-worshiping priest leading others in idolatry—of a full tribe of people! For the Levite it is time to leave and go with the Danites; it is time to expand his work even as Dan seeks to expand its inheritance.

Much like using the idea of assuming the Lord's *blessing* as a justification of our covetousness, the providence of God and the *opportunity to expand* one's work provide common facades to stand in front of our covetous storefronts. Unfortunately, one can claim "the providence of God" for almost anything. But we must think of providence properly. Providence—the Lord's rule of all things to provide for his creation and guide all things to the end of his glory—does not absolve humans of their choice to sin, including the choice to covet. For the Danites to claim providence properly, they should have offered Laish an opportunity for peace.

Similarly, one does not need to think of *expansion* as the Lord's will whenever such opportunities present themselves. Expansion can lead to increased idolatry, as in the case of the Levite and the Danites. The Danites might have had to search high and low to find another stray Levite and search even harder for an Aaronic priest. If the Levite does not expand his ministry here—so to speak—idolatry in Dan would have a huge hurdle to clear.

There is nothing wrong with growing in the grace of God in Christ without expanding materially or financially. It is human to desire to expand materially and financially. Yet no teaching in Scripture requires an increase in influence, reach, or products. Nothing in Scripture demands or even promises expansion of church property, an uptick in baptisms or membership, or an increase in the reach of one's media platforms. The expansion that is a certain work of the Spirit is *deepening—deepening in the knowledge of God and love for him and one's neighbor.* That is the expansion one can seek without coveting.

Loss

JUDGES 18:21-26

The Danites depart from Micah's house with everything that is theirs—women, livestock, and possessions—plus Micah's tools of idolatry. Once the Danites are far away, with the warriors taking up the rear guard behind their families and possessions, it seems that hearing of the loss of his priest and shrine artifacts is too much for Micah to bear. He or someone else in town with a strong sense of justice musters the men to chase after the warriors and get them to return what they took from Micah.

Micah does not seem concerned about facing hundreds of fully armed warriors. His only concern is for the stolen items and his household priest. His words reveal his real issue: "What do I have left?"

The idols and priest would not have had any significant monetary value. Micah was paying the priest, and he could have found another blacksmith to fashion idols for him, for idols were plentiful in Israel during this period. So Micah is not concerned about the monetary loss. Instead, he worries about the loss of the ability to use divination to seek blessings—albeit a divination he thinks the Lord is blessing (see 17:13).

The Danites—themselves lost in their covetousness for a place of inheritance—do not take kindly to Micah's feeble attempt to bring a mob of his neighbors against the Danite warriors in order to recover his idols and his priest.

Keep in mind that the writer earlier emphasized that this is a horde amounting to six hundred fully armed warriors who are shielding the back of the caravan going to Laish, standing between Micah's citizen-militia and the warrior's families, spoils, and possessions. Micah is letting his desire to gain more via divination fuel his inability to accept loss of his goods at the hands of trained warriors. His covetousness deceived him into thinking he and his neighborhood could overtake and defeat the Danite fighters.[58] Further, as Younger notes, "Micah is concerned about the loss of gods who could not even protect themselves or their

---

[58] If Micah had intended to negotiate, he could have done so alone. The gathering of others displays an attempt to gather a force that can confront his opposition.

maker" (Younger, *Judges-Ruth*, 342). He doesn't think of how foolish it is to rescue gods that are not strong enough to keep from being stolen by mere people.[59] He is refusing to accept loss because his desire for prosperity blinds him.

Unfortunately for Micah, the Danites are glad to open his eyes to his real situation. First, *his covetousness has him either out of control or out of his mind,* for he has raised a battle cry against the Danites.[60] To this end, the warriors tell Micah to shut his mouth and say nothing else to them.

Second, *his covetousness is about to provoke angry men to attack him as retribution for his foolish threat toward the Danites.* The NASB translates the "angry" of the CSB as "fierce." Other translations have "short-tempered" (NLT) and "hot-tempered" (NRSV). The word carries the idea of "bitter of soul."[61] Micah is about to be confronted by brutish people without scruples of soul. Third, *his covetousness is about to cost him his life, the lives of his family members, and the lives of his neighbor-militia and their families.*[62]

Covetousness can mask the real dangers we face. Having now seen that the threat from the Danites is too much for his personal militia to engage further, Micah finally accepts the loss and returns home. Sometimes our inability to accept the loss of our potential to prosper is rooted in previous traumas. Sometimes it is fueled by a need for justice. Sometimes it is a matter of pride. Yet many times it is due to covetousness. We need to let go of our material and financial goods or at least hold them loosely enough to let them go. We do not have to talk to management like we are fools, nor do we need to risk the ire of people

---

[59] "The gods made with human hands cannot defend either themselves (cf. 6:28–32) or their makers! The man who had installed a god in his own house finds his house plundered" (Block, *Judges, Ruth*, 508).

[60] "The Danites' pseudoinnocent/ignorant question is intentionally insulting, 'What's the matter with you that you have called out your men to fight?' The verb, *zāʿaq*, which the NIV translates expansively as 'called out your men to fight,' means 'to call for help, to summon (the militia), to raise a battle cry'" (Block, *Judges, Ruth*, 507–8).

[61] Block, *Judges, Ruth*, 508–9, writes, "Although the speakers intend the expression *ʾănāšîm mārê nepeš*, 'men bitter of disposition/soul,' to intimidate Micah into immediate retreat, it represents an apt characterization of the Danites. These men are brutes before whom any right-thinking person will step aside. By threatening to take the lives of Micah's household as well as his own life, they escalate the threat and also confirm their own inhumanity."

[62] "Approaching the Danite vandals, Micah's people shouted after them, but they were rebuffed with threats of brutality not only against them but their families as well" (Block, *Judges, Ruth*, 507).

who might turn on us in greater anger or possibly cause harm to those we love. Instead, we can let go of our goods and live to tell about it.

Company
JUDGES 18:27-31

The people of Dan turn from Micah to continue toward their intended conquest. They meet the unsuspecting, unprotected, and isolated people of Laish and annihilate them with the sword, burn the city, and give them an evil treatment that could have been Micah's fate. Then they rebuild over the ash heap of the previous people. How could they be so cruel and wicked in their coveting of the territory of Laish? The three things to follow reveal one last justification of covetousness: *They are in good company*, or, to say it another way, *they seem to have the approval of God's people*.

First, *they name the place "Dan" after their ancestor.* The tribe is made up of the descendants of Jacob's son, and their character demonstrates elements of the fulfillment of the prophecies made about their progenitor's offspring: *Dan is a tribe that attacks like a snake, with the potential to become a great predator like a lion cub.* But they name the city after Dan "who was born to Israel," which would give him honor. It is as if they were saying to themselves, "Dan, the son of Israel! Dan, the son of Israel!" Their pride was in Dan, and they named the city after their honored ancestor as if he would have approved of their actions. If Dan is honored, the covetousness is justified, along with all the sinful decisions and actions made in the process of overcoming Laish.

Second, *they appoint Jonathan the descendant of Gershom as priest.* Although the weight of the manuscript reading is in favor of reading "son of Moses," whether from Moses's line or Manasseh's is not most important.[63] What is important is that he is from a line of one praised for his association with Israel. The Danites are saying either "Moses's grandson approves of the idol," or "Manasseh's grandson approves of the idol." Both are approval by association.[64]

---

[63] Some LXX manuscripts and the Vulgate read "Moses" (מֹשֶׁה). But a few MT manuscripts insert the Hebrew letter nun (נ) above between the first two letters of the name, indicating "of Manasseh" (מְנַשֶּׁה). This seems to be an attempt by a well-intended scribe to distance Moses from the sins of the Danites. For more, see Butler, *Judges*, 398.

[64] "*Certainly the Danites trumpeted the fame and family of their priest*, but the Jerusalem tradition held on to Aaronic priesthood, not Mosaic" (Butler, *Judges*, 398; emphasis added).

Third, in the region of Dan, *the worship of the idol of Micah continues to coexist with the presence of the Lord's tabernacle until the Philistines capture the ark and take it from Shiloh* (see Block, *Judges, Ruth*, 513–14). After the change of venue, when the house of God at Shiloh no longer serves as a place of worship, the followers of the idol of Micah retain a tribal priesthood until the Assyrian conquest in 722 BC. By some means, the Danites seem to reason that the Lord is approving the presence of the worship of Micah's idol *alongside his presence in the house of God.* Even when the ark is captured, the Danites seem to reason that the Lord wants them to continue in their idol worship.

Collecting together the supposed approval of Dan, Moses, and the Lord, the Danites have justified their coveting by the approval of good company. If the company has strong character and the company approves, then Dan can appeal to the company's approval for their choices. Dan presumes the approval of two great followers of the Lord—two people great in Israel. Dan reasons that they have the approval of God himself. But the reader can see that company approval does not justify idolatry, especially since the justification stands on a faulty process of reasoning.

It is baffling to watch a believer justify any sin or foolishness by company association. "That pastor does 'X' [morally questionable thing]." "My friend who is a Christian does 'Y' [foolish decisions]." "People at my church do 'Z' [worldly leisurely activity]." Or, "Joe's/Jane's parents are Christian and they let her do 'A' [sinful behavior] or don't require Joe/Jane to maintain 'B' [Christian standard or practice]." These words are thrown in the faces of believers as another believer's justification for unwise or sub-Christian doings. Teens and young adult believers use such excuses to justify participation in sexual sins. College-student believers use similar excuses to justify joining a fraternity or sorority known for ungodly behavior and giving time for service to the organization that could be given to serving the Lord. Adults use that line of reasoning to participate in cultic activities of religious lodges and to walk away from their families—in pursuit of their ideas of happiness—when they lack biblical justification to do so.

The same holds true for justifying coveting. Many believers' use of a questionable means of financial investment or approval of the questionable practices of get-rich-quick business that uses so-called Christian principles does not give good justification for one's participation in those things. All the other believers might be blinded by covetousness, greed, and financial anxiety. Neither does saying, "Well if the Lord doesn't approve, why doesn't he stop me or close this means of gain," supply a solid argument for continued coveting.

The Lord has his purposes and timing. In the Ten Commandments the Lord revealed disapproval of having other gods in his presence or the crafting of images of other gods. At the time of the crafting of Micah's idol, the Lord was already disapproving of the idol. Yet he did not bring full judgment against the idolatry until hundreds of years later with the coming of the Assyrians. If the Danites had concluded that the silence of God meant approval, they would have been wrong. When we conclude that the silence of God means approval rather than a display of his patience, we are wrong.

Close

Offering, security, blessing, providence, expansion, loss, and *company* act as shining facades over covetous storefronts. But when we hold up these justifications before Jesus and his work on the cross, we readily see the weakness of these excuses.

Jesus offered the greatest offering one can give to the Lord without needing more materially or financially. As the Lamb of God, he gave himself to pay the penalty for our sins. The Lamb of God pointed to the widow giving her meager coins in offering and said, "This poor widow has put more into the treasury than all the others" (see Mark 12:42-44).

Jesus, judicially separated from the Father as the offering for sin, thus being at the greatest moment of insecurity in the history of the universe, cried out to his Father, "My God, my God, why have you abandoned me?" (Matt 27:46). Yet he did so in full assurance of the faithful provision of the God who promises to provide for those who seek first his kingdom and promises never to leave or abandon us (Matt 6:33; Heb 13:5).

Jesus, beholding the providence of God, had before him as option B for the Father to take away his cup of wrath from Jesus, potentially summoning thousands of angels to slaughter his enemies and rescue him from their unjust trial and inflicted suffering. But Jesus embraced option A—to obey the will of the Father by being wounded for us, seeing providence as an opportunity to do what pleases God.

Jesus expanded by empowering his own to proclaim his resurrection from the dead. The path to expansion meant humbling himself, having no place to lay his head, experiencing Israel rejecting him, watching all disciples leave him at his greatest hour of need. Jesus would embrace loss, becoming poor so that we might become rich in the things of God. The only company that mattered to Jesus was that he did what he saw his Father doing.

Jesus went to the cross to cancel out our coveting and to give us power to live for him. We must go to him to unjustify our covetousness so that the thing we covet most is him.

Review and Discuss

1. What should alert the Danites to dismiss the word of the Levite priest in Micah's home?
2. In your own words, describe what motivates the Danites to pursue taking Laish.
3. What would be the right treatment of the people of Laish and why?
4. What aspects of the law are the Danites breaking by taking Micah's household idols for themselves?
5. Name several ways you have experienced others using expansion as an excuse for coveting. When have you justified an increase in material or financial wealth by using the expansion excuse?
6. Why is it rare to hear believers speak of downsizing or losing as a sign of God's blessings on them? Why might having less be more of a blessing than having much?
7. What would it take for you to cap your lifestyle at its current level and to sacrificially give all future material or financial income toward the expansion of the gospel in the world?
8. What would a congregation's repentance from and denunciation of covetousness in faithful practice do for increasing their witness in the world? If you placed coveting in your rearview mirror, what freedom would that give you in service to Christ?
9. How does Jesus's life show anticovetousness in the path leading to our salvation?
10. What prayers can you offer daily to embrace the anticovetous character of Jesus?

The Personal Ethics of Family Life

JUDGES 19

Main Idea: The Levite's inconsistency in his personal ethics as he jour-
neys from Bethlehem to Ephraim results in the concubine's death at
the hands of wicked men and ends with the concubine's dismembered
body and with calls for Israel to make a judgment on the wickedness, as
offers of hospitality by the father-in-law and the old man are rejected.[65]

I.   Sanctify Marriage without Substitutes (19:1-3).
II. Seek True Happiness for Our Children's Marriages (19:4-10).
III. Seek Healthy Churches Full of Hospitality (19:11-15).
IV. Invite Younger Believers Away from Fellowship with Darkness
     (19:16-21).
V.   Do Not Propose Sex with Women as a Solution to Men's
     Hypersexuality (19:22-26).
VI. Act with Urgency and Consistency toward Abused Women
     (19:27-30).

It is easy to lament secular society's so-called assault on the family or
assault on family values. We show concern because we do not want to
see the erosion of our own families—the turning away of our children
from the faith toward acceptance of lifestyles and worldviews that are
sub-Christian.

However, Scripture lays blame for the erosion of the family at the
feet of the church. The story of the sojourning Levite and the dismembered concubine reveals that the problem does not lie in the world's
rejection of our values. The fault lies with the people of God being

---

[65] I am not so sure that Judg 19:1-2 creates a "gap." The element of "there was no
king in Israel" is pregnant with thoughts from the entire book. It seems to be impossible
to read the phrase as a gap waiting to be filled when the history of the period of Judges
provides plenty of gap fillers. However, what happens with the concubine before dawn—
whether she is dead on the doorstep, too ashamed to move, or simply asleep—constitutes
a gap. The reader does not hear from the narrator or the character what happened.
Instead, one must ask whether the unnamed Levite kills the concubine or finds her dead.

called to a holy standard of living but making choices that make the standard seem like simple advice to be rejected.

Sanctify Marriage without Substitutes
JUDGES 19:1-3

The plot of Judges 19 intends to show how a Levite acts when Israel is without a king. Immediately one observes a consequence or danger the kingless episode gives as a foreshadowing of items to follow: a Levite "acquired" a female companion who is not a virgin,[66] signaling that both the priesthood and marriage—Israel's key religious and social structures—are at stake during the period of the judges.[67]

The narrator employs a series of successive gaps to show that the Levite's character does not match his relationship to the tribe of the priesthood. He does not inform the reader as to why the Levite has been sojourning in Ephraim, yet Ephraim will become significant to the episode later. Neither does the writer explain what the Levite does to cause the concubine to leave him in order to return to her father's house.[68] Nor does the writer explain why the Levite waits four months before going after his wife (or what happens during the period of the four months in Bethlehem). The gaps invite the reader to consider reasons behind the *oddity* of these actions. All answers would be speculative because the text offers no answers. However, the gaps manifest behavior inconsistent with the high standards the law gives for the priesthood, thus allowing the reader to consider, at minimum, that the Levite's actions are inconsistent with expected Levite behavior. He does not care about what God's Word teaches about marriage.

---

[66] In reading the MT and LXX of Judges 19, one sees that the English texts translate the words (אִשָּׁה פִילֶגֶשׁ) simply as "concubine," when there are two terms present. "Woman, concubine" would be more accurate; the LXX has γυναῖκα παλλακὴν, following the Hebrew.

[67] The priesthood is associated with the law, and marriage is the key to having a family under the law. So it might be better to say that both the law and the family are in jeopardy.

[68] The LXX reading says that the concubine became angry with the Levite. Butler notes, "Following the LXXA (compare OL) ὠργίσθη, 'grew angry,' and Vg. along with *Tg. Jonathan, wbsrt lwby*, 'she despised him,' and deriving וַתִּזְנֶה from a second root that appears only here in MT" (*Judges*, 105). Butler therefore translates the phrase as "His concubine found him *repulsive*."

The concubine who becomes the wife goes back to her old ways and is unfaithful to the Levite. For four months she retreats back to her father's house after her unfaithfulness. For four months the Levite does not attempt to reconcile a problem in a marriage. It is as if he is content to live with a wrecked marriage.

When he finally goes after her, he does speak kindly to her in apparent attempts to bring her back home. But she somehow convinces him to join her father's home rather than go be in her own home with her husband. The husband with his servants goes to the father's house rather than carrying the wife back to repair their own home. The father-in-law is happy to see the couple reunited, but he should be encouraging them to go make their marriage work in their own home.

Like the Levite, concubine, and father-in-law, we also substitute an alternate version of marriage for God's standard. Like the Levite, we do not make enough priority of a strong marital relationship to seek to repair one that is hurting. Yes, one believing spouse might seek counseling, but the other Christian spouse does not. Then dysfunction reigns, and our children and friends get the message that a strong marriage is not really important to being in Christ.

Like the concubine, we run from our failures and throw ourselves into our families of origin when our marriage is broken rather than going back in confession and contrition to those we have harmed. This makes marriage something of lesser status than the bond to the family of origin. It makes it so that society says to married people, "Don't allow your marriage to pull you away from your family."

Like the father-in-law, we rejoice in low standards of marriage for our children. Yes, we want to see them with those they have married. But we should want to see more than a lack of divorce or separation. We should want to see them striving and thriving.

Seek True Happiness for Our Children's Marriages
JUDGES 19:4-10

The man stays with his father-in-law three days, taking advantage of the hospitality offered. Seemingly, however, he understands that he needs to be with his own wife in their own home and has no intentions of overstaying and getting the cold shoulder. So on the morning of the fourth day, he rises to depart with his wife, servant, and saddled donkey.

The father-in-law—identified also as the girl's father—wants them to stay longer for reasons unstated to us. At minimum, it would seem he thinks the couple's marriage would be better off in his presence than wherever they will make their home. He will use trickery to force them to stay longer. He will act as if he wants to enjoy them, binding the son-in-law in feasting for much of the day, inviting him to merriment, while offering the son-in-law to depart at evening. Then, when evening draws near, the girl's father will suggest it is too late to travel and press the son-in-law to stay for another evening and get more rest and depart the next morning. The ploy works once.

On the fifth day, the father-in-law attempts the same feigned fellowship and merriment when the son-in-law tries to depart. The ruse seems to work for half a day. But when evening draws near and the father attempts the second half of the ploy, the son-in-law refuses to stay. He will not be pressured into staying in the father-in-law's home again. With his wife, servant, and donkey, he departs in the evening, not staying the night, risking even a DUI to make his way to Jebus.

As parents, we want the best for our children. But the best, when it is not a matter of Scripture, is a matter of preference. No matter how well-meaning our attempts to help our children's marriages prosper, when we try to force them to live within our confines of marriage health—as the father-in-law attempted to do—it will not work because it is unethical to do so. It is ethical for us to allow our Christian children and their spouses to go live their marriages as they wish.

The people who marry our children can see when we really just want to control their lives because we are fearful for our own sons and daughters—like the man identified specifically as "the girl's father" in this scene (v. 6). They know when we want real fellowship with them versus the invitation to lunch that we offer to be nosy or to force our agendas on them. They can recognize real care for their well-being rather than an attempt to cover up a concern that the in-law spouse is about to make things go well for our child.

One of the blessings the Lord kindly has given me is parents who have accepted my wife as if she were their own, precious child. This is not something my wife had to earn while she was my girlfriend or fiancée or in the early part of our marriage. Acceptance with love is something my parents offered from the beginning while also caring for my best interests. That acceptance has continued when allowing us the freedom to make marital and parenting mistakes. Rather than imposing their wishes on us—for there are times we have done things vastly differently than they would have done them—they have given us the freedom to learn, to grow, and to figure out how things work.

Yes, they have offered advice and wisdom. Because they have allowed freedom as the norm in our relationship, when they offer wisdom that seeks to correct something we have done, we listen, because this is not the norm; they have to be concerned if they are expressing disagreement. If they had expressed disagreement as the norm, at some point we would be inclined to ignore or avoid the negativity toward our marriage or parenting.

Freedom does not guarantee our children and in-laws will have marital success and bliss. Freedom is ethically correct. Feigned love and care while attempting to make someone conform to your views is one way to build resentment among your children and in-laws. Many avoid the church for this reason. The world can smell our control facade ten miles away, and it makes them say of our family values, "Nope. I don't need those. I'm good."

Seek Healthy Churches Full of Hospitality
JUDGES 19:11-15

As the trio travels, the servant suggests that they lodge in Jebus as the evening approaches. Jebus is known to us and the original readers as Jerusalem, the home of the Jewish people. But at the time of the events in Judges, it was the city of the Jebusites, a people foreign to the Abrahamic covenant. The servant's request would take the traveling family to a city of foreigners. This provokes an ethical response in the man married to the concubine: he will not go to a city outside the people of the covenant.

This ethical stand seems strange coming from a wandering Levite who married a concubine and allowed her to disappear from their marriage for four months even though he seems to have known her whereabouts. But blind spots and unintended hypocrisy in our ethics come with being fallen creatures. We cannot keep God's law perfectly; we are not perfectly ethical.

Still, the man decides not to find lodging and possibly future housing in lands controlled by a noncovenant people. Therefore, he rejects the offer to stay in Jebus, and they press on toward Gilead in Benjamin and leave open an option to turn to Ramah.

Upon arriving in Gilead, they intend to spend the night. However, it appears that Lallapalooza, Coachella, or the soccer draft weekend is in town, for all the guest housing seems to be taken.[69] Or at least there is some reason they are left standing in the square. The choice to be among their people rather than in a place that is full of foreigners still leaves them without a place to lodge.

Wisely, the man passes by Jebus, a place that will in the future be a place he should be able to find lodging but now is filled with foreigners—people who could harm his marriage and/or attempt to turn him back from his marriage. Only recently has he started on the road to repair the adultery and separation. He needs to go to a place that has people who will hold up the Lord's standard for marriage. He needs to go to a place where he can find God's people more than in name only.

If and when the man gets to such a place, finding hospitality should be the norm. One measure of a people's ethics toward family is what they do with their homes. If their homes are places open to serve others in kindness, their homes are good for supporting marriages. The man should be able to find a safe place for his family and servant.

Invite Younger Believers Away from Fellowship with Darkness
JUDGES 19:16-21

The appearance of the old man offers hope to the stranded travelers. Acting in accordance with the Melchizedekian priesthood, the man intercedes into the situation of those in need of help and mediates a service of peace. The writer first describes the old man as one coming from working in the field, bringing him on the scene with no beginning or mention of parents. The old man works in this town, so he knows it well.

The second description identifies the man as someone local to Ephraim—the place from which the man and his companions were sojourning originally (see v. 1). There is a geographical connection between the old man and the younger man, which might make the old man trustworthy in the eyes of the younger and make the old man

---

[69] Lalapalooza is an annual four-day summer music festival in Chicago. Coachella Valley Music and Arts Festival is an annual rock festival held at the Empire Polo Club in Indio, California.

sympathize with the traveler. Gibeah is just a place in which the old man of Ephraim has found work.

Third, the old man will have behavior distinct from the men of Benjamin. He will honor the Lord by means of his offer of hospitality, whereas the men of Benjamin will dishonor the Lord in their lust.

Upon seeing the traveler in the square, the old man investigates the traveler's itinerary. He is not being nosy or a busybody; instead, he is showing care for the travelers' well-being, as the later scene will reveal. The old man extends peace to the travelers and offers to serve them by opening his home to them. A few things about the man's offer are significant.

For one, the old man seems to offer so that the travelers can continue on their way to the house of the Lord. While the reader knows that the younger traveler has some ethical lapses as a Levite, the old man does not know that when he makes his genuine offer. The man might not have offered hospitality if the traveler had said that he had heard of the ways of the men of this town and came to join them. The mention of travel to the Lord's house seemingly makes the man see in the traveler a fellow follower of the God of Israel.

Also, the old man offers hospitality despite the traveler's self-sufficiency. The old man does not need the traveler's provisions for the traveler's animals. The issue for the old man is not affordable lodging. The issue for the old man is that the younger traveler has a place to lodge with another who loves the God of Israel. Although unknown to the reader, the old man, moreover, does not wish for the traveler to take his chances in the square with the relativistic people of Benjamin. Getting out of the square concerns the darkness that is falling on the land.

What one sees in the old man is an older saint who offers hospitality to a younger seeker of the Lord so that the younger sojourner will not need to receive hospitality at the hands of the evil Benjaminites. His ethical sensors recognize the danger of the traveler staying in the square and finding hospitality in the town from others who would not care that the traveler is seeking the Lord.

It is ethical to care about the well-being of others. In this scene, it is ethical for the older saint, with knowledge of the ways of the people of the town, to offer the younger sojourner housing in his home rather than allow him to be forced to take housing among the rabble. An older sojourner who knows the God of Israel does what is right toward the younger sojourner because housing with those of darkness is dangerous.

In the same way, older saints must offer hospitality to younger seek-ers of the Lord. The goal of such hospitality is to provide the peace that cannot be gained in fellowship with darkness (see 2 Cor 6:14–7:1; Eph 5:7,11; 1 John 1:6). In the home of the old man, the Levite will learn of the ways of the Lord, maybe even being challenged to live a life consistent with his tribal identity. However, if he had gone to the home of a Benjaminite or stayed in the square to rest, he would only have learned the ways of darkness and fallen victim to them. The old man intends to provide the younger traveler a means to see righteousness rather than experience fellowship with those in darkness. The old man does not want the younger sojourner to be prevented from going to the house of the Lord.

Do Not Propose Sex with Women as a Solution to Men's Hypersexuality
JUDGES 19:22-26

Until one reads in the four Gospels of the rejection, false accusation, mocking, spitting, flogging, abandonment, and crucifixion of the Son of God, there is no more grotesque event of evil in the pages of redemp-tive history than these next scenes in this story. Scripture does not hide or veneer-coat the depravity of humankind; neither does it minimize men's historical and perpetual abuse of women. This passage comments on the vulnerability of women in a society that has a relativistic morality, challenging the church to be different as followers of Christ—the God who gives dignity to women equal to that of men and who loves women as much as he loves men.

Without question, this passage is condemning sexual deviance of men, sexual abuse of women, and rape. However, because the writer presents a *biblical* morality, the story does not stop at the level of actions. This passage condemns the worldview that sees sex with women as the solution for men's sexual deviance, not putting the onus of the cure of men's sins on women. This passage also condemns the worldview that sees women's lives as something less valuable than men's lives, the view that sits in safety, silence, and fear while women continue to be abused and ignores the brokenness sexual abuse causes women in this present age. The onus to change the worldview and the action of men falls on the two persons identified as "master" in this passage ("owner" in vv. 22-23 and "master" in vv. 11-12,26-27). The heads of household need to act as masters in the protection of the women in their care and not simply wear the title of "master."

The old man and the traveler seem to be enjoying themselves in fellowship within the hospitable walls of the old man's home. Yet the fellowship will be interrupted by men intending to rape the traveling visitor. The men are sexually deviant. Like sexually deviant men, they intend to exert power over their victim, as their surrounding of the house shows. They have no intention of letting the traveler escape.

Until now, the old man seems to be a faithful follower of the Lord, offering the hospitality consistent with God's will for his people (see Job 31:32; also Lev 19:33-34; Deut 10:19). However, in the face of this threat by the horde of wicked men encroaching on his home, he waffles on his commitment to the law of God. He rightly stands for the protection of his houseguest, but wrongly he offers the two women in his house as substitutes available to rape in place of the man. The old man makes the offer without permission from either woman, with total disregard for his daughter's life, without compassion for his daughter's sexual innocence and purity, and without care for the dignity of either woman (for even a concubine has dignity in the eyes of God as one made in the image of God).

All the old man's ethics go out the door in a flash under the guise of doing right toward the traveler in his home. It would have been right for the old man to keep reasoning with the wicked men, barricade his home, protect the women with the same force he attempted to protect the male guest, and sacrifice his own life to protect the others if necessary. That proposal is scary for any of us, but it is the job of the master of the house. The women should not have to protect him; it is his job (and the job of the other male) to protect the women.

The men of the town are so wicked that the offer of the virgin and the concubine will not suffice. They will have their way with the male guest. We are not told the words and actions of the Benjaminites' rejection of the old man's offer, but we can imagine them pressing the door, banging on it fiercely, attacking the exterior of the rest of the home, and getting louder with yelling toward the inhabitants of the house. There is a fearsome mob outside the home demanding the male guest of the home be given over to rape for their sexual fulfillment—not of one man but of all the men surrounding the house. They intend a gang rape of prison proportions. Certainly, this is terrifying to the sojourning Levite, for his dignity and life have been threatened. He alone is the intended victim of this twisted crowd of men.

Terrified, and already relativistic in his thinking, the Levite finds a way to save his own hide at the expense of another. He will grab his concubine with force and throw her out the door to the men like one throws a piece of meat to a pack of wild dogs, on which the dogs might gorge themselves until even the shank bone is devoured. What the CSB translates in verse 25 as "took her outside to them" rightly reflects the sense "caused her to go outside to them" of the Hebrew.

The old man and the Levite then remain in the house as the deviants outside rape the woman and put her through hours of abuse under the cover of darkness. As Mitzi Smith writes, "The young woman's terror in the night will not interfere with the Levite's business in the day" ("Reading the Story," 26). She screams and no one comes to help. She tries to escape only to run into another man with evil intentions at every turn. Exhausted, battered, humiliated, terrified, most likely bleeding, bruised, filled with dirt, and naked, the woman only escapes the torture at dawn when the evil Benjaminites do not wish for their deeds to be seen in morning's light. For the several hours of the entire length of the long night, the two men stay indoors with talk of hospitality rules and other justifications for their cowardly disregard for the life and well-being of the Levite's wife. He has exploited her as if she were still merely a concubine in his eyes. The two men's ethics are in full view of the old man's daughter.

In sad irony, with the little strength she has after being abandoned and abused, she makes her way back to the threshold of the door of the men who willingly trafficked her. She comes to a door that should have been the opening to a place of safety for her from the terrors of this society. Instead, that door opened the way for the society of Benjaminite men to dehumanize her without outcry or defense by her husband and male host—two men who were supposedly followers of the God of Israel. She comes back to the door of two people whom the writer identifies with the covenant people of God. Here are two men who know what is right but who do not act with courage to do what is right. They only think of themselves; they have not thought of the one now lying at their doorstep broken by their silence and weakness. The result of the men's inconsistent ethics lies in full view of the entire society in the light of the morning that dawns upon the concubine.

I wonder how our daughters grow up watching a world in which men demean women and ignore the harm caused by men's hypersexuality. What do they learn when we *are slow to* or *do not* speak up against pornography, work for the end of human trafficking, or fight for women's equal pay, positions, and representation in the workplace without women having to offer sexual favors to advance in their professions? What do our daughters learn when the men in their lives make few comments to our sons about the words they use to describe women and maybe even fewer about a predator's abuse of an Olympic gymnastics team?[70]

What they learn from us are warped ethics—*ethics that selfishly consider men's worth to be more than that of women and that consider women's lives to be cheap, degradable objects made for the fulfillment of men's sexual deviancy.* They are learning about our personal ethics because our response to women's mistreatment is a statement of what we deem to be right or wrong for men to do toward women. What they are learning by such ethics is enough to turn them off toward and even against men the rest of their lives. Men's ethics help make the feminist agenda and turn many women toward sexual relationships with other women. There is no need to point fingers at critical theories or liberal philosophies taught in classrooms. Men's silence models enough teaching for young girls that men's warped ethical teachings do not need help from any formal lectures or textbook readings.

Act with Urgency and Consistency toward Abused Women
JUDGES 19:27-30

The master of the concubine gives full display of his complete selfishness and total disregard for his wife. It is evident that he believes his life is of more worth than hers. The next morning, he arises and intends to continue on his journey without so much as a thought for what happened to his wife. If the woman had not been in his way at the doorstep, he would not have considered her at all. Even when he does, he acts as if nothing happened—that there is no significance to her being thrown to a horde of sexually deviant men for them to abuse for several hours.

---

[70] See Abigail Pesta, "An Early Survivor of Larry Nassar's Abuse Speaks Out for the First Time," *Time Magazine*, July 18, 2019, https://time.com/5629228/larry-nassar-victim-speaks-out/, accessed April 19, 2021, for more on Larry Nassar's abuse of the girls of the US Olympic Gymnastics Team.

He continues as normal, as if the abused lady should jump into normal routine with no mention of the evil committed against her and not one word of compassion toward her pain and trauma.

This story of the man and his concubine-wife in Judges 19 has many parallels to that of Sodom and Gomorrah in Genesis 19. The reader, therefore, should anticipate a scene in which hospitality is offered, evil men approach, hospitality is rebuked, and angelic beings appear to rescue the Abrahamic relative needing hospitality, as in Genesis 19. However, in Judges 19, hospitality is offered, evil men approach, hospitality is rebuked, but no one intervenes, demonstrating the guests to be acting in discord with the Abrahamic covenant. Instead of intervention, the host offers his own daughter and the guest's concubine.[71]

In comparison to Lot in Genesis 19, rather than a Moabite offspring as a result of the poor choice the male figure makes, in this story the narrative relates the death and dismemberment of the concubine. Although Lot escapes Sodom and Gomorrah, this man does not escape being Canaanized like the nations around him. His system of ethics reflects no compassion or concern for another.

The man will dismember the dead wife, further degrading the abused and dehumanized woman. Effectively, he is doing the same as the Benjaminites, who divided her and sent her throughout all the Benjaminite men to be reduced to a piece of meat for their devouring. Yet in the man's outrage over the woman's rape and death, he fails to see that he can seek for Israel to have alarm and avenge her death without chopping her body "limb by limb." He needs an urgent response—one he should have had as soon as he awoke. He should alert others to the horror of the acts of Benjamin. But it would have been ethical for him to honor her in her death, burying her, and then to send verbal notice to the tribes of the disgrace of the sins of Benjamin.

The reference to the day of redemption—the exodus (v. 30)—allows the reader to compare present Israel to those who were redeemed from the hand of Pharaoh. The nation of Israel has devolved so miserably that they are acting like the generation that needed redemption from idolatry and oppression in Egypt. As the tribes' leaders take counsel to decide what to do with the dismemberment, irony abounds, for they should be taking counsel to decide how to act toward all the sins of

---

[71] Rhetorically speaking, this is another example of the rejection of family in the episode.

Israel. Even in evaluating this event, no discussion is necessary: the law prescribes the judgment needed (see Deut 22:22,25-27).

Conclusion

In reading the horrible story of Judges 19, one still sees the light of the gospel shining through. Typologically, one discerns the concubine's father acting in the role of a Melchizedekian priest when he intervenes in the man's plans to bring him joy. Coming on the scene without father, mother, or the beginning or ending of days, the father steps in to rescue this family. The family, however, drawn into the Canaanite worldview, as evidenced by the Levite's marriage to the concubine, rejects the offer of the Melchizedekian priest.

Similarly, the old man will come in the same vein, having no mention of father, mother, or the beginning or ending of days, interceding to protect the sojourning family from the lurking evil of Benjaminite society. While the first intercession does bring the man and his family into the home of the old man, the second intercession fails to stop both the evil of the Benjaminites and the man's working out his own plan of saving himself. The ethics of the man, shaped by the worldview of the Canaanites, makes his wife save him rather than him save her.

Benjamin and all the people of the judges period might be going down to the moral collapse and destruction of the family. But Jesus's sacrifice provides for the righteousness of the members of entire families. His personal ethic considers the family's need and our individual needs above his own. Jesus has the personal ethic we need for our family lives to honor him.

Reflect and Discuss

1. What is the problem with the Levite's waiting four months before going after his wife?
2. How can one tell that the concubine's father has good motives toward the daughter and son-in-law based on his actions?
3. Where do you see your church succeeding or failing at providing hospitality to young families?
4. If a believer is displeased with or embarrassed by the size, condition, location, or age of his/her home, how can he/she still practice hospitality toward young families in one's local congregation?

5. What are a few things a local assembly could do to encourage the faithful practice of hospitality between older saints and younger families?

6. What are some examples of younger believers fellowshipping with darkness of which older saints should intercede personally and lovingly to help younger believers avoid?

7. What can you and/or church members do locally to put an end to human sex trafficking and pornography—two industries fueling the abuse of women around the world?

8. Thousands of rape kits in US police stations remain unprocessed.[72] As those who love your neighbors, what can your local congregation do to help these rape victims have their dignity restored and to pursue justice on their behalf?

9. If a man is sexually deviant, what are some problems with thinking marriage will cure his deviancy?

10. In a modern sense, how does the church show disregard for the abuse, pain, and dehumanizing of women?

---

[72] "Rape Kits Are Sitting on Shelves, Untested," *Scientific American*, July 2020, https://www.scientificamerican.com/article/rape-kits-are-sitting-on-shelves-untested/; Barbara Bradley Hagerty, "An Epidemic of Disbelief," *The Atlantic*, August 2019, https://www.theatlantic.com/magazine/archive/2019/08/an-epidemic-of-disbelief/592807/; Pagan Kennedy, "The Rape Kit's Secret History," *NYT*, June 17, 2020, https://www.nytimes.com/interactive/2020/06/17/opinion/rape-kit-history.html; Steve Reilly, "Tens of Thousands of Rape Kits Go Untested across USA," *USA Today*, July 16, 2015, https://www.usatoday.com/story/news/2015/07/16/untested-rape-kits-evidence-across-usa/29902199/; Ali Watkins, "Old Rape Kits Finally Got Tested. 64 Attackers Were Convicted," *New York Times*, March 12, 2019, https://www.nytimes.com/2019/03/12/nyregion/rape-kit-tests.html.

From Accusation to Exile

JUDGES 20

Main Idea: We must address all accusations of one family harming another with a proper investigation and conflict-resolution process to avoid an all-out war in church that leaves everyone harmed.

I. **Accusation Starts toward Exile (20:1-10).**
    A. One side, ready for war, acts on accusation.
    B. The other side sits back without confession.

II. **Accusation Heads toward Exile (20:8-11).**
    A. We start by determining we have a war to win.
    B. We don't determine we have a family to help.

III. **Accusation Escalates toward Exile (20:12-17).**
    A. The accused rejects submission bullying.
    B. The accused returns superior battle planning.

IV. **Accusation Moves toward Exile (20:18-26).**
    A. Despite prayerful attempts at obedience
    B. Despite attempts that repeat antiquated ways of handling conflict
    C. Despite attempts that eventually give way to brokenness before the Lord

V. **Accusation Verges on Exile (20:27-37).**
    A. The accuser does not seek the peace of God.
    B. The Lord provides victory through smaller resources and the accused's missteps.

VI. **Accusation Turns into Exile (20:38-48).**
    A. The congregation signals for ambush.
    B. The congregation forces the accused to flee and stay away with the little family they have left.

After the assassination of Archduke Franz Ferdinand of Austria-Hungary by Serbian nationalist Gavrilo Princip on June 28, 1914, Austria-Hungary hoped to use the incident as justification for settling the question of Serbian nationalism once and for all ("World War I").

The speed with which the assassination escalated into a world war is amazing, as one encyclopedist notes:

> Convinced that Austria-Hungary was readying for war, the
> Serbian government ordered the Serbian army to mobilize
> and appealed to Russia for assistance. On July 28, Austria-
> Hungary declared war on Serbia, and the tenuous peace
> between Europe's great powers quickly collapsed. Within a
> week, Russia, Belgium, France, Great Britain and Serbia had
> lined up against Austria-Hungary and Germany, and World
> War I had begun. ("World War I")

WWI—the Great War—lasted four years and took the lives of more than nine million soldiers. More than twenty-one million soldiers also were wounded, along with ten million civilians being injured. If they had come to the table to talk terms of peace, they could have avoided the first modern, global-scale war, maybe even steering away from what would become WWII.

While some wars have started with two hating factions each sitting on powder kegs with their fingers on trigger devices, others have started from false accusation. On August 4, 1964, when US Navy destroyers *Maddox* and *Turner Joy* reported that they were under attack by communist torpedo boats while steaming eleven miles off the coast of North Vietnam, in waters between Hainan Island and Haiphong, the two warships returned fire and reportedly drove off the raiders. *Military History* reports what follows:

> Within minutes of this second skirmish however, President
> Lyndon Johnson was in front of the national media
> condemning what he characterized as repeated acts of
> aggression by Hanoi. He then vowed retaliation. Hours
> later, 64 American warplanes struck a series of targets in
> North Vietnam. On Aug. 10, Congress passed the Gulf of
> Tonkin Resolution granting the president wide latitude
> to wage war in Indochina. . . . A full on air campaign
> followed the initial strikes and by the following spring,
> American combat troops were on the ground in Southeast
> Asia, joining more than 20,000 advisors already in country.
> Subsequent investigations revealed that the Aug. 4 raid

> by North Vietnamese attack boats *probably* never actually
> occurred. The destroyers had likely detected only false
> radar returns or "ghosts"; no enemy torpedoes were ever
> fired. ("Damned Lies")

Ten years later, the US would emerge from the end of that incident with 2.7 million soldiers having fought in Vietnam, fifty-eight thousand of whom would never return home, and Vietnam would lose three million people of its own. The relationship between the US and Vietnam would remain strained for twenty years after the end of the war. What a difference there might have been in the history of the US and Vietnam if someone had investigated rather than going to war on an assumption.

Missing the opportunity to make peace, going to war on misinformation, looking to end nationalistic ideals of a border state, region, or people—these beginning points of conflict are common on an international scale. But they also are common on an ecclesial scale. That is, church members have been known to go to war against one another, with devastating consequences to the church. This is true in fights over budget, staffing, calling of a pastor, building a new edifice, or changing vision. It is especially true when one family in a congregation accuses another family in the congregation of gross wrongdoing, and we do not go through the proper investigation and processes to resolve concerns at the lowest level before going to war that will leave one or more families never returning to church again. As we come to the penultimate chapter in Judges, we see this happening in Israel as we follow an accusation of wrongdoing that will lead to Benjamin's exile.

The chapter will show sinful actions and negative outcomes. Stories like this one intend to teach by negative example with the hope of preventing believers from making the choices the characters in question made. Like a lit Krispy Kreme sign that alerts all to fresh doughnuts rolling off the conveyer belt, this chapter holds up a huge flashing neon sign that says, "Do not handle a similar situation the way those in the story handled it in history! To please the Lord, do not do what they did." This chapter gives six ideas of what the church must do differently from Israel and Benjamin when there is an accusation of wrongdoing by one family against another, so that no one has to choose exiling themselves from the larger body because everyone went to war rather than resolving the conflict properly.

Accusation Starts toward Exile

JUDGES 20:1-10

One Side, Ready for War, Acts on Accusation

We now find ourselves on the other side of the concubine being severed and distributed throughout all Israel. Enraged by the message, the entire nation—the entirety of the congregation in Canaan—travels from their tribal territories to assemble at Mizpah. The author stresses the distance some tribes have come over the matter at hand. Once gathered, a force of four hundred thousand men is put before the people as those who are prepared to address the internal problem in Israel with the sword. Where in the previous cycle of narratives we might have expected a sixteen- or even forty-year wait in oppression before going to war against the Philistines, we have hundreds of thousands in Israel immediately ready to go purge evil in their midst, backed fully by the entire population of the eleven tribes. Yet it is to go against a brother under the same covenant and worshiping the same Lord, and not an uncircumcised enemy.[73]

The Other Side Sits Back without Confession

Parenthetically, the writer inserts that Benjamin is aware that all the rest of the nation has gone up to Mizpah and they did not get an invitation to the dance. It would not have taken a genius in Benjamin to figure out the topic of discussion, nether could it be kept from them on all the trade routes. They are aware that the tribes are coming to address what Benjamin did to the concubine. Benjamin could prevent the four hundred thousand from even needing to assemble if—with knowledge of the gathering—they go to the gathering and confess their failure and

---

[73] The structure of the passage intends to show a war between *brothers*. Trent Butler writes, "This is an extended holy war battle report featuring an ambush, but a report with an edge on it, for the holy war is not against Canaanites but against a tribe of Israelites" (*Judges*, 438). Similarly, with emphasis akin to this present writer, Dale Ralph Davis says, "It is a unity of Israel against Israel. The story itself breathes an air of tragedy, for three times it remembers that all Israel and Benjamin are 'brothers' (vv. 13, 23, 28). No, Benjamin's wrong cannot be ignored, but there is a sadness about it nevertheless. And it becomes a sadder sadness when one begins to ask: Now why couldn't Israel ever get that united against the Canaanites or the Midianites or the Ammonites or the Philistines? Why is it that when Israel can really get itself together it is against—Israel?" (*Judges*, 214).

ask for mercy in the righteous handling of the wrongdoing. This entire episode could be put to rest in verse 3 if the men of Benjamin stopped ignoring the problem, acting like they did not know about the deliberation, humbled themselves and admitted wrong, and accepted the will of the congregation in mercy.

Instead, the Benjaminites apparently stay in Benjamin, not sending a delegation to meet with Israel along the way. Israel, then, is forced to ask the Levite—one from another brother tribe—what happened. It is now the word of one brother accusing another brother of wrongdoing within the full congregation of Israel. Conveniently, the Levite leaves out his complicity in the crime, painting Benjamin as the singular, egregious, murderous, sexually deviant member. His only roles are victim, postmortem butcher, and herald of outrageous wrongdoing. On this basis he will act in the role of the court and demand a judgment against Benjamin rather than say, "Maybe you should go investigate for yourself and see if my claims are true." In Israel, no one could be put to death except on the basis of two or three witnesses; a single witness was not sufficient (Deut 17:6; 19:15).

Accusation Heads toward Exile
JUDGES 20:8-11

We Start by Determining We Have a War to Win

Israel does not investigate. They instead move closer to war, acting "united," the text says. They are going to escalate something that will end with Benjamin's exile. They are so determined that they make plans for supplying provisions to the troops without anyone returning home from Mizpah. They are in this for the long haul.

We Don't Determine We Have a Family to Help

The writer emphasizes here that they are united in their decision to prepare for war; they act as one man; seemingly, not one cool head voices disagreement with the plan for war. One way or another, the four hundred thousand fighters are going to purge the evil from Benjamin. Everyone feels this way; no one pauses to say, "But Benjamin is our brother. Let's see if there is another way we can help them without going to war."

Unfortunately, more than once, I have found myself in the middle of friction between two colleagues. I try not to be in such a position, but sometimes we just end up caught between two colleagues, two family members, or two friends. What I usually find interesting in conflicts between believers is how simply the conflict could be resolved if one person would back down in humility. (I say "between believers" because genuine humility comes by a working of the Spirit of God; see Gal 5:16-23.) Instead of backing down, however, even believers become entrenched in a win-at-all-cost-protect-myself-and/or-my-position stance rather than one that says, "How can we love God and one another here? How can we act like people who have been made brothers or sisters by Christ satisfying God's wrath against us and adopting us into his family? How can we right wrongs and end hostility as the Lord did for us?"

Accusation Escalates toward Exile
JUDGES 20:12-17

The Accused Rejects Submission Bullying

Imagine now the show of force when the entire congregation of Israel with four hundred thousand sword-bearing soldiers comes to the gates of your city. This does not look like an ambassador's entourage or a UN peacekeeping force. Instead, this looks like a plan to scorch the earth and make Benjamin's name no more. The request is a demand to give up the guilty men or else face the force of Israel's might. Facing all Israel, Benjamin has no due process, no Miranda rights, no city-of-refuge cards to play for the offenders, no lawyers on retainer to call to intervene on their behalf. Their options are to give up the offenders or be on the wrong end of the *cherem* principle in Gibeah—the way Israel should have brought it upon the nations. Israel will come with the sword; the sword is not an act of mercy.

Benjamin has two options. They can give up the men at Israel's show of brute strength and hope for peace. Or they can take their chances at war and see if they will fare better than Cushan-rishathaim, the Moabites, Jabin, the kings of Midian, the Ammonites, or the Philistines (3:10,21,31; 4:24; 7:25; 8:21; 11:33; 16:30). Benjamin chooses the latter; they will not be bullied into submission by Israel. They muster twenty-six thousand warriors of their own, with an additional seven hundred men of their special forces—left-handed aces from the tribe that is "son of the right hand."

The Accused Returns Superior Battle Planning

The ability to sling with the left with exactness displays their level of fighting skill that gives them the advantage over regular fighting forces. Benjamin is banking on having a superior military even though it has a much smaller fighting force. As Dale Davis explains,

> Most soldiers were probably right-handed and carried their shields on their left arms. That would provide normal defense against right-handed slingers, but lefty slingers would be hurling at a different angle toward the unguarded side, and, if these left-handers could hit a hair (v. 16), they could surely smash a right ear. (*Judges,* 214)

It almost seems that Benjamin has spent years planning for the day, or that Benjamin suspected they would have to face a foe mightier than them, alone. They might not ever have suspected that these forces would be needed against people of their own congregation.

Israel brings their force of four hundred thousand veteran warriors—men who have experienced war and who will not give way when they see Benjamin's special forces. Certainly, these battled-hardened soldiers are not going to retreat from an army that is little more than one-fifteenth their size—not with their entire nation backing them. The eleven tribes cannot possibly give in to the one tribe's crimes and back down from warriors of only one tribe. Both sides are going for a win; peace talks are not a consideration at this point.

Once knives are out, it often becomes hard for believers to talk themselves away from full-scale escalations. Ill-spoken accusations and retorts have the force of saber-rattling. Add a few churchwide email exchanges—which is an ungodly thing to do, as it fosters divisions and preempts the role of the elders—and you move to what looks like British carriers headed to the Falkland Islands.[74] Throw in a church business or membership meeting to allow for discussion that will turn into side-taking with accompanying finger-pointing, shouting, clapping, booing, and accusations against fellow members, and a congregation can find

---

[74] The reference is to the Falklands War, April 2–June 14, 1982.

itself at the sort of brinkmanship that threatens to tear a church apart or, at a minimum, send a family or families out the door with great pain from mistreatment and wounding.

On church conflicts and splits, Emmitt Cornelius notes, "Leadership must seek divine wisdom in order to avoid creating or exacerbating a crisis situation." He further writes of his own experience with an escalating church conflict, "Our problem wasn't that we didn't seek outside help; rather, we waited too long. By the time we reached out for help from others, the combative members were adamant that only their solution was acceptable, and they refused to include mediators" ("Anatomy"). The tendency toward believers becoming adamant (rather than humble), coupled with the saving of face on the part of some and leaders not responding with wisdom that avoids escalation, puts many assemblies in the unfortunate position of inevitable war against brothers.

Accusation Moves toward Exile
JUDGES 20:18-26

Despite Prayerful Attempts at Obedience

Israel will enter the war with an inquiry to the Lord. The irony of their pausing now to ask this question is evident, as it echoes the first question in the book of Judges (1:1-2), and here it is followed by yet more evidence of their recurring rebelliousness.[75] The inquiry itself does not intend to discern the will of the Lord but to gain permission or approval to do what they already desire and intend to do.[76]

---

[75] Davis writes, "Israel asks Yahweh, 'Who should be the first to go up for battle with the sons of Benjamin?' and receives the reply, 'Judah first' (v. 18). This inquiry and answer cannot fail to remind us of the opening scene of the book when Israel asked Yahweh who should lead the attack on the Canaanites and received the same answer (1:1–2). Sadly, Israel must now battle their own brothers, who, by their solidarity with the Gibeans, had become neo-Canaanites" (*Judges*, 215). Similarly, Daniel Block writes, "Indeed one may recognize in the narrator's crafting of this account a deliberate echo of 1:1–2, suggesting that in his mind Israel was now engaged in a similar kind of holy war. Tragically, however, now the enemy is a tribe of fellow Israelites, who by their conduct have demonstrated themselves functionally and spiritually Canaanites" (*Judges*, 559).

[76] "On the surface the fact that the Israelites approach God for guidance in the conduct of the war appears hopeful. But the manner in which the narrator casts the inquiry raises several concerns. First, the Israelites do not ask, 'Shall we go up against our brother?' but 'Who shall go up first?' Their decision seems to have been made without reference to God. Second, in contrast to 1:1, which otherwise employs the same formula

Despite Attempts That Repeat Antiquated
Ways of Handling Conflict

What follow in the story are the first two war encounters in two successive days. Within three days the war takes such a turn that a tribe is exiled. In the first two days, however, one cannot tell that the fighting will end that way. The first two days it appears that Israel will have to live with Benjamin in their midst as the perpetrators who would not back down in war—that the war will continue until Israel's fighting forces have been reduced to a size nearer to that of Benjamin's numbers. Benjamin will kill twenty-two thousand Israelite warriors without any loss of their own troops. The next day Benjamin will kill an additional eighteen thousand Israelite troops without loss of a single Benjaminite warrior. At this rate, Israel will have lost a hundred thousand troops in a week's time, and the mental toll might be immeasurable.

Despite Attempts That Eventually Give Way
to Brokenness before the Lord

The two days of losses bring Israel to a place of brokenness. The writer emphasizes that all Israel went up to Bethel with the army, all Israel wept as before, yet this time all Israel also fasted, offered burnt offerings, and offered peace offerings before the Lord. They are broken of any thought of being successful on their own. Brokenness does not mean they want to honor the Lord. They just know that what they are doing is not working. Their strategy will still be one of war rather than of diplomacy. They see fighting as the only resolution and do not see the possibility of reconciliation. Even though they later ask, "Should I once more march out to fight against the sons of Benjamin, my brothers, or should I quit?,"[77] they weep over the loss of war, not over the loss of a brother.

True brokenness by a congregation is what we need when members of the body of Christ are at odds with one another. Brokenness means that a congregation is brought from a place of confidence of victory to a place of humility, weeping, fasting, acknowledgement of the need for the Lord to deal with their sins,[78] and seeking a relationship of peace

---

for oracular inquiry, here the narrator refers to deity by the generic designation 'God,' *Elohim*, rather than by the personal covenant name, Yahweh" (Block, *Judges, Ruth*, 559).

[77] Author's translation. The Hebrew has "I" (a singular collective) and "my brother" (singular).

[78] This is the intention of burnt offerings in Lev 1:1-17.

with the Lord.[79] Routine congregational life should not continue without acknowledgement of a deep rift within the local body. Just as biological families experience confusion, paralysis, sorrow, and a deep sense that all is not well when one adult sibling is at odds with another, so too a local assembly should feel a sense of dysfunction and disruption—of sorrow and helplessness—when a breach between Christians seems irreparable. Speaking to individuals who are at odds with other believers, Jesus guides us away from continuing in common worship practice as if nothing were wrong:

> So if you are offering your gift on the altar, and there you remember
> that your brother or sister has something against you, leave your gift
> there in front of the altar. First go and be reconciled with your brother
> or sister, and then come and offer your gift. Reach a settlement quickly
> with your adversary while you're on the way with him to the court,
> or your adversary will hand you over to the judge, and the judge
> to the officer, and you will be thrown into prison. Truly I tell you,
> you will never get out of there until you have paid the last penny.
> (Matt 5:23-26)

In the eyes of Jesus, no true worship is taking place before the Lord if there is an offense between two believers that has not been addressed with an attempt at reconciliation. Instead, for Jesus, the threat of judgment looms large over those who will not be reconciled quickly. Instead of staying entrenched in a position to win a war against a brother, we should seek brokenness—individually and corporately.

Accusation Verges on Exile
JUDGES 20:27-37

The Accuser Does Not Seek the Peace of God

The mention of the ark of the covenant and Phineas calls to mind a faithful Israel: impressions of marching around Jericho with the ark and the mental image of Phineas zealously ramming his javelin through the disobedient Israelite man and his Midianite woman. On that challenging day in history, God fought for Israel, and there was a great victory.

---

[79] This is the intention of fellowship offerings in Lev 3:1-17.

On that previous day of weeping in history, Phineas's zeal for the Lord stopped the plague of judgment from devouring more Israelites. It would seem that in going to the place of the ark and Phineas that Israel is hoping for an outcome like Jericho or like crossing the Jordan, or that Israel is hoping to stop God's judgment against them in battle.

Inquiring of the Lord once again about battling their brother, Benjamin, Israel this time receives word that the Lord will provide victory; the Lord will deliver Benjamin into the hand of Israel.

The Lord Provides Victory through Smaller Resources and the Accused's Missteps

As Israel draws up for battle on a third day, if you were in Benjamin, you might be confident that you would again defeat your adversary. Israel has fewer soldiers and two actual losses before them. Benjamin might even sense coming vindication toward Israel approaching them with force because they acted on the accusation of another brother within the congregation of the people of God. While initially Benjamin has success over Israel that seems akin to the wins of the previous two days, the final outcome for Benjamin will be disaster. The author tips us to the coming ambush by mentioning that Benjamin has been drawn out of the city into open places. With words of overconfidence, Benjamin heads into a trap in which defeat is certain.

To be clear, it is not Israel who wins here. The Lord is bringing this civil war to an end. Israel has twice tried to win but lost. This time the Lord does something. But keep in mind that Benjamin is brother to all the people against whom he is fighting.

Twice the writer will mention the Lord as the victor (vv. 28,35). The Lord wants his people to stop. The Lord has Israel bait Benjamin into overconfidence. Benjamin's forces relinquish the shelter of the city, they assume past victories mean certain success, and they miss their adversary's signal from the city. When they can see their defeat is near, they just run. Israel's chase reveals that this third-day effort still is not an attempt to win back Benjamin. There will be no such attempt. Israel had sought peace with the Lord before Phineas, but they will fail to seek peace with Benjamin en route to accomplishing justice for the wrong done to the Levite and his concubine.

This entire scene is filled with messy despair as 25,100 Benjaminite warriors lose their lives. This is the greatest one-day defeat in this three-day war and represents a loss of 94 percent of Benjamin's fighting troops. The Lord uses Benjamin's missteps to defeat Benjamin. But the Lord really is bringing an end to the war between the brothers while rightly passing judgment against Benjamin for the wrong they did to the Levite and the concubine. Truly, however, when brothers are at war, there are no real winners. Benjamin loses, and Israel loses because Benjamin loses. The victory is pyrrhic for Israel. A tribe of their own brothers—people of their own flesh, family, covenant, calling, and Lord—is on the verge of extinction.

Accusation Turns into Exile
JUDGES 20:38-48

The Congregation Signals for Ambush

Keep in mind what this story is saying and where it is headed: Benjamin, a brother in Israel, will be exiled because an accusation was made against the tribe by a family member of the Levites, and Israel responded with a stance to go to war rather than starting with investigation and resolving the offenses at the level of personal conversation and reconciliation. Now we arrive at the point where we find six hundred surviving men of Benjamin hiding in the wilderness.

This is Benjamin—the tribe of the one named "Son of My Suffering" by his mother but renamed "Son of the Right Hand" by his father as his mother's soul departed for glory (Gen 35:18). This is Benjamin—the tribe of the one whom Jacob refused to send to Egypt for fear that his life would be lost like Joseph's. That same Benjamin is the one who brought Joseph to tears in Egypt upon his sight, to whom Joseph gave a double portion of the meal for the brothers, on whose neck Joseph wept.

This is the tribe of Jacob's prophesied ravenous wolf who would devour its prey—as is evident in their first two days of victory against Israel. When this prophecy is fulfilled completely, we look for the day this tribe will divide the plunder of their enemies when tribute is made to the one with the ruling staff from Judah (Gen 49:10,27).

This is the tribe of Benjamin—no mean tribe—the tribe of whom Moses said, "The LORD's beloved rests securely on him. He shields him all day long, and he rests on his shoulders" (Deut 33:12). We are looking for a day when this people will have absolute safety from all enemies and will be a sanctuary of God, protected by the Most High himself.

The Congregation Forces the Accused to Flee and Stay Away with the Little Family They Have Left

Yet at this point in history in the book of Judges, it appears we are about to lose this highly favored tribe. He looks so much more like a son of sorrows than an exalted son at the moment. He has been forced to flee from the people of God even though he is a brother previously spoken of well by the Lord.

One of the most unfortunate, sorrowful, even evil things that happens in the local body of Christ is that we harm families, and they never return because we force them away. Who can blame them for leaving? Who—in the vein of Benjamin—would return to a place where people came after them with four hundred thousand warriors before even hearing their side of the story? Who would return to a place where terms for peace never were offered, but only vengeance is offered?

Who wouldn't stay exiled from a people claiming to be the people of the Lord, claiming the Lord for themselves but turning on their own far faster than they would turn on the world? Israel would stay in oppression sixteen to forty years before crying out to the Lord, but when it came to fighting Benjamin, it seems like they assembled for war in less than a week! They couldn't even take a month of Benjamin's reported evils, but Israel worshiped Ashtoreths, Molech, Baals, and Chemosh for decades before crying out to the Lord for a judge. How could it be safe for Benjamin to return to the assembly of the Lord? How could it be safe for a family against whom a congregation went to war to stay in or return to a congregation when they received little to no grace, mercy, kindness, or consideration in addressing an accusation made toward them? How could anyone expect those treated like Benjamin to stay where the people of God are making clear that they are not welcomed into the family equally, like all the other tribes, based on how the body handles a conflict?

We can tell of countless stories of family members forced to stay exiled from a local assembly because the assembly botched the way it handled a disagreement, accusation, or even removal from membership of a family or one of its members. I have a friend—a former elder in his congregation—whose wife was badly wounded and would not return to church for ten years after a controversy with accusations of wrongdoing against the church's elders. I have another friend who refuses to return to ministry due to harm caused by members wrongly exerting their monetary power and business clout in controversies with accusations against him of being incompetent for a job in which he was serving well. I have another friend who feels a congregation only desired to use his gifts for their selfish purposes and showed no real care for his desires, passions, or concerns but accused him of not addressing his concerns correctly—the ultimate irony. Now he is skeptical toward all churches. Another friend was accused of having a problem with his sexual orientation—a greatly false accusation—but the damage was done before anyone thought to have a simple, kind conversation over what they thought they were seeing.

History allows us to look back and say, "That conflict probably could have been avoided if X party had simply done Y." The problem is, we don't have history to tell us how significant going to war over any of the aforementioned controversies will be. We have no idea of the full ramification of what will be lost, what will be the costs, and what relationships might be broken—possibly broken forever.

Yet the grace toward all of us is that the most wrongly accused man in history—Jesus, the righteous—provides grace both to handle wrongdoing in a manner that minimizes the chance for exiling a family and also to recover from the pains when a controversy is not handled correctly.

Exiled from the hearts and minds of the generation he came to save, Jesus was treated like Benjamin. Rather than sitting with him to examine his claim, the Jewish leaders of Jesus's day lay in wait to trap Jesus (Mark 3:2; see also Mark 3:6; Luke 11:54; 20:20; John 8:6). Rather than resolving their concerns over his actions and claims, they looked for further ways to accuse him (Mark 12:13). Rather than enjoying Passover with him and all the people of God, the chief priests and scribes looked for ways to arrest him and kill him (Mark 14:1).

So eager to go to all-out war against Jesus and secure their victory at whatever the cost, the chief priests are glad when Judas comes to offer to betray Jesus (Mark 14:10-11). They rejoice, celebrate, and high-five one another for the opportunity to kill their perceived enemy. They do not see Jesus as brother from the tribe of Judah, from the house of David, from the family of Joseph and Mary—an Israelite brother with their shared hope of the redemption of Israel. Once the war begins, all they can see is an enemy to depose.

We are so thankful, however, that Jesus, in going to the cross, saw the situation with the eyes of mercy. He whom Israel would not receive as king in their eyes acted as King in redemption.

Review and Discuss

1. What are some factors that contribute to conflicts between Christian sisters and brothers?

2. When have you witnessed a congregation miss an opportunity to make peace over a small conflict only to witness it escalate into a larger conflict?

3. What is significant about the parenthetical statement of Benjamin's knowledge of the gathering of the tribes?

4. How did you feel when you read of four hundred thousand brothers about to go to war against a much smaller tribe of their own? Why do you think they come with determination and so many troops?

5. Why does it become hard to back down from a conflict once knives are out?

6. If a conflict between two families in your congregation began today, what wise, God-fearing men and women should your church look to in order to move the families toward a resolution? Who among you has conflict-resolution training and experience via their professional experience or through a ministry like Peacemaker Ministries?[80]

7. What is the significance of the writer's saying that all Israel went up to pray and weep?

8. Why do you think the Lord allowed Israel to experience two defeats before a victory? Why might the Lord have allowed Israel to crush Benjamin on her third attempt rather than instruct Israel to seek peace?

9. When have you witnessed a family forced away from a church because the congregation could not resolve that family's conflict charitably? What role did you play at that time? As you reflect on that conflict now, what are your thoughts and feelings?

10. What role should you play if families in your congregation come to a conflict they cannot resolve on their own?

---

[80] See more on this conflict resolution ministry at Peacemaker Ministries, https://www.peacemakerministries.org, accessed June 24, 2022.

The Law of Marriage Tribalism

JUDGES 21

Main Idea· Believers live by man-made laws rather than grace when they withhold their children from marrying believers of other ethnicities.

I. The Law of Marriage Tribalism Can Exist while Honestly Seeking the Lord (21:1-4).
II. The Law of Marriage Tribalism Can Hide behind Other Equally Strong Laws (21:5-7).
III. The Law of Marriage Tribalism Allows Us to Place Others at a Deficit to Protect Our Self-Righteous Interests (21:8-12).
IV. The Law of Marriage Tribalism Allows Us to Ambush Others while Proposing Grace for Our Potential Guilt (21:13-22).
V. The Law of Marriage Tribalism Puts Others in a Position to Accept Unrighteousness while Allowing Us All to Think Everything Is Right with God (21:23-25).

It is commonplace now to see biracial couples on TV commercials enjoying life as a family. But a few short years ago, this just was not so. In May 2013, Cheerios launched the first interracial TV ad with a couple and their daughter enjoying the breakfast cereal. Despite interracial couples appearing on TV for more than a half century prior to this, the ad still sparked controversy. The comments section below the ad on YouTube was so filled with racist vitriol that it had to be closed. Old Navy and State Farm also dealt with racist commentary online after posting Twitter spots that showed interracial relationships (Kaufman, "A Sign of 'Modern Society'").

Larry Chiagouris, a professor of marketing at the Pace University Lubin School of Business, speaking on the phenomenon of the appearance of interracial couples in TV commercials, says,

> For the longest time, ads presented the typical American household as Caucasian, heterosexual, two children and two cars in the driveway. There's still a part of the world that's like that, but there's a large portion that is nothing like the "Father Knows Best" Americana image. It's taken the advertising

community, and particularly their clients, a long time to come to grips with that. They're risk averse. ("World War I")

Slowness in coming to grips with interracial marriage is a nice way of speaking of the reality behind the response opposed to the advertising. More direct and to the point of the objections are words in a comment found on Reddit after the Cheerios commercial launched: "Shoving [multiculturalism] down our throats when we know it fails . . . awesome" (Rivas, "Cheerios Ad").

More than fifty years removed from the decision in *Loving v. Virginia* that ruled unconstitutional all race-based legal restrictions on marriage,[81] the mixing of races in marriage in America still causes indigestion to us. For some, there is the simple belief that races should not mix, and it is best to marry someone of your own race or ethnicity. For others, there might be a hatred for a different ethnicity or nationality based on past warring between two people groups.

For yet others there are the issues of perceptions of self-hatred, seeking social elevation, proclaiming another group is equal to or better than your own people in innate worth, or that the other gender in another people group is of greater beauty than people within one's own group. An African American man's choosing a wife of European or Asian descent sparks all these sorts of sentiments in the hearts and minds of many African Americans, especially as the number of available single, professional, college-educated, middle-class African American women continues to increase.[82]

---

[81] *Richard Perry Loving, Mildred Jeter Loving v. Virginia, 388 U.S. 1* (1967); Warren, Earl, and Supreme Court of The United States. *U.S. Reports: Loving v. Virginia, 388 U.S. 1* (1966). Periodical, accessed June 24, 2022, https://www.loc.gov/item/usrep388001.

[82] See Madeline Baars's research into this topic: Madeline Baars, "Marriage in Black and White: Women's Support for Law against Interracial Marriage, 1972–2000," *Intersections* 10, no. 1 (2009): 219–38. Also, see Roland G. Fryer Jr., "Guess Who's Been Coming to Dinner? Trends in Interracial Marriage over the 20th Century," *Journal of Economic Perspectives* (Spring 2007): 71–90; Derek Hawkins, "'God Called My Bluff': A Christian Blogger Faces Fury over a Post about Her White Daughter's Marriage to a Black Man," *The Washington Post*, August 11, 2016, https://www.washingtonpost.com/news /morning-mix/wp/2016/08/11/god-called-my-bluff-a-christian-blogger-faces-fury-over-a -post-about-her-white-daughters-marriage-to-a-black-man, accessed December 15, 2020; and Zhenchao Qian, "Breaking the Last Taboo: Interracial Marriage in America," *Contexts* (Fall 2005): 33–37. The point of the trouble of a white daughter marrying a black man is evident in the removal of the controversial post by Gayle Clark, "When God Sends Your White Daughter a Black Husband," *The Gospel Coalition*, August 8, 2020, https://www

The problems of interracial marriage become more complex when the church supports the separation of the races. Bob Jones University was not alone among Christian colleges having a clause against interracial dating or supposedly biblical justification for identifying interracial marriage as sinful.[83] Other Christian institutions had similar policies, proposing theological justification for their stances.

But the problem is not always in need of biblical support. Some believers, affected more by social thought than Scripture, just cannot imagine one of their *daughters*, in particular, sharing a bed with a man of another race or ethnicity. The mores that prevent such joining of their daughters' bodies with a man of a nationality or color different from one's own are just fine for them, often allowing such persons to think they are being Christian in all areas of life while failing to see they are living by a law that displeases God.

In the last chapter of Judges, one sees Israel blindly suffering from this law of marriage tribalism. It is this final issue of Canaanization—of being conformed to the world—that the writer of Judges addresses here.

This chapter is about *Israel's attempt to show compassion to Benjamin's need to continue as a tribe without breaking their oath to refrain from giving their wives to Benjamin*. How do I justify this as the subject of Judges 21? A topic this controversial warrants justification that it is the idea in the passage.

First, the plot of the story begins on the trajectory of the oath to refrain from giving their wives to Benjamin (v. 1). The writer presents this as the first thought in the chapter and launches all subsequent ideas in reference to the first theme. If one's reading of the story were interrupted by a phone call between verses 1 and 2, the reader would be

---

.thegospelcoalition.org/article/when-god-sends-your-white-daughter-a-black-husband, accessed December 15, 2020. The *Relevant Christian* site reposted the original article: http://www.relevantchristian.com/the-gospel-coalition-blog/8632-when-god-sends-your -white-daughter-a-black-husband.html, accessed December 15, 2020.

[83] See "Bob Jones University Drops Interracial Dating Ban," *CT*, March 1, 2000, https:// www.christianitytoday.com/ct/2000/marchweb-only/53.0.html, accessed December 10, 2020; *Bob Jones University v. United States*, 461 U.S. 574 (1983); Sarah Jones, "Bob Jones University Would Probably Like You to Forget It Once Banned Interracial Dating," *The New Republic*, February 17, 2017, https://newrepublic.com/article/140724/bob-jones-university -probably-like-forget-banned-interracial-dating, accessed December 10, 2020; Kenneth S. Kantzer, "The Bob Jones Decision: A Dangerous Precedent," *CT*, September 2, 1983, https://www.christianitytoday.com/ct/1983/september-2/editorial-bob-jones-decision -dangerous-precedent.html, accessed December 10, 2020.

left wondering whether the men of Israel will be faithful to their oath against Benjamin.

Second, twice the writer mentions the desire of Israel to show compassion to the people of Benjamin (vv. 6,15). In both mentions of compassion, the impetus for their desires is a tribe being separated from the rest of Israel. In both mentions, a question follows about securing wives for the men of Benjamin who survived the war with Israel (vv. 7,16). The question seeks a compassionate response to Benjamin's plight.

Third, the oath receives greater mention than any theme in the chapter, appearing three times explicitly (vv. 1,7,18). The theme appears implicitly a fourth time in the concern over incurring guilt for securing wives via the festival at Shiloh. *Guilt* is in question because a de facto law concerning giving wives to Benjamin has been established by the oath.

Fourth, the entire narrative moves toward making sure every man in Benjamin has a wife so that the tribe will not be wiped out in the generations to come. The assumption is that Benjamin must have wives from within Israel rather than the nations, of which the literary irony is great. Here Israel decides to follow the stipulations of the covenant that call her to refrain from giving the daughters of Israel to the nations and taking daughters from the nations for wives. Yet if no tribe in Israel can give a daughter to Benjamin, there appears to be no solution, even though—ironically—Israel has been giving her daughters to the nations throughout the book. But Israel does keep working until they have a wife for every man in Benjamin.

Fifth, the chapter moves toward a close only after Benjamin has secured wives. Once they obtain wives for every man, Benjamin continues in a normal course of living. Israel, too, ceases from asking the Lord for solutions and from proposing questions and solutions to the problem in Benjamin with respect to the oath.

It also is important to both establish and justify the author's subject for this passage, since the application to which it points will be controversial. The passage focuses on not breaking an oath against giving the daughters of Israel to the men of Benjamin in marriage. The application of the passage seeks to understand how this idea speaks to a modern audience.

As discerned from my introduction, I propose that his passage's application addresses *the church's attempt to show concern for believers of minority ethnicity without being willing to allow people from the majority ethnicity to wed the minority ethnicity's children.* What this passage is getting at is the error in thinking one group compassionately is helping a minority group while saying to that group, "We will never give you our daughters to marry." Israel even sought grace before God for their actions without seeing their solutions to Benjamin's plight are only right according to their standards. This examination of the passage will help us guard against making and accepting a law of marriage tribalism by considering five things.

The Law of Marriage Tribalism Can Exist while Honestly Seeking the Lord
JUDGES 21:1-4

In Judges 20, Israel arrives at Mizpah to confront the tribe of Benjamin for the crime against the concubine. While in Mizpah, Israel makes a law that is unrecorded and also unknown until chapter 21. The law to which all the men of Israel swear is that they will not give their daughters to the men of Benjamin in marriage.

The oath means that no one in Israel can break the stated rule for any reason. Its institution intends to punish the tribe for their abuse of the concubine by withholding any of Israel's daughters from the possibility of such mistreatment. If Benjamin's existence depends on receiving daughters from the other tribes, *tough*; that will not be allowed. The rule, however, is unnecessary, for the Mosaic law had ample measures to address adultery and rape in Leviticus 20 and Deuteronomy 22 without cause for tribalism.

Even in making a law that separates one tribe from the rest of the people of God, the people seek the Lord. They have instituted a man-made rule that disregards the Lord's plans for Israel on the earth, yet they go before the Lord with contrition, inquiry, and offerings in worship. They are seeking peace with God while ignoring the problem of their rule.

The Law of Marriage Tribalism Can Hide behind Other Equally Strong Laws
JUDGES 21:5-7

As the people are making offerings, they ponder a question related to another issue that arises because of another oath they have made. If a tribe did not take responsibility to come to Mizpah to fight in the face of the outrageous sin in Israel, that tribe was to be cut off from Israel. At this point the tribe goes without naming, for the writer is focusing on the fact of a second oath; the identity of the tribe will come later. While seeking to have compassion on Benjamin out of one side of her mouth, Israel is calling for the death of a different tribe and holding to the oath against Benjamin with the other side of her mouth. The Israelites are lawmaking hypocrites.

It is baffling to think of how people in the church worship together for years, earnestly seeking the Lord, while yet occasionally thinking within, *I really hope my daughter will grow up to marry someone of her own race—her own people.* Singing, shouting, clapping, crying, tithing, affirming sermons, witnessing baptisms, and taking the Lord's Supper did not reveal the need to repent over such ethnocentric, worldly, ungodly thinking. The inability of years of sermons to dislodge marriage tribalism from the believer's heart should make us wonder what gospel message was preached.

If Jesus did in fact die for the sins of people from all nations, his death then purchases all persons equally. One is not purchased more or less than another; one is not more of a brother or sister in Christ than another. The cause for tribalism is something other than the gospel, for in Christ there is neither Jew nor Greek when it comes to obtaining salvation (Gal 3:28-39).

"Oh, let's be practical," you say? "The mixing of races in marriage causes so many concerns in society." But isn't practicality the problem of Israel and Benjamin? Who would want to give their daughter to a people like Benjamin? But why should someone want a daughter from anyone in ancient Israel as they are portrayed in Judges, for they are an idolatrous people who love the nations and fail to destroy the nations.

The man-made law looks good, as man-made laws tend to do. But the scenes show how easy it is to love the Lord with a blind spot to this area.

The Law of Marriage Tribalism Allows Us to Place Others at a Deficit to Protect Our Self-Righteous Interests
JUDGES 21:8-12

The people of Israel return to the question of which tribe was absent at the confrontation with Benjamin. The people of Jabesh-gilead—a subset of the people of Gilead, associated with the tribe of Manasseh—had failed to send a man to the war. Thus, they were due payback for their failure to assemble against Benjamin. Again, the hypocrisy of the tribes is obvious, as so often they enjoyed their Canaanite neighbors rather than assembling to destroy them and their idols.

The plan of recompense assembles twelve thousand men from the tribes to go against Jabesh-gilead to slaughter the residents. As a multiple of twelve, the number itself, although completely historical, seemingly intends to indicate that all Israel was complicit in the sins of murdering the people.

The slaughter of the women who had lain with men—even the married and widowed ones—seems to be an act of judgment that lays blame on the innocent. En route to reducing the population of Jabesh-gilead to virgins only—for the sake of being compassionate to Benjamin according to their man-made oath—Israel overlooks the innocence of the women being murdered. These acts reduce and harm Jabesh-gilead in an attempt to bless Benjamin while allowing Israel to keep the oath made at Mizpah.

When it suits the interest of the people, they will make a way to find daughters for the men of Benjamin, despite the oath. It appears that one oath can trump another, revealing again the man-made, earthly nature of the oaths. When the Lord makes covenants, he does not need to break faithfulness in one to keep a second and does not ask us to do so. His law is true and will not be broken by him. It can be completed to give way to another, like the Mosaic being completed in Christ and giving way to the new. But nothing in the Mosaic covenant needed to be ignored to accomplish all that is promised in the new covenant.

Christian institutions that have held to marriage tribalism or bias against interracial marriage (and the dating that leads to such marriage) were unable to see the harm they performed against the students. Inherently, the love for the God who sent his Son to die for all people is being denied. Loving one's neighbor as oneself is being ignored, for to love as one loves oneself is to treat the other the way you wish to be treated. For marriage, this means to be able to love and be loved by whom you will—by the one who catches your eye, deepens in friendship, matures you as a person, affirms your worth, lights up your emotions, and inspires hope to build a life, all within the parameters of the creation order and God's stipulations on believers being bound with other believers.

The Great Commission faces a challenge, too. When a Christian proclaims the gospel to a culture outside of the US, I would love to see that Christian be receptive to the question, "Why does Jesus frown on marriage between two people for whom he died and rose again if they are of two different ethnicities?" If there is an answer to that question that does not deny the gospel and all the implications of the gospel, it escapes me. If Jesus's death changes a person from unredeemed to redeemed in an instant, the suggestion that two redeemed cannot get married because they are not from the same tribe is not at all related to Jesus's death and resurrection for us. It is social, earthly, secular, worldly—from the depths of hell.

The Law of Marriage Tribalism Allows Us to Ambush Others while Proposing Grace for Our Potential Guilt
JUDGES 21:13-22

The eleven tribes from Israel give women from Jabesh-gilead to the men of Benjamin in an effort to be compassionate. Imagine this conversation: "Benjamin, here. Please accept these wives from Jabesh-gilead. We feel so badly about slaughtering your 25,100 warriors and all the people in your cities, making it so that you might cease to exist as a people. We can't go without a tribe in Israel. After all, we are God's people. All of us should exist. Here are women we gathered by going to war against Jabesh-gilead. Sorry that we are short a few hundred."

The writer recognizes the sovereign hand of the Lord that made the breach. That, however, does not get the tribes off the hook for finding wives for Benjamin. The tribes recognize their conundrum when they are short wives to give but stand by their oath with all their self-righteous might. They even have invoked a curse on anyone who will break the rule, thus wrongly ascribing the rule to the decree of God, for only the Lord could enforce a curse invoked on another. They think they need a solution that will keep them from coming under a curse.

In some sort of brainstorming meeting of the elders of Israel, they remember a yearly feast at Shiloh. While not considering at all the harm they will do to the people of Shiloh, they command the men of Benjamin to do something similar to what Israel just did to Jabesh-gilead—to ambush the unsuspecting wives in order to steal them from their families and take them for themselves. Then the problem of there not being enough wives for all the men of Benjamin will be solved at the relatively little expense of ambushing Shiloh.

In actuality, the problem is not solved. Israel only has created a bigger problem for itself—one finding its origin in the law of marriage tribalism.[84] Shiloh, as part of the territory of Ephraim, was a member of the people who had made an oath to refrain from giving wives to Benjamin. If Benjamin secured wives from Shiloh, Ephraim would be guilty of breaking the oath and would thus invoke a curse on itself (even though the reader understands that the Lord has not established a curse for this law). The tribes, themselves, would be guilty, too, for being complicit in the solution.

Once again, the most obvious and righteous course of action to resolve Benjamin's wives and continuance dilemma would be to rescind the oath against giving their own daughters to Benjamin. It is somewhat shocking that Benjamin does not propose this solution to the rest of the tribes, since the tribes claim to have so much compassion for them. That is, if they really wish to be compassionate toward the different tribe, why not give up their own daughters and offer their best and most precious items to Benjamin rather than approving of taking the best others have to offer?

The depraved heart figures out a way to embrace law and remove itself from the impasse created by its own sinful law. Israel plays a game of technicalities to convince herself that she has not broken any law—not hers, and certainly not the Lord's. First, they will make an appeal of grace to the men of Shiloh who will lose daughters and sisters. They are recognizing the right of the near kinsmen to avenge wrongdoing in the family, but they will ask them to let go of that right with an appeal to grace. They want Shiloh to employ grace to Benjamin's wrongdoing even though they themselves will not be gracious to Benjamin with their own daughters.

Second, they will free themselves from guilt because they did not take wives for Benjamin as spoils of war. But this seems odd, because they just gave Benjamin wives as spoils of war from the battle with Jabesh-gilead. In their tortured logic, *intentionally* taking wives from Jabesh-gilead is within the acceptable limits of marriage tribalism, but

---

[84] Daniel Block notes, "The elders again try to sanctify their strategy by calling this event a 'festival of the LORD.' But the narrator's refusal to specify which festival is in mind suggests that in his view this is another symptom of the Canaanization of Israel" (*Judges, Ruth*, 580).

only encouraging the taking of wives from Shiloh is not. Theft of wives for the sake of keeping the oath is righteous, but promoting theft of wives from within Israel is not. The cognitive dissonance of the suggestion is astounding. Even if it means harming people within the eleven tribes—harming themselves!—and committing acts of evil against other women and their families, that is more desirable than simply giving their daughters in marriage to a people with whom that have refused to give their daughters in marriage.

Third, the men of Shiloh will be free from breaking the covenant by the same passive distancing that removed Israel from guilt. If the men of Shiloh were uninvolved in the giving of their daughters because their daughters were taken, then they cannot be held responsible for the oath. All they have to do is look the other way at the theft of their own precious daughters for Benjamin while the rest of Israel continues to put their daughters on untouchable pedestals when it comes to marriage to the men of Benjamin.

What may be the most amazing aspect of this scene is the total ignorance of Israel toward their own sins: they have made a wicked law in withholding their daughters from that one tribe of people, they have stolen wives from Jabesh-gilead without remorse, they have encouraged the theft of the virgins of Shiloh, and they have taken the place of God to exonerate both Shiloh and themselves from any guilt over their actions. They have forgotten that the reason they went to went to war against Benjamin was over the report of the abuse to the Levite's concubine.[85] How easy it is for us to be ignorant of our sinfulness and the harm we are doing to others when we are feeling so righteous about having kept our daughters from marrying Benjaminites!

The Law of Marriage Tribalism Puts the Others in a Position to Accept Unrighteousness while Allowing Us All to Think Everything Is Right with God
JUDGES 21:23-25

The writer masks the graphic nature of this final scene with terseness of speech: "The Benjaminites did this and took the number of

---

[85] "It does not seem to matter to the elders that these same Benjaminites have only recently defended their fellow tribesmen after they had gang-raped a young woman" (Block, *Judges, Ruth,* 581).

women they needed from the dancers they caught" (v. 23). When you unpackage what happened, something gruesome is evident. In taking the wives from the field, the unsuspecting, dancing virgins are yanked from their homes forever and forcibly raped. This is not happening to one concubine—which would have been one woman too many; this is happening to two hundred women. Let's assume, for the sake of argument, half of the dancers have one sister. That leaves a hundred and fifty homes without daughters and sisters at the table and no recourse to avenge the kidnapping and raping of the maidens.

The men of Benjamin go back to their homes as if nothing happened, and normal life resumes. The women have to accept their trauma and new positions in life because all Israel has backed the Benjaminites' crimes as legally acceptable. Save the people of Shiloh possibly, no one in Israel shows the outrage over evil toward the women of Shiloh that they showed toward the concubine's rape and dismemberment. In smugness they go home to normal life with the partially completed conquest of their inheritance, being satisfied that they have done what is right.

The double refrain of "In those days there was no king in Israel" (see Judg 17:6; 18:1; 19:1) and "everyone did whatever seemed right to him" (also 17:6; cf. Deut 12:8) to close the book gives the reader a chilling effect. Why doesn't Israel recognize their need to return to the Lord and submit to him as King? David Beldman writes,

> What set the cycle of judges in motion was a generation that
> emerged after Joshua "who did not know the Lord or the
> work that he had done for Israel" (Judg 2:10). The "work"
> here refers to Yahweh's redemption of Israel from Egypt,
> his giving of his instruction on Sinai, his leading his people
> through the wilderness, and his conquering of the Canaanites
> and gift of the land. The Israelites in Judges had forgotten
> Yahweh—they had deserted their king. Their behavior
> demonstrates again and again that they were ignorant of the
> "Manifesto for a Holy Nation and a Priestly Kingdom" (i.e.,
> the Sinai covenant), which had been issued by King Yahweh
> himself. The crisis in Israel "in those days" was not merely that
> they lacked a king, but that they lacked a divine standard for
> the order of their society. (*Deserting the King*, 55)

Everyone in Israel, including in Benjamin and Shiloh, goes home satisfied that they have done what has pleased the Lord. Yet everyone has blood on their hands! Everyone just sanctioned the total destruction of the lives of two hundred women while acting as if they were being righteous toward one concubine and all their own daughters! The reader should be struck with the callousness of all Israel and wonder, *Are we like our forefathers in Israel?*

We think we are doing something great in helping people while we are holding back from them our most precious gift: our own children. We cannot imagine our daughters lying with people who do not look, smell, or have folkways and ideologies like us. This attitude smacks of arrogance, elitism, feelings of superiority, unwarranted fears, and beliefs in false narratives about other races. This thought might come from African American believers not wanting a child to marry a white child because of the history of racism or what the marriage connotes about the goodness of one's own race in relationship to another. Or this thought might come from Japanese and Chinese believers due to conflicts that go back through Sino-Japanese wars to wars dating back many dynasties. Whatever form it takes, the we-will-not-let-our-child-marry-your-kind statute (because we think this is right in our own eyes) is as unrighteous now as it was when practiced by ancient Israel.

Believers are tied together by the death of Christ for our sins. The blood of Christ's death should be thicker than all familial and ethnic ties. Truly, this passage shows that one of the real tests of the end of our racist thoughts and of whether racial identity is more important than identity in Christ is how we feel about our children marrying people outside our ethnic groups. We should not think we are making any form of racial progress while this wall against interracial marriage remains. For the world to maintain this wall is one thing. For believers to maintain this wall is to show how we have been Canaanized by the world just as much ancient Israel was.

Can you embrace giving your daughter away to someone who does not look like her father or brother, or your husband, father, sons, or brothers? Sure, we will be compassionate to others to a degree, and even say you can marry someone from one of the tribes, but not with any willingness on our part. If someone from another tribe just grabs your son or daughter at a dance without your sanction while your child is away from home in college or the military, nothing can be said or done; we can absolve ourselves from guilt over that.

Unfortunately, in Judges 21 the minority tribe has been relegated to having to accept a situation and solution generated by the wrongdoing of others and thereby join in the moral breach.[86]

Here we close the book on a Canaanized people who have deserted their Redeemer-King, the Lord, thus falling into a lifestyle of doing everything with the eyes of relativistic morality.

The law of marriage tribalism reveals Canaanite thinking in us—thinking that shows we, like ancient Israel, need to acknowledge Christ as the King over every area of our lives. Unfortunately, often we enjoy this law without recrimination in the body of Christ.

Review and Discuss

1. Historically, why has interracial marriage been a cause for disagreement in the US?
2. Personally, how do you feel about interracial marriage? How does your love of Christ shape your view?
3. Think of a close friend or loved one in an interracial marriage. How did you respond when you first heard of that couple dating? How did you feel when you heard they were engaged? What has been your relationship with them since they engaged?
4. How does a stance against interracial marriage contribute to racial conflict in society?
5. What false ideas does Christian rejection of interracial marriage cast on Christian faith and practice? What false ideas does Christian rejection of interracial marriage cast on God?
6. Could one believe that Christ will enter interracial marriage when he weds the church and still be on solid theological footing? Explain your answer.
7. Why do you think the tribes were able to return home with ease rather than with concern about bloodshed on their hands?

---

[86] Barry Webb concludes, "In effect the men of Shiloh are asked to accept the rape as a *fait accompli,* just as Micah had to accept the plundering of his shrine by the Danites (18:22–26)" (*An Integrated Reading,* 196). Victor Matthews argues that the men of Shiloh "have no real choice given the political decision of the elders of the other tribes" (*Judges, Ruth* [Cambridge: Cambridge University Press, 2004], 200; cited in Butler, *Judges,* 466).

8. What stereotypes and fears would you need to address within yourself if your female loved one were about to enter an interracial marriage? What are the origins of these stereotypes and/or fears?

9. After reading the exposition of Judges 21, is there anyone with whom you need to make apologies, seek reconciliation, and make restitution? If so, do not delay. Begin the process today.

10. If a fellow believer in your sphere of influence speaks out against interracial marriage, how will you respond charitably to them?

11. Are there any bylaws, covenants, confessions, teachings, or attitudes among the leaders in your congregation that need to be challenged, changed, or removed based on Judges 21?

Ruth

Mysterious Mercy to Satisfy
Our Deepest Longings

How a Sovereign God Loves—
A COVID-19 Pandemic Sermon
RUTH 1

Main Idea: A believer's seeking of provision for an empty life receives providential, unrecognized kindness when the Lord disciplines one's dependence on the wrong things for life fulfillment in order to draw the believer back to Christ of Bethlehem as the Redeemer.

I. Mysterious Mercy Is at Work when We Choose the Wrong Means of Fulfillment (1:1-2).
II. Mysterious Mercy Is in Force when We Depend on the Wrong People for Our Fulfillment (1:3-13).
III. Mysterious Mercy Is Guiding Us when We Turn to Places that Show Evidence of God's Blessing (1:14-21).
V. Mysterious Mercy Can Provide Hope when We Rest in What the Faithful Perceive to Be Blessings (1:22).

God moves in a mysterious way,
　　His wonders to perform;
He plants his footsteps in the sea,
　　And rides upon the storm.

Deep in unfathomable mincs
　　Of never failing skill;
He treasures up his bright designs,
　　And works His sovercign will.

Ye fearful saints fresh courage take,
　　The clouds ye so much dread
Are big with mercy, and shall break
　　In blessings on your head.

The familiar lines of the 1773 hymn "Conflict: Light Shining out of Darkness" by William Cowper intend to comment on what Scripture seems to reveal about the working of the providence of God in our darkest life experiences. Somewhere in mines known only to the Almighty, he forges out designs of his will that bring gloomy clouds upon us. Ominous as the clouds are to the sight of his saints, the torrential rains they bring will be floods of mercy showering upon us. How both can be true is but the mystery of God and his wonders.

We moderns have the benefit of quipping the first line as a common adage in order to gain a sense of comfort when unforeseen circumstances occur. For example, you wanted to work from home, but telecommuting was not an option for your job; then the Coronavirus plague hit, and all you could do was work from home. "God moves in a mysterious way," we say.

Or again, the inability to gather in your church's building for worship combined with a kickback on energy bill costs during the pandemic allows for ample time and budget to make needed upgrades to the church's sanctuary and broader church campus. "God moves in a mysterious way," the assembly affirms.

In another example, the city's repair of the street in front of your neighbor's home gets you and the whole block a new and much needed sidewalk and repairs to your easement, at no cost to you or your neighbors. Here, then, one inserts the refrain, "God moves in a mysterious way!" Who knew the city's error in street repairs—errors that clogged traffic on your block for weeks—would make a beautification project to last you for years? "Yay!" to the mysterious-way-moving God.

But what happens when the outcome is different? For example, you want to excel at your job or school, the Coronavirus hits, and now you have to become worker, homeschooler, circus entertainer, and sharer of bandwidth with spouses, children, and parents around the clock with no end in sight. If the resurgence in Coronavirus cases in your city means your school district will go to online learning only, indefinitely, should one drop "God moves in a mysterious way" in this space?

If a choice to pursue graduate studies delays or almost nixes your opportunity for marriage, or doesn't yield the job satisfaction a graduate education promised, do you break the "in case of emergency" glass and grab the "God moves in a mysterious way" extinguisher to put out these fires? Where does one stamp the concept behind the "mysterious" adage when one cannot get near a dying loved one in a nursing homes during a quarantine, when one's role as a first responder continues without optimal PPEs, when your business or job is lost during a pandemic or destroyed by riots, when insurance costs and discretionary income make dramatically bad turns in the aftermath of the election cycle, or even when social distancing reveals to you that you actually have few true friends?

Bringing together the working of a good and loving God, tragedy and pain, and our deepest unfilled longings and unanswered questions is not a journey for the fainthearted. Yet it is a journey we must take if we arc to love God as he is and enter into loving our neighbors in our and their enigmatic despairs—in their and our "Why like this, God?" moments and seasons.

Mysterious Mercy Is at Work when We Choose the Wrong Means of Fulfillment
RUTH 1:1-2

Enter Naomi. If ever there was a person who stepped into this tension with both feet, it is the ancient Israelite wife of Elimelech. Elimelech and Naomi are like you and me. A famine of pandemic proportions hits Judah (for that's the only kind of famine there is), and they simply want to obtain food for their family. They decide they no longer will remain sitting ducks in a starvation movie, so they make a move to Moab. We cannot discern whether the family's decision materialized because Elimelech made a choice for the family, or Naomi pushed for the family to be practical, or there was a joint decision in favor of Moab. But try to imagine a conversation between the married couple:

- Elimelech: Nay, you know that Moab introduced idolatry and immorality wholesale to Israel. We can't go there.
- Naomi: But Ell, what else can we do? My boys are going to starve!

Or maybe the conversation sounded like this:

- Naomi: Ell, a Moabite cannot even enter the assembly of the Lord, according to the law of Moses. Have you forgotten what they did in the Balaam incident?
- Elimelech: But Nay, I don't have any way to give this family food if we stay here while this famine shuts down everything!

See? They are just like any modern couple making tough decisions for their family's well-being.

Going to Moab is no small matter. Literarily, the writer tips us to this immediately by saying, "During the time of the judges" (v. 1). That was a time when everyone was doing what was right in his or her own eyes rather than in the eyes of the Lord, and relative morality was the rule of the day. We are shocked that a man whose name means "my God is King" with a wife who is named Pleasant would go live among a people that, based on the *cherem* commands in the law of God, should be devoted to destruction (Deut 7:2-5; 20:17). Yet one gains some sympathy for them when one realizes that Elimelech and Naomi have endured this famine for a long time, for shortly after birth their sons are given the names Sickness (Mahlon) and Wasting (Chilion). The boys must be at least preteens by the time of the sojourn to Moab, for the family only lives in Moab for a decade, and during that time the boys become old enough to marry. Thus, they have been sick and wasting for a long time. It looks like Elimelech and Naomi had been trying to wait on the Lord and endure, but they do not see signs of the Lord showing up in their famine-afflicted life.

Mysterious Mercy Is in Force when We Depend on the Wrong People for Our Fulfillment
RUTH 1:3-13

The reader should assume that things start out well in Moab for this family—that they find food, work, and a place to live—for they settle in Moab.

Then, maybe without warning, the first tragedy strikes. Elimelech, the primary breadwinner, dies. This was not part of the Moab recovery plan. The hope for provision in Moab takes a huge blow.

However, the surviving family still has good chances for survival and thriving because there are two sons who can work and take care of their mom, the widow. Each boy marries a woman from Moab, and things seem good in the company of the Moabite women, whose names mean "fawn" and "friend."

Again, like something worse than a setup in a Dickens or Austen classic, both sons are ripped from Naomi's life. The writer emphasizes that Naomi is left without her sons or husband so that the reader feels the sense of desperation and gloom that hangs over Naomi's life. Naomi's family had no food or prospect of provision when they left Bethlehem for Moab. Naomi now has no prospect of provision in Moab because she has no one to work to earn income for the family, and she has lost the husband and sons she loves. Her grief is even greater than the gaping hole in her family's provision scheme.

Hearing that the Lord has blessed his people in Bethlehem with provision, Naomi makes a turn from Moab back to Bethlehem. The famine is over, there are crops growing, and food is available. Naomi knows that the Lord is the one who sends rain for crops to grow. She needs to go back to Bethlehem, for she might find hope for her abject despair where the Lord is working among his people.

But what should Naomi do about the two *Moabite* daughters-in-law? Truthfully, they could make life harder for Naomi, for they would be additional mouths to feed, they could bring their Moabite idolatry with them, and immediately people would question Naomi's return with Moabites. Her people might choose not to help her as long as the Moabites were with her; they might not want to spend their Israelite resources on Moabites when there are covenantal mouths to feed.

No problem—jettison the girls. They have mothers to whom they can return, they will not wait for Naomi to have more sons, and there is no prospect of Naomi's marrying again. They have been kind to Naomi in her widowhood, so Naomi wishes the Lord's kindness—the Lord's *chesed*—the Lord's mercy on them in return. There is no hope in staying with Naomi because, says Naomi, "The Lord's hand has turned against me" (v. 13).

How dare Naomi see her situation as the working of the Almighty! It is one thing for Naomi to see the Lord's visitation in the return of crops to the land, for this is within the provisions of the Mosaic code (Deut 28:3,8,11; 30:9-10). It is fine for Naomi to call on the Lord for his mercy to be on two Moabite daughters-in-law who showed kindness to a widow in Israel because the Abrahamic covenant calls for blessing on those who bless the members of Israel, and the law stipulates care for widows (Gen 12:3; 27:29; Deut 14:29; 24:19-21; 26:12-13). But now Naomi attributes her messed-up life to the direct rule of the I AM? *Careful, Pleasant One; it sounds like you are about to write lines to a strange hymn.*

Naomi's attribution does not make assessing our own lives easy. Your marriage to the love of your life came crashing down like a house of cards. Gone is the Cinderella, happily-ever-after story for which you longed. That was not supposed to happen to you because you were the upright guy, the faithful one, or the good girl, and you made every sacrifice of your whole self for the other person.

Or think of the Hallmark card parent. You only want your children to love Jesus, but there is one atheist or agnostic among the adult siblings. Most, if not all, of your offspring see in your nieces and nephews all the material success any parent could hope for their children. But that one of yours is so far from how you raised him or her. The apostasy, rebellion, or rejection of you or the family influences your relationship, how they are raising your grandchildren, and what you do when the family is gathered for special days. You were not supposed to have this dysfunctional dynamic in your home.

Naomi looks at something almost as bad as it can get in this life and says, "The LORD's hand has turned against me." She sees her life as the blueprint of God. She holds up her life for all of us to evaluate and to conclude that what we are looking at in our own lives when they are like hers is a God who is taking his hand—the power of his rule—and is saying, "You want to find a satisfied life in Moab, but I am putting a stop to it, even using three tremendous tragedies and a really bleak outlook to do so."

Mysterious Mercy Is Guiding Us when We Turn to Places that Show Evidence of God's Blessing
RUTH 1:14-21

Kissy, kissy, hug, hug. Tearful goodbyes are said so that Naomi finally can walk with her despair back to Bethlehem by herself, for her chances of survival seem better that way. While Orpah takes the golden parachute, Ruth will not have it. Forsaking Moab's gods, Ruth has become a proselyte to Israel and committed to the well-being of her mother-in-law. "For wherever you go, I will go, and wherever you live, I will live; your people will be my people, and your God will be my God" (v. 16).

Effectively, Ruth pledges to Naomi, "I will go where you go, camp where you camp, even if in homeless places. Israel, not Moab, is now my people. Your God, the Lord, is now my God." This Moabitess who was outside the covenant people of Israel, forbidden to enter God's sanctuary, and from a people doomed to be destroyed now enters into the covenant people of Israel (Deut 23:3; Neh 13:1-2; Isa 15:1; Jer 48:42; Mic 6:5). In doing so, *the Abrahamic promise for all nations breaks upon Ruth's and Naomi's heads.*

What can Naomi do now? She has been silenced by the determined devotion of Ruth. She must wonder why the Almighty would send her back to Bethlehem with a Moabite mouth to feed.

Naomi has additional theological and spiritual evaluations of the situation. The excited throng remembers the Naomi who left Bethlehem with husband and sons and now stares when witnessing her return with only a Moabitess companion. While they remember the pleasant woman who once resided among them, Naomi informs them that a different woman is returning: "The pleasant woman you remember is no more; I am bitter. I'm not happy, I'm not glad, I'm not joyful, and I'm not going to cover up my hurt. 'Mara' (meaning "Bitterness") is my new name, that is how you will address me, and I want everyone to know why I am bitter: *the Lord has dealt bitterly with me, testified against me, and brought calamity on me;* I went out full with a husband, two sons, and hope of a better life in Moab; I am returning with no husband, no sons, and a Moabitess daughter-in-law. You do the math. I am empty."

The first term, *made me very bitter,* indicates that El Shaddai—"the Almighty," God the sovereign King—actively worked to make Naomi's life bitter.

Has opposed me uses courtroom language to picture the Lord standing against Naomi in court saying, "Naomi, here is the judgment I make against you."[87]

Afflicted is a familiar term we see hundreds of times in the OT. Job uses it when he says, "Should we accept only good from God and not *adversity?*" (Job 2:10; emphasis added). Jeremiah uses the term when the Lord says,

> *For I am already bringing* disaster *on the city that bears my name, so how could you possibly go unpunished? You will not go unpunished, for I am summoning a sword against all the*

---

[87] Robert Hubbard notes, "Her language, however, borrows a term from Israelite law and applies it metaphorically to her situation (has testified against me). Significantly, it portrays her as a defendant in a legal action who has already been found guilty and punished (i.e., her misfortune) but who knows neither the charges nor the testimony against her. Since only Yahweh controls such things, he must have given witness against her—and there is no more incontrovertible witness than he! Hence, her 'bitter' straits: though preferring to offer rebuttal, such reliable testimony required her simply to endure her punishment" (*Book of Ruth,* 127).

inhabitants of the earth. This is the declaration of the LORD *of
Armies.* (Jer 25:29; emphasis added)

And again, when the Lord says,

*"Just as I watched over them to uproot and to tear them down, to
demolish and to destroy, and to cause* disaster, *so will I watch over
them to build and to plant them"—this is the* LORD*'s declaration.*
(Jer 31:28; emphasis added)

Amos uses this term when the Lord also says,

*If a ram's horn is blown in a city,
    aren't people afraid?
If a* disaster *occurs in a city,
    hasn't the* LORD *done it?* (Amos 3:6; emphasis added)

Naomi sees the Lord actively bringing about the deaths of her husband and sons, making her a widow, and leaving her with the burden
of a Moabitess companion as the Lord's making a judgment against her
choice to go to Moab.[88]

There is not a linear correspondence between all suffering or
tragedy and one's personal sin. All tragedy is not judgment. That is an

---

[88] Almost in contrast to his previous comments concerning Naomi's outlook on her
situation, Hubbard challenges any view that suggests Naomi perceived her circumstances
stem from judgment, commenting, "But one must avoid attributing Naomi's suffering to
some heretofore unmentioned sin, whether done by her, her family, or Israel as a nation.
The narrator gives no grounds for doing so. Rather, Naomi's words point to the mysterious and often (from a human perspective) unjust workings of God. Finally, one must
realize that her outburst in fact assumes a positive view of God, namely, that he controls
the universe, normally with justice. Her case is an exception—though not a rare one—
but such is the mystery of God" (*Book of Ruth*, 127). However, as Hubbard already noted,
the terms Naomi uses are terms for legal judgment. Repeatedly in this chapter Naomi
ascribed the events to the direct hand of God, including the legal striking down of her
husband and sons.
    Daniel Hawk offers a better commentary on Naomi's circumstances, saying, "Naomi,
however, is not without faith. Even though she holds Yahweh responsible for her suffering, she does not abandon him. Rather, her suffering drives her back to the place of
Yahweh's visitation. He shapes her people's identity and thus her own. She cannot abandon Yahweh, even when she believes he has turned against her. Both her return and her
protest express her devotion to Yahweh. She clings to him even though she believes he
has turned against her. Naomi thus joins those whose anguished complaints manifest an
unshakable commitment to God, one that mirrors the devotion of a Creator who refuses
to abandon those who turn away to other relationships (Pss 22:1–2; 60:1; 74:1; Jer 15:15–
18; 20:7–18; Lam 3:1–44; cf. Mark 15:34)" (*Ruth*, 63–64).

American thought—that America should be judged for her sins. "Oh, the Coronavirus is judgment for America's sins," so the thinking goes. That is a false perception of America as a theocratic nation that has vassal status under God her suzerain. Or it wrongly stems from a transference of God's judgment of political nations during the old covenant age to judgment of political nations in the present age, even though believers reside throughout the nations in this age differently from how Israel dwelt among the Gentile nations as God's son.

The United States of America is not Israel, nor is the US another political nation given wholesale to worshiping gods that are not gods. So to impose the Coronavirus as a judgment for moral laxity is a huge assumption with many theological problems. Yet it is American to attempt to make such correspondences, as if the US were God's city on a hill.

Your tragedy might not be a judgment for a sin or sins. It could be, but you don't know, especially if you are living before the Lord in earnest efforts of grace to please him. This is part of the mystery with which we live. *It is part of the mystery of God's love for Naomi and us.*

In order to keep from going off the rails of the doctrine of the Lord's providence, this present writer mused to himself, *If George Floyd's mother were sitting in front of you, would you still write these words?* This passage and this message have significant implications concerning the injustice in the death of George Floyd and all his mother's pains.[89] Would one say to George Floyd's mother, "This is part of the mystery of God's love for us"? This sermon has implications for the death of this present writer's oldest son, Eric Jr., who would be twenty-five years old at the time of this writing had he lived and had this writer had days to throw him in the air, play ball with him, watch him graduate from college, and see him marry and have children of his own.

The Lord's love is not restrained by our actions. God chooses from all eternity past to set his love on his own forever. This love never changes or ends. It is the work of a totally good and absolutely holy God. So goodness always comes to us as part of the package of love. When you hear the story of Jesus's death on the cross to satisfy God's wrath against sins we have committed, and when you hear of his resurrection from the dead that offers life after death and power over sin to those who

---

[89] George Floyd was murdered in Minneapolis, Minnesota, during a police arrest, May 25, 2020.

believe, and then you turn from living life apart from God to trusting Jesus, you then begin to *experience* the love that God has set upon you since eternity past.

A good, holy, loving God is not in the business of glibly using family members as pawns in a game to get us to know him better. He is in the business of judging people, for that is his prerogative. He rules over all death; we expect and almost even demand to die in peace at an old age, never to die from tragedy or to bury the young. We are like Orual in C. S. Lewis's *Till We Have Faces*, who screams at the council of the gods, "The girl was mine. What right had you to steal her away into your dreadful heights?" (p. 291). But avoidance of bereavement and absence of tragedy are not promised in a fallen world. Only death is promised because of our sins. Never is the Almighty being unfair toward us in tragedy. It might feel unfair, but it is not unfair.

Changing the terms of our perspective on the Lord's sovereignty in tragedy by saying, "He allows it," does not help; it worsens every tragic dilemma. Everyone wants a God sovereign enough to *prevent* pain. But when pain occurs, we don't want him to be so sovereign that he *inflicts* the pain, even if it is mediated through secondary means of human evil. However, if the Lord is in glory looking the other way while we are writhing in pain, then he is ignorant of things going on in his universe, is intentionally ignoring them, or is not acting because he is powerless to do anything. That would mean we are at the whims of Satan, the forces of creation, and evil people, and the "he allows it" God can't help us.

Instead of a "he allows it" God, we want the God of the Scriptures—the one who *caused* the Chaldeans to come against Judah and accomplish all that Deuteronomy 28 promised, including women eating their own children and the afterbirth (Deut 28:53-57; 2 Kgs 6:28-29; Jer 19:9; Lam 2:20; 4:10; Ezek 5:10). That sovereign God held the Chaldeans accountable for the evil afflicted on Judah without doing anything evil himself (Hab 2:6-8,20). God never does evil because he cannot. But he has decreed mysterious designs that intentionally use the evil of others to accomplish his mysterious good and holy will.

In life's tragedies, we prefer to know the God who took the life of Eric Jr. through the secondary means within this fallen creation that caused a lethal birth defect. That sovereign God remains worthy of our praise and undying love toward him. Not everyone can accept Naomi and Job's God, who is Jesus's God—the one pleased to bruise Jesus on the cross (Isa 53:10). May we love this God all the more, for only he can bring grace upon grace in our pains and our deepest longings for a fulfilled life.

Mysterious Mercy Can Provide Hope when We Rest in What the Faithful Perceive to Be Blessings
RUTH 1:22

Naomi is blind to much of what the Lord is doing in her life. Naomi is the recipient of *unrecognized mercy when the Almighty testifies against her.* The Lord returns Naomi to Bethlehem at the time of the barley harvest—the best possible time that she could find provision for herself and Ruth. While Naomi thinks she went out full, she actually was leaving Bethlehem *spiritually* empty because she thought her hope was in Moab rather than in the Lord's ability to sustain her through a famine. Now she thinks she is coming back empty, but the Lord has put her in a position where she now has her hope in him alone. Although great tragedy has struck her in the human realm, she is in a far better position now that her soul is following the Lord. In her tragedy she is coming back full.[90]

The writer of Ruth is trying to show us that the Lord's striking down with tragedy and giving of mercy are in fact the same thing in the lives of believers. It is not that tragedy strikes and then the Lord responds by jumping in to offer mercy. It is that the sending of the tragedy from a good God is the sending of mercy—mysteriously but certainly.

Mercy is the hand in the glove of tragedy. Mercy is the head on the coin of which tragedy is the tail. Mercy is the two parts of "H" and the one part of "O"—the hydrogen and the oxygen—in your tragic waters. It is the mass and square of the speed of light in all tragic energy in your life; mercy cubed is your tragic energy. Mercy is every note of every

---

[90] Hawk's comments seem to agree: "The chapter concludes on a note of closure and anticipation (v. 22). The reference to the harvest complements the opening reference to a famine (v. 1), reversing the 'fullness to emptiness' trajectory of Naomi's speech and foreshadowing better things to come. The beginning of the barley harvest is also the time of the celebration of Passover and the Feast of Unleavened Bread, festivals that recall Yahweh's saving acts and Israel's journey to the Promised Land. In the course of the story the absence of food has been displaced by the absence of men, and the absence of men has been displaced by the absence of God. The chapter closes, however, with a glimmer of hope that Naomi's situation—and her relationship with God—may take a turn for the better" (Hawk, *Ruth*, 64).

octave of tragedy; it is warp and woof, knit and sateen. It is brick and mortar; it is flavor and texture! Tragedy is the merciful, powerful, holy, righteous working of a good God—a God we barely understand on this side of eternity. When we are in eternity, never will we say, "I know all there is to know about God; now what?" Or "I already knew that about you, God." Instead, we will be awed and blown away by the beauty of his fearful majesty every moment. There will not be a nanosecond of boredom in all of eternity with him. *Naomi and we have received nothing that is not mercy from this great God.*

Application

In responding to the meaning of Ruth 1, a few obedient actions would seem to flow from experiencing the mysterious mercy of a loving, holy, good God. First, *self-examination in tragedy is good.* But it only is good if we remember that El Shaddai is a good and merciful God. Otherwise we might begin to look for sin behind every experience of pain, persecution, suffering, hurt, disappointment, and calamity. Even if tragedy forces self-examination and reveals sin, you cannot determine whether any one tragedy relates to that specific sin or sins.

Second, *when it comes to walking with God, we must think in terms of an open-ended journey rather than a closed system with commonsense outcomes.* Closure is just not promised, if by "closure" you mean you must have a neat bow on the package of life and everything gets to make sense according to our relative sensibilities. That's not promised. Yes, Proverbs 3:5-6 is true: if you trust the Lord completely, he will direct your paths. Yes, Matthew 28:20 is true: he will be with us always, even to the end of the age. But neither Proverbs 3 nor Matthew 28 promises us that we will be able to see the outcomes we desire. They only promise the Lord's guidance and presence, which should be enough for us.

Ruth 1 is trying to free us from bargaining with God or putting him in our debt, domesticating him to a controllable monarch. We must accept God as who he is and not make God in our own image.

God is not that all-powerful boss who blames a company misfire on his employees. He is not the man or woman who turns into a different person when inebriated because his or her day was awful or because you had a bad day of chores or at school. He is not a dad who is trying to make you tougher by slapping you down anytime you get nearer to reaching a bar of success. God is not a capricious wizard, Superman's Mxyzptlk, John Picard's Q, or a tiger who needs to stay on his side of the boat. He is a good God through and through—a wonderful, merciful, kind, loving, and gracious God! He is shrouded in mystery because he is infinite and we are finite. Yet before they died, Jacob, Job, Joseph, Naomi, and the whole cast of the people of God in Scripture would have affirmed that God is good in all things at all times, with no "but" to follow. Even Paul, who was beheaded, and John, who was exiled, clung to God as good in imprisonment and exile. Paul says, "Everyone deserted me. . . . But the Lord stood with me" (2 Tim 4:16-17). John ends the Apocalypse by saying, "The *grace* of the Lord Jesus be with everyone" (Rev 22:21; emphasis added). Grace only comes from a good God. Hold on to that God when tragedy does not make sense.

Third, *during your trials, tragedies, and pains, plan to be a faithful participant in your local church community*, in both smaller intimate forms and in the whole-church gatherings. The COVID-19 pandemic revealed the need for proximate, vibrant, abiding community and made us long to have such as soon as we could once again love our neighbor in person. The revelation of our need for community increased in our pain. We are not wired to suffer alone or to face disappointment, tragedy, or despair alone.

To be faithful to our gatherings as believers after personal calamity strikes requires us to dispel thoughts about people in the body of Christ leveraging our pains against us. Such thoughts should be left to the devices of those outside of Christ and outside the church. *In Christ*, and in his church and congregations, pain should find comfort, mercy, grace, steadfast companionship, prayer, words of hope, notes of encouragement, and humility on the part of each of us because even we who are without pain at the moment have an unknown date on the books when the bottom drops out in a suffocating form.

Among those in your local assembly, your testimony of pain should not receive, "I'm sorry your life sucks. Go figure it out on your own and come back when you have pulled yourself together." Neither should it receive stares from people wondering what part of the story you left out and what sin you are not confessing. We need to rid ourselves of such *graceless* thinking. That thinking is like walking up to the cross on good Friday, looking at Jesus, and saying, "I wonder what you really did." You would pass Sanhedrin 401 with that attitude. But it would not look like the grace and mercy of one who leaves the ninety-nine for one missing sheep and rejoices when he finds it.

Close

Of course, we know Naomi's life did not end here. Ruth meets Boaz, and Boaz weds Ruth and takes in Naomi as the near kinsman redeemer when the other schlep bows out of his responsibility.

At the end of Naomi's life, it would be tempting for us to say, "OK, I see now. It all worked out." Well, did it?

Do you think Naomi never had pain again as a widow and mother who lost both of her sons? Do you think she never wrestled with the fact that her grandson was not really her own son, even though she was totally happy for Boaz and Ruth?

Yes, this is speculation. But what we do not have to speculate about is that Naomi does not get another husband in this story, and she does not get to enjoy her two sons or other daughter-in-law.

Naomi is blessed; Naomi gets a son in the form of a grandson. But the writer is pointing us to the fact that Naomi's hope does not lie in a grandson named *Obed*, a great grandson named *Jesse*, or even a great-great grandson named *David*. Even though Naomi never saw that being grandma to Obed would put her in the genealogy of Jesus, her hope is the same as ours: it is in a *Son*.

In the healing of the nations, a holy God first announced that Son to Adam and Eve when the Lord told the serpent in the garden, "He will strike your head, and you will strike his heel" (Gen 3:15).

In kindness, that Son is the hope of Abraham when the Lord says to him, "All the peoples on earth will be blessed through you" (Gen 12:3).

With goodness, that Son gets a cryptic mention when God tells Pharaoh to let go of his *Son*, so that Hosea could leave room for Matthew to say, "Out of Egypt I called my Son" (Hos 11:1; Matt 2:15).

Lovingly, the Lord makes a covenant with David so that he will have a Son who will always have the right to the throne of Israel (2 Sam 7).

Mysteriously, forty-one generations after Adam—fourteen from Adam to David (including one generation with a Moabitess named "Ruth"), fourteen from David to the deportation, and fourteen more from the deportation to Mary and Joseph—that promised Son was born and wrapped tightly in cloth; that Son was given because God loved the world; that Son took on our sins and defeated eternal death for us so that we could become sons of God. And just as mysteriously as he came to us in the history of redemption by God's good's hand, so now mysteriously he rules in tragedy and triumph by God's good hand.

Judge not the Lord by feeble sense,
　　But trust him for his grace:
Behind a frowning providence
　　He hides a smiling face.

His purposes will ripen fast,
　　Unfolding every hour:
The bud may have a bitter taste,
　　But sweet will be the flower.

Blind unbelief is sure to err,
　　And scan his work in vain:
God is his own interpreter,
　　And he will make it plain. (William Cowper)

Review and Discuss

1. If you were the leader of Naomi's family before they decided to depart for Moab, what are some things with which you would have wrestled before making the decision to go? What should the family leader have reasoned in order to make the case to stay in Bethlehem?
2. What do you think Naomi felt upon receiving notice of the death of her sons? What might she have prayed for in the days immediately following these second and third deaths in her family?
3. What do you think makes Orpah choose to remain in Moab rather than go to Bethlehem? Would you fault Orpah for her thoughts and feelings contributing to her departure?
4. When you read Naomi attributing the death of her husband and sons to the hand of the Almighty, how do you feel about her words? How do you feel about the most painful events in your own life?
5. Why do some believers find it difficult to attribute tragedy directly to God, despite seeing Naomi, Job, and several others do so in Scripture? What is it about our human experience that wrestles with saying in tragedy, "God directly caused this," and affirming the Lord as the direct sender of evil?
6. What theological problems might one encounter if the God of Scripture is not so sovereign as to send tragedy but only sovereign in a way that allows tragedy?

7. What potential problems could Ruth's identity as a *Moabite* have caused for Naomi? How would Naomi's status as a widow have worked to the benefit of Ruth and her status as a *Moabite*?

8. What does Ruth's inclusion in the genealogy of Jesus indicate about God's plan of redemption of the world?

9. How does Naomi's care for the Moabite daughter-in-law and Ruth's loyalty to Naomi contribute to an evangelical theology of racial relations? With what race-related thoughts and feelings might Naomi and Ruth each have wrestled as they returned from Moab to Bethlehem?

10. Based on Ruth 1, in your own words, explain how a sovereign God loves people through tragedy.

Reaping Prosperously in a Man's World

RUTH 2

Main Idea: A single Christian woman living in a world that advantages men finds hope for provision in wise and faithful trust in Jesus's kindness toward women.

I. **A Woman Hopes in Having a Good Reputation with Good Men (2:1-7).**
   A. The foreshadowing of hope in a kinsman (2:1)
   B. The gleaning in hope in the field of the kinsman (2:2-3)
   C. An inquiring of hope in the blessed man who blesses men (2:4-7)

II. **A Woman Hopes in Men Concerned about Both Women's Well-Being and Honoring God (2:8-13).**
   A. Boaz's concern for Ruth's safety around young men (2:8-9)
   B. Ruth's humble acknowledgment of favor as a foreigner (2:10)
   C. Boaz's communication of blessing for Ruth's faithfulness (2:11-12)
   D. Ruth's acknowledgment of favor as one not Boaz's employee (2:13)

III. **A Woman Hopes in Men Who Foster Women's Public Equality without Men Interfering (2:14-16).**
   A. The invitation to Ruth to share at the table with men (2:14)
   B. The instruction to the men to supply and not hinder Ruth (2:15-16)

IV. **A Woman Should Bring Glory to the Kindness of Men and the Lord while Still Acting with Wisdom toward Men (2:17-23).**
   A. The blessing of Boaz upon return with abundance (2:17-19)
   B. The blessing of the Lord upon recognition of his kindness (2:20)
   C. The obedience of Ruth upon reception of wisdom toward men (2:21-23)

I n 2019 Hasbro addressed the perennial issue of the pay gap between men and women by creating a new Monopoly game. In the updated version of the classic board game, women players earn more than men

(Asmelash, "In the New Game of Monopoly"). While the attempt to level the playing board and present a world of corrected inequalities was admirable, some critics noted, "This concept perpetuates the idea that women need an advantage to be equal to men instead of simply being equal—an idea that companies hopefully do not emulate" (Jansen, "Societal Influences").

On average, women in the US make 18 percent less than men (Hegewisch and Tesfaselassie, "The Gender Wage Gap"). Over the course of a year, the average working woman loses $10,122 as a result of the gender pay gap ("The Simple Truth"). Women make up 47 percent of the workforce, but only 4.8 percent of S&P 500 companies have female CEOs. Men are promoted at 30 percent higher rates than women during their early career stages. Women are paid seventy-nine cents on the dollar of their male colleagues, and it's even worse for women of color. Fifty percent of women in STEM fields eventually leave their jobs because of hostile work environments (Gender Equality Fund, "Gender Equity"). The pay gap actually increases for women at higher education levels ("Women Are Paid Less than Men").

Women have many forces in society that work against their gaining equal pay. Gaining equal pay is not simply about fairness. Equal pay affects mobility in society, respect, retirement wealth, the ability to influence political and social movements. In short, it affects satisfaction in life. The contributing forces to the present inequity include views of women as inferior in intellect or leadership abilities, the pull and duties of motherhood, media portrayals of ideal woman leadership, workplace harassment and abuse, and both men and women who just do not even see any issues of misogyny, sexism, chauvinism, or the oppression and hatred of women at hand.

The situation becomes all the more complicated for Christian women, especially the single Christian woman. While Scripture holds a standard of humble, Christlike complementarianism as a model for the wife in a home and women in the local assembly, misteachings of complementarianism leave women feeling stifled, undervalued, unappreciated, overtasked and unsupported, and unable to thrive as female beings. The lack of a male companion can give single women feelings of a second- or third-class membership status as evangelical messages—formal and informal—communicate that "single" is a synonym for "incomplete." The ability for a Christian woman to find felt and real satisfaction and success in this life has many hurdles.

What if there were something the church could do about helping women gain equality and satisfaction in a world that advantages men and disadvantages women? What if that way depended on both men and women working for the good of women in the same vein as Jesus?

Boaz and Naomi both work toward helping Ruth gain the provisions she needs to survive and thrive. They help her reap prosperously in a setting in which men are the reapers, men are in charge, women follow behind men in reaping, women do not have a place at the table with men, and women are vulnerable to physical assault and charges of being sexually promiscuous. Despite the wall built against the hope of Ruth's prosperity, the efforts of Boaz and Naomi prevail on behalf of Ruth. Following this story, one discerns four things needed for women to reap prosperously in a world that advantages men.

A Woman Hopes in Having a Good Reputation with Good Men
RUTH 2:1-7

Ruth gleans behind the reapers in the field of one in whom she hopes to find favor. Her work catches the eye of Boaz, the relative of Naomi's husband Elimelech, eventually. The story starts differently.

The Foreshadowing of Hope in a Kinsman (2:1)

The author begins by informing the readers that Naomi has a relative. The description of him as (1) "on her husband's side," (2) "prominent man of noble character," and (3) "from Elimelech's family" foreshadows the hope of a near kinsman with means to redeem. He has the character to make him worthy of marriage and of good standing in the community. He is from the clan of Naomi's husband, so seemingly he would have been familiar with Naomi's family leaving Bethlehem, the passing of the husband and sons, and the return of the widow with the family's name. The reader anticipates a rescue for Naomi before one reads of Ruth going to glean.

The Gleaning in Hope in the Field of the Kinsman (2:2-3)

The writer describes Ruth as "the Moabitess." These words are juxtaposed against the family and clan identity of Boaz, interposing an ethnic obstacle that might be a challenge for the prominent man of noble character who most certainly is a Bethlehemite. Ruth seeks permission to glean grain because she is under the household of her mother-in-law and in a strange land. Rightly, she is hoping for favor that will allow her to gain food for the household so that they might survive, and Naomi is permissive and supportive.

Ruth will glean behind the harvesters, naturally, as the workers drop portions of grain while gathering the produce. The workers cannot possibly gather or carry 100 percent of what has grown. The law dictated that they were to leave a portion of the harvest for the needy to glean:

> When you reap the harvest in your field, and you forget a sheaf in the field, do not go back to get it. It is to be left for the resident alien, the fatherless, and the widow, so that the LORD your God may bless you in all the work of your hands. When you knock down the fruit from your olive tree, do not go over the branches again. What remains will be for the resident alien, the fatherless, and the widow. When you gather the grapes of your vineyard, do not glean what is left. What remains will be for the resident alien, the fatherless, and the widow. (Deut 24:19-21; see also Lev 19:9-10; 23:22)

There are provisions for both the resident alien and the widow within the Mosaic law. So Ruth is free to glean behind the harvesters. In an incredibly odd sort of way, she comes to glean in the field of the aforementioned, prominent, noble Boaz, whom the writer again states is from the clan of Naomi's husband.

An Inquiring of Hope in the Blessed Man Who Blesses Men (2:4-7)

True to the stated character, when Boaz finally enters the scene, he is a man who follows the Lord, shows care for his workers, and is blessed by those under his care. It would not have been hard to notice an additional woman gleaning in the fields, especially one from Moab. So the blessed man who gives blessing to his workers inquires of the identity of the young lady in his field following the reapers. He learns from the male servant in charge of the harvesters—for no woman would have been in charge of those men in ancient Israel—that Ruth is (1) the Moabite who returned with Naomi her mother-in-law, (2) one who asked permission to glean, and (3) one who has been faithful in the field with little rest. The writer makes a deliberate threefold comparison to Boaz's description so that the goodness of Boaz and the goodness of Ruth are both evident in Boaz's knowledge of Ruth.

It is unfortunate that discussions about women's prosperity—or lack thereof—tend to blame the victim. Such discussions might suggest that all women need to do to be equal is work as hard as men do. Any thought about how much harder a woman had to work just to gain a place in the company is not part of the discussion. Like the saying among African Americans, "You have to work twice as hard to be twice as good to get half the pay,"[91] so we place the responsibility for overcoming educational, occupational, and financial disparities upon the backs of women.[92]

Ruth is a hard worker of solid character, as evidenced in her requests to Naomi and the head of the field servants and in her faithfulness to glean with little rest. But her reputation and work ethic will mean nothing going forward if this story lacks a man with the character and power of Boaz to use his influence to make a path of prosperity for Ruth. A lesser man could tell the head of the servants to get that Moabite out of his field lest he have to share gleanings with her, and Ruth's character and work would have meant nothing.

A Woman Hopes in Men Concerned about Both Women's Well-Being and Honoring God
RUTH 2:8-13

Boaz's Concern for Ruth's Safety around Young Men (2:8-9)

Boaz turns to address Ruth directly. One quickly discerns his care for her as a woman. Tenderly, he calls her "my daughter," just as Naomi did when she gave Ruth permission to glean in unknown fields. For

---

91 For more on the "twice as good" idea among African Americans, see Britni Danielle, "Michelle Obama's 'Twice as Good' Speech Doesn't Cut It with Most African Americans," *The Guardian*, May 12, 2015, https://www.theguardian.com/commentisfree/2015/may /12/michelle-obama-twice-as-good-african-americans-black-people, accessed January 6, 2021; Courtney L. McCluney, Kathrina Robotham, Serenity Lee, Richard Smith, and Myles Durkee, "The Costs of Code-Switching" *Harvard Business Review*, November 15, 2019, https://hbr.org/2019/11/the-costs-of-codeswitching, accessed January 6, 2021; and Danielle Young, "Black Hollywood's Thoughts on Working Twice as Hard to Get Half as Far," *Essence*, September 26, 2019, https://www.essence.com/entertainment/black-holly woods-thoughts-on-working-twice-as-hard, accessed January 6, 2021.

92 See Julia Gillard, "Women Still Have to Work Twice as Hard as Less Competent Men to Succeed—Just Ask Hillary Clinton," *The Independent*, November 13, 2019, https:// www.independent.co.uk/voices/hillary-clinton-julia-gillard-gender-equality-women-work -equal-pay-success-a9200791.html, accessed January 6, 2021; Antionette Kerr, "Why Are We Still Telling Black Women to Work Twice as Hard?," *Women Advance*, August 22, 2019, https://www.womenadvancenc.org/2019/08/22/why-are-we-still-telling-black-women-to -work-twice-as-hard, accessed January 6, 2021.

this foreigner and widow who is a stranger to Boaz, these would have been endearing and fear-removing words. Similarly, he tells her to glean exclusively in his field—a field in which, earlier that morning, Ruth had never before been seen or worked, and which she could not identify specifically as belonging to a relative or a prominent person. She could have landed in the field of a tyrant who would have demanded favors or a miser who would have asked her to glean in another field. But he makes the fields of his prominence available to her.

Boaz further tells Ruth to stay near his own women workers and follow them. The women workers will know where and how to glean, so Ruth will not have to play any office politics in order to get a share of the gleaning pie. Moreover, Boaz has instructed the young men not to interfere or harm Ruth, for she would have been vulnerable and an easy target as a woman—a Moabite woman. But Boaz looks out for her physical safety in the male-dominated work environment. He is not being biased, a misandrist, filling quotas, or practicing tokenism in doing so. Ruth herself will describe his actions as "favor."

If all that effort to give Ruth a real chance at successful gleaning wasn't enough, Boaz tells Ruth to drink water already drawn by the men when she finds herself thirsty. Ruth does not even have to lift a finger at a well to get her own water. Boaz provides for her to benefit from the work the men already have done. Many corporate offices need a Boaz.

Ruth's Humble Acknowledgment of Favor as a Foreigner (2:10)

Easily one can understand how Boaz's unforeseen kindness would overwhelm the young foreigner who put her hope in Naomi's God—the God of Israel. That act of faith could have landed her in poverty. Even here she could have heard words of rejection and experienced mistreatment. But blessing comes as the first words from this powerful man to this stranger. Ruth rightly responds in humility, falling on her face before Boaz, as one undeserving of such kindness. Her question about favor as a foreigner makes sense, as she would not necessarily know his motives or the poverty stipulations of the Mosaic law.

Boaz's Communication of Blessing for Ruth's Faithfulness (2:11-12)

Boaz's reply is intensely theological and equally compassionate and assuring. Whereas Ruth sees favor coming from Boaz, Boaz sees himself as an instrument of the Lord to reward Ruth for her faithfulness to the

Lord and to her mother-in-law. Certainly the full reward will go beyond the blessing of the gleaning. But Boaz blesses Ruth based on his understanding of how he, a believing member of Israel, should act toward another with faith in the same God. He is not ignoring her gender or being gender blind. Instead, he has recognized what she has done as a believing woman, and he responds as God's conduit of blessing to this female servant. He is the figure to whom Ruth comes so that in doing so, like a baby bird or chick, she comes under the pinions of God for safety and care.

Ruth's Acknowledgment of Favor as One Not Boaz's Employee (2:13)

Ruth again recognizes the favor of Boaz in his attribution of the kindness to the Lord and his reward. This time she goes one step further to recognize the authority, comfort, and kindness of Boaz.

Boaz does not seem to feel any sense of needing to choose between showing kindness to Ruth and being obedient to God. Instead, he understands that in seeking Ruth's human, female, earthly care he is doing the work that is spiritual—work that is from the Lord and honoring to him.

Often however, in contemporary Christianity, we sometimes see a conflict between the gospel and doing practical good on behalf of women. Our solution to the trouble of women being disadvantaged is, "Just preach the gospel," because the preaching of the gospel will change individual hearts toward a righteous treatment of all women. But such naivete ignores centuries of women fighting to find a semblance of equality in everything from voting to playing sports and joining country clubs, to being considered qualified to be executive leadership, and even to having roles in the church that, although not ordained positions like elders and pastors, are positions that maximize their gifts, abilities, experiences, insights, and unique skills that will be a blessing to men and women.

As men, being concerned about the well-being of women goes far beyond physical safety and financial security. It does not overlook protecting women from workplace and ecclesial predators, but it does more. It does the metaphorical heavy lifting to make a way of blessing for women, seeing ourselves as working to do the will of God in the process. Boaz never asked Ruth to get her own water.

A Woman Hopes in Men Who Foster Women's Public Equality without Men Interfering
RUTH 2:14-16

The Invitation to Ruth to Share at the Table with Men (2:14)

Boaz's actions already go beyond minimal aid to the Moabitess widow. Now however, he will give a mealtime invitation to Ruth to eat with him until she is satisfied. The typology of the "vinegar sauce" in this passage almost screams to the reader, as one looks backwards to the vinegar Nazirites needed to avoid (Num 6:3) and forward to the sour wine the Lord would take to wet his mouth enough on the cross to cry aloud and say, "It is finished!" (John 19:29-30).[93] Boaz's invitation looks like the Lord's invitations to dine with him, while he and Ruth both drink the wine that points toward the Savior's redemption of Israel.

The experience is public, not private. All the men at the meal can see that Boaz invites Ruth near, offers to her to dip in the same sauce in which he and the men are eating, shares the roasted grain with her, and allows her to eat until she is satisfied with some left over. One hears Matthew 14:20: "Everyone ate and was satisfied. They picked up twelve baskets full of leftover pieces."

The Instruction to the Men to Supply and Not Hinder Ruth (2:15-16)

Still before the young men and not simply in the hearing of Ruth, Boaz instructs the reapers to let her glean without harming her or putting her to shame. They are told not to insult her or censure her. Among the men, Ruth has the ability to work freely without fear of being limited or stifled.

In the process of writing the commentary on this passage, the present writer found similar thought expressed by *The Gospel Coalition* writer:

> Righteous integrity in the workplace begins with looking for
> ways to protect and bless the employees under your care,

---

[93] The Hebrew word for "vinegar sauce" is used only two other times in the OT: Num 6:3 and Ps 69:21. The Greek term that translates the "vinegar sauce" of Ruth 2:14 is used in Num 6:3 and Ps 68:22 (68:22 LXX = 69:21 MT) in the OT, along with Prov 25:20. In the NT, it is used in Matt 27:48; Mark 15:36; John 19:29-30. In Luke 23:36 the term appears as the wine Jesus refuses to drink to relieve suffering.

not turning a blind eye to their vulnerabilities or needs. The aim of Boaz's words and actions were twofold—to protect Ruth from harm (Ruth 2:9b) and to help her to be productive (Ruth 2:9c, 15–16). Boaz was unequivocal in his instructions to his men, and to Ruth herself, to ensure she wouldn't be harassed (Ruth 2:9b). He was equally forthright in his direction to proactively care for her and the other women (Ruth 2:9c). He created an environment where her work would be easier. Because of Boaz's proactive direction, Ruth's work environment was more than just physically safe. She was equipped with what she needed to work well and to feel welcome. Policies that protect people from harassment or abuse are right and good. They create a basic level of safety so people can do their jobs. Bosses who implement additional policies that equip people to perform their jobs do even better. . . . Boaz's work values were more than hollow sentiments crafted by Human Resources that hung on a breakroom bulletin board. They bounded and shaped all his actions. (Starke, "Be a Boaz")

Each semester I strive to invite at least one woman to guest lecture in each of my courses. During a postlecture, casual Q and A session, I once had to stand between two male students and a senior-aged, accomplished theologian who was female. Their disagreement with her views on topic were allowable, but their physical approach toward her in a natural, unknowing, intimidation stance was not. I asked them to back away. Sadly, I had anticipated that some of the male students from outside of honor-shame communities might attempt such actions.

Recently, as another budding theologian explained to me what she intended to give in her lectures in my course and asked me if she was within proper parameters, I said to her, "It is important that I not control or dictate what you will bring to the lecture. If I do, your gifts and expertise will be reduced. We do not need reduction; we need you to bring the full use of your gifts and abilities to the lecture, and the students need to experience the fulness of your scholarship. Moreover, the male control of women in the academy we are attempting to defeat by your presence will be lost hypocritically if I tell you what you may and may not say. I need you to lecture as the Spirit of the Lord leads you to lecture." This seems to be a gracious path toward allowing her to grow into success as a scholar and experience satisfaction as a woman. She does not need my interference or approval. She needs my encouragement and the creation of an environment in which she can thrive without suppression.

A Woman Should Bring Glory to the Kindness of Men and the Lord while Still Acting with Wisdom toward Men
RUTH 2:17-23

The Blessing of Boaz upon Return with Abundance (2:17-19)

After her day's work, Ruth returns to Naomi with six quarts of barley and her box of leftover food from the meal—far more than either of them seemed to have expected from the first day of work as a foreigner in unknown fields! Naomi's line of questioning in response to all Ruth brings understandably leads to both identification and blessing of the man who showed such kindnesses to Ruth. It is the Lord's blessing Naomi wishes on the yet unidentified landowner. Then Ruth reveals to her mother-in-law Boaz as the man of kindness.

The Blessing of the Lord upon Recognition of His Kindness (2:20)

There is some ambiguity in the antecedent of "he has not abandoned his kindness." The Hebrew is unclear as to whether it is the Lord or Boaz. This allows for the possibility that Naomi refers to both the Lord and Boaz. Boaz has not abandoned kindness to the living (Ruth and Naomi) or the dead (Elimelech and his sons), and the Lord has done the same through Boaz. The Lord is exalted as one merciful by his use of Boaz toward Ruth. When Naomi identifies him as a close relative and family redeemer, Boaz begins to step into the foreshadowed role of the kinsman redeemer. Of this role in Israel, Daniel Block writes, "As a kinship term it denotes the near relative who is responsible for the economic well-being of a relative, and he comes into play especially when the relative is in distress and cannot get himself/herself out of the crisis" (*Judges, Ruth*, 674). Block indicates that the kinsman redeemer had five responsibilities according to the Mosaic law:

> (1) to ensure that the hereditary property of the clan never
> passes out of the clan (Lev 25:25–30); (2) to maintain the
> freedom of individuals within the clan by buying back those

who have sold themselves into slavery because of poverty (Lev 25:47–55); (3) to track down and execute murderers of near relatives (Num 35:12, 19–27); (4) to receive restitution money on behalf of a deceased victim of a crime (Num 5:8); and (5) to ensure that justice is served in a lawsuit involving a relative (Job 19:25; Ps 119:154; Jer 50:34). (*Judges, Ruth,* 674–75)

The writer of Ruth combined the role of the kinsman redeemer with the law of levirate marriage in which a widow without a male heir would wed her husband's brother in order to produce an heir for the family (Deut 25:5-10). If Boaz fulfills these roles, Naomi (who would most likely be the target for the levirate marriage) and Ruth will find themselves redeemed rather than destitute.

The Obedience of Ruth upon Reception of Wisdom toward Men (2:21-23)

There are many good men in the world like Boaz. Many men will work against the historical and social grain and intentionally and courageously strive for the full life enjoyment of all women. But the existence of Boazes does not negate the existence of men who intend to harm women and the real threat they pose to women's ability to obtain satisfaction in the workplace and all of life.

Boaz instructs Ruth to stick close to his men because he models for his men how to treat women and instructs his men to go the extra mile for Ruth's welfare. He forbids them from hindering her work. This is a significant provision for Ruth.

What happens next is a work of discipleship from a mother-in-law to a daughter-in-law. It is older female wisdom being passed to a younger female. The text is emphasizing the woman-to-woman discipleship role based on the repetitive use of "mother-in-law" and "daughter-in-law" in 2:17-23:

- She picked up the grain and went into the town, where her *mother-in-law* saw what she had gleaned (v. 18).
- Her *mother-in-law* said to her, "Where did you gather barley today, and where did you work?" (v. 19).
- Ruth told her *mother-in-law* whom she had worked with (v. 19).

- Then Naomi said to her *daughter-in-law*, "May the LORD bless him because he has not abandoned his kindness to the living or the dead" (v. 20).
- So Naomi said to her *daughter-in-law*, "My daughter, it is good for you to work with his female servants, so that nothing will happen to you in another field" (v. 22).
- And she lived with her *mother-in-law* (v. 23).

Where the author simply could say "Naomi" or "Ruth," instead there is emphasis on the relationship between the two women. As mother-in-law, Naomi observes the gleanings, inquires into the identity of the field owner, infers blessing on the Lord and Boaz, and instructs Ruth to adhere to the words of Boaz so as not to be abused in the field of another. As daughter-in-law, Ruth responds with the identification of the field owner, obedience to Naomi's wisdom, and continuous dwelling in Naomi's home. In this mother-to-daughter-like relationship, Naomi tells Ruth to listen to Boaz because men in other fields might see her as a target for their earthly desires, and she could be harmed. Every young woman needs this sort of exhortation from an older, mother-like figure in her life, even if that figure is the mother-in-law.

Application

Two important applications grow from this chapter if our children will be courageous, Christian change agents who strive for the equity of women in the world and especially in the workplace.

First, *we must tell our daughters that they are complete in Christ without being married and/or affirmed by men.* We need to emphasize this from her earliest understandings and reemphasize and reinforce her completeness daily. We never want our daughter to think she is not equal to men by suggesting she needs male approval to be a whole person. Telling her she is complete does not intend to create hatred toward men. Instead, it intends to create a wall against self-hatred for being born biologically female. She is made in the image of God with as much dignity as anyone born male. She must know within herself that she should not accept inequitable treatment in any arena because she is a woman. She should receive all opportunities, support, and recognition that her male counterparts of comparable positions receive.

Second, *we must teach our sons that they are not God's gifts to women and that women are not their enemies.* Emphasize to your sons the need to operate differently in worlds of men and women. In the world of men, your Christian son needs to walk in humility but also needs to know that he will need to be fearless. Fearlessness is not brash; Jesus was fearless without being brash.

In the world of women, he will need to be humble, compassionate, sensitive, safe, and appear powerless. Teach him that he never can raise his voice or hand at a woman, or frown at a woman, even if he will need to be ready to engage physically against other men in certain arenas. Raise your son to be a person in whom every woman would feel safe confiding and every man could respect him for his courage and steadfastness. This is the picture we have of Jesus in the Gospels as the Jewish leaders took offense at his words, but lepers and the blind, and many women, could touch him and be touched by him.

Close

The Jesus who calls us to salvation provides salvation equally for all people. He could challenge Nicodemus to be born again by believing on the Son of God and challenge a woman from Samaria to confess him as Messiah. Jesus healed women and their children, commended women's faith in him, enjoyed the financial support of women, freed women and men from their sins, and appeared first to women after rising from the dead, sending them to tell the disciples he is alive. Jesus gave hope to women who lived in a world of men. Jesus calls those who live like Boaz to do the same.

Review and Discuss

1. What efforts has your congregation made to help women achieve practical equity in your assembly without violating Scripture's teaching on the roles of men and women?
2. What efforts have you and members of your congregation made to help women achieve practical equity in pay, executive positions, and respect within greater society?
3. Why is it important for the church to strive for the equity of all women in the world?
4. How would being from Moab create an extra hurdle for Ruth to thrive among the men? How does being an ethnic minority make the task of achieving equity in society a greater challenge?

5. Why do women experience a blame-the-victim response to discussions about equity in pay or occupational opportunities? As believers, how should we respond to discussions that promote the false idea that women are at fault for a lack of equity in society?
6. Practically speaking, in your congregation, what are three or four concrete actions you would like to see male leaders take to create equity within your assembly?
7. What is the theological significance of *equity* being at the center of a chapter's idea in Scripture?
8. In your own words, describe what Boaz did to bless Ruth.
9. How can you help your brothers in Christ grow in their protection of women in their workplaces and in their heavy lifting on behalf of women and women's achievement of workplace equity?

Resting by Faith

RUTH 3

Main Idea: I must walk by faith rather than manipulation to fully enjoy resting in Christ.

I. **Resting by Faith Involves Not Advantaging Ourselves at the Goodness of Others (3:1-5).**
   A. The timing of advantage (3:1)
   B. The motive of advantage (3:1-2)
   C. The plan of advantage (3:3-4)
   D. The agreement with advantage (3:5)

II. **Resting by Faith Includes Not Manipulating Provision before the Presence of God (3:6-13).**
   A. The obedience of manipulation (3:6-7)
   B. The adjustment away from manipulation (3:8-9)
   C. The provision apart from manipulation (3:10-13)

III. **Resting by Faith Incurs Abundant Blessings while Awaiting the Return of the Redeemer (3:14-18).**
   A. The blessing of an honorable name (3:14)
   B. The blessing of large provision (3:15)
   C. The blessing of testifying about the provider (3:16-17)
   D. The blessing of waiting for the redeemer (3:18)

Early in the Christian life one learns the importance of walking by faith. The use of "walking" language in the NT abounds as a way of describing "living."[94] Believers, while walking through the course of life, are to *live* by faith in the Word of God because the Lord has shown he is true. Walking by faith is the means by which Christ sanctifies his own as we live in obedience to the Scriptures.

Often later in one's Christian life one encounters the concept of rest, even though it is a large theme in Scripture. God rested on the seventh day of creation, the Sabbath work ordinances command rest

---

[94] Romans 6:4; 8:4; 13:13; 2 Cor 5:7; 10:3; Gal 5:16; 6:16; Eph 2:10; 4:1,17; 5:2,8,15; Col 1:10; 2:6; 4:5; 1 Thess 2:21; 4:1; 4:12; 2 Thess 3:11; 1 John 2:6; 2 John 6.

on the seventh day of the week, the Israelites were to give the land rest one year of every seven but failed to do so and wound up in captivity for their failure, and the writer to the Hebrews informs us that the promise of God's rest remains for the people of God.

Resting involves more than the dead being at peace from the troubles of this world. Rest is an all-encompassing idea that includes ceasing from labors. The Lord ceased from his labor on the seventh day, he called his people to do the same on the seventh day of the week and one year out of every seven for the land, and we look forward to the day of eternal rest in Christ. The dead have ceased from the labors of this world.

When the Israelites were resting, especially in the year of the land's rest, a good question would be, How does anything get done if no one is doing labor? Or, more poignantly, If no one is doing labor, how then do we provide for ourselves? Inherently, resting means not working, and not working means not eating, not paying bills, not saving, not increasing in wealth, and seemingly not having needs met that normally would be met through the wages one earned from laboring.

The thought of simply trusting the Lord for provision might be met with a "but" (i.e., "I know the Lord will provide, but . . ."). Thoughts of laziness, poverty, late bills, repossession, eviction, and a decreased credit score immediately come to mind. "Yes, the Lord wants us to trust him, *but* he also wants us to use common sense" might be the sentiment some feel toward trusting without working.

Just as much as the Christian life consists of walking by faith, the Christian life consists of *resting by faith—of trusting the Lord for provision without working for it or trying to manipulate one's circumstances to make provision happen.* Ruth learns this truth and teaches it to Naomi. Their story is challenging us to glorify the name of Christ as the provider of salvation. Her story will oppose our stories of trying to make provision happen apart from trusting the Lord's kind processes of provision through our Redeemer.

Resting by Faith Involves Not Advantaging Ourselves at the Goodness of Others
RUTH 3:1-5

The Timing of Advantage (3:1)

Naomi's plan for Ruth to find rest through Boaz seeks to leverage Boaz's kindness, and she gains a promise to obey from Ruth. Rightly, the CSB does not translate a time marker at the opening of this chapter because the Hebrew text does not reflect one. However, the ESV and NASB supply "Then" as the opening word, and NET supplies "At that time" in order to recognize a time shift implied from the events in Ruth 2.[95] What the supplied helping terms clarify for us is that Naomi is taking advantage of the good fortune Ruth reports at the hands of Boaz.[96] What she does is like being with your best friend when you have a chance happening in the store of running into the dream date you have been eying for months, and the best friend conveniently finds a way to leave you in the aisle alone with the potential date. Naomi thinks she sees something coming together and rather than reading into the fortune "Pray," "Get more info," "Let's see if Boaz will do more," or "Ruth, just go back and keep being faithful," Naomi reads, "Time to go into action."

It is important for the reader to understand that what happens in the story would have happened without Naomi's scheming. Naomi should know better than this by now. Her husband schemed a way to provide for the family apart from the Lord's commandments, and that didn't work out as they planned. She did not scheme Ruth to come with her; in fact, she actually was pushing Ruth away because her plan was to go back to Bethlehem and try to fend for herself, to never again worry about providing for either of her daughters-in-law. But the reader already can see that the scheme of God to move Ruth to tag along is working out for Naomi much better than anything she could have planned.

Naomi did not scheme the timing of her return to be at the barley harvest, nor did she scheme the field in which Ruth landed to be Boaz's; neither did she make Boaz inquire of Ruth's identity, protect her, offer her a seat with the boys at the table, or fill her up with gleanings enough to care for her and Naomi! Naomi really should have paused and rethought any blueprints to make provision come about, for she already had seen that the Lord has a blueprint for successful provision that is much greater and better than anything she could draft.

We too need to stop hitting the default button of "scheme a plan" when we are in circumstances of need. Yes, there is a fine line between *waiting in anxiety* and *acting in faith,* and there is an equally thin line between *being patient* and *making excuses for being paralyzed into inaction.* Knowing the will of the Lord when it seems like an opportunity is

---

[95] See the first footnote on Ruth 3:1 in the NET.

[96] One can discern this based on the flow of the story without the helping terms.

presenting itself takes great prayer and counsel, as anyone who has ever been offered a less-than-opportune-job when laid off from work knows. The urge to work it all out in our head how we will bring about provision needs to leave room for the sovereign, miraculous, unpredictable goodness of the Lord to break into our situations. Waiting on that breaking in, however, should not be reason to negate wise council, faithful prayer, and even practical steps like getting a second health opinion or posting a résumé.

The Motive of Advantage (3:1-2)

Naomi now is on a quest to find the "rest" she told Ruth she might be able to obtain back at her mother's home in the arms of a new husband (see Ruth 1:8-9,11-12). She tries to be coy about her scheming by introducing her question about providing for Ruth with the tender term, "My daughter." Rest will consist of a home in which Ruth will find care from a husband. Naomi indicates this will be her task, even though everything is stacked against her as a widow who has been in a far country and against Ruth as a Moabitess.

Naomi speaks of Boaz as both the near kinsman and of his nightshift schedule. The mentioning of the young female servants might be a way of drawing attention to the kindheartedness of Boaz toward his women workers. Or, since Naomi is working out her own plan, it could be a way of speaking of potential competition and the need to make use of Boaz's status as a relative. Naomi is going to fit a square Moabite peg into a round hole of the hope for rest despite competition and the occupational standards of nighttime threshing-floor work being for men only.

The Plan of Advantage (3:3-4)

Naomi, therefore, hatches a three-part plan that is just as earthly and manipulative as it could be, especially since the previous episode showed us that Boaz is a man of honor through and through. First, *she objectifies Ruth by telling her to make herself beautiful.* She wants Ruth to draw Boaz in by alluring him with scent and attire. Second, *she tells Ruth to be sneaky.* Naomi knows Ruth has no business being at the threshing floor at night. So Ruth will have to keep her presence unknown from Boaz (because as an honorable man he would tell her to go home). In Naomi's plan, Ruth needs to wait until Boaz is satisfied with food and drink and asleep from the satiation and exhaustion from work. Only then should Ruth, who has observed the exact place he is lying down—while also staying clear from the sight of anyone else—approach Boaz.

Third, *she tells Ruth to make an advance toward Boaz.* It is possible that she is only suggesting that Ruth make a marriage proposal, even as odd as that would indeed be in the ancient Near East and Israel. One does not need to read into this instruction a sexual solicitation. Following Naomi's advice, Ruth, who has demonstrated herself faithful to Naomi and the Lord, would be making an innocent but intentional request. There is no hint of anything more being proposed than for Ruth to uncover the legs and feet of Boaz and place herself under his cloak. Still, this would be Naomi's manipulative version of a request for marriage.

The Agreement with Advantage (3:5)

Ruth, the younger, agrees to do everything Naomi planned out for her. If she believes Naomi has her best interest in mind, it makes sense for Ruth to follow the plan. Even if the plan amounts to trying to stretch the goodness shown to an extent beyond the initial boundaries of its intention, so be it; it is the apparent means to survival.

A few times in life I looked before I leaped when in a desperate situation. What looked like a benign door of opportunity opening through one means was just a small mirage on the way to a true oasis. In a recent attempt to purchase a new home, my wife and I found ourselves in a quandary in which our home had sold but we were unable to have a contract accepted on a new home by a seller. As the time for our move neared an only-thirty-days-left window, we panicked (inadvertently) and made an offer on a home we had seen that was not where or what we hoped for in a home. However, the price was significantly lower than the ranges we were considering for purchase, and we reasoned that having a home in hand was better than having to scramble to place our household belongings in storage and locate a place to rent until the next buying season.

Almost a week later, we placed an offer on a home that was closer to our desire in style, size, lot, and price. Moreover, this home was in an area over forty miles from the location in which we had been searching for homes, yet it turned out to be perfect in terms of the location we needed for travel. Only as this opportunity came to fruition did we realize that we had been attempting to secure our own rescue by taking advantage of the lower offer before us because it seemed that our backs were against a wall. The Lord needs no such advantages to sustain his own.

Resting by Faith Includes Not Manipulating Provision before the Presence of God
RUTH 3:6-13

The Obedience of Manipulation (3:6-7)

Ruth has no problem with obedience. She heads to the threshing floor. The writer affirms that Ruth "did everything her mother-in-law had charged her to do" (v. 6). She waits until Boaz is satisfied with food and drink and "in good spirits" from them. The writer notes that Boaz lay at the end of the pile of barley in order to show Ruth has "[noticed] the place where he's lying," as Naomi instructed in verse 4. As Naomi also instructed, she keeps herself in secrecy, not letting Boaz know she is there (see Ruth 3:3). She uncovers the feet of Boaz and does nothing else until he speaks, as instructed. Naomi's plan was for Ruth to find rest through *offering* a marriage proposal. She will manipulate the kindness of Boaz into the perfect scenario for a levirate marriage.

The Adjustment Away from Manipulation (3:8-9)

Then something unexpected happens. When Boaz awakens at midnight, he is startled to find a woman at his feet. It is dark and he cannot see her or her attire. He may have been able to smell her perfume, but that would not have identified her the way you immediately recognize your mother's favorite scent on another woman in a crowd. So he has to stop and ask her identity.

If Boaz were not a man of integrity, there would not be any asking of a name. A woman on the threshing floor at this hour would be vulnerable, and it would be within Boaz's earthly sensibilities to think she is offering herself like a prostitute. But this noble near kinsman, having no ill intent but only having a fear of the Lord God of Israel, asks the identity of the woman in order to begin to discern what is happening.

That turning and asking by Boaz will change the situation for Ruth. That is, once Ruth is in the presence of the righteous Boaz, powerful landowner and near kinsman, she drops Naomi's plan for rest in favor of one that appeals to Boaz to act: she presents herself as a servant rather than an available maiden, she appeals to come under his care in the way in which he has described her coming under the Lord's care, and she recognizes him as the family redeemer rather than trying herself to redeem the family. In short, she stops trying to manipulate rest once she encounters the presence of Boaz. Ruth's obedience to Naomi's plan for rest through Boaz adjusts to an appeal to him as redeemer upon encountering him.

The Provision Apart from Manipulation (3:10-13)

Now Ruth's hope of redemption rests in the hands of Boaz alone. She is but a servant; Boaz can reject her appeal because she was sneaky, intentional, and even manipulative of his goodness for her own ends. But the appeal is an act of faith that receives blessing from Boaz because of Ruth's choice of him.

Boaz pronounces blessing on Ruth, again being compassionate to alleviate any fears she might have of his power and authority. He follows his blessing by praising her for choosing him over younger men. He again tells her not to fear for her redemption, speaking tenderly to her with the words *my daughter*. He gives his word that he will spread his wings over her—a metaphor for offering care and protection—which he does by pursing her redemption with an offer to the near kinsman. The righteous Boaz recognizes that the nearer kinsman has the rights and responsibilities toward building up the line of Naomi. If the nearer kinsman learns of Naomi and Ruth, they will be redeemed, and Boaz will have secured their purchase.

Boaz also leaves open the possibility of personally redeeming Ruth if the nearer kinsman shows himself to be derelict in his duties. Boaz's redemption plan considers far more than did Naomi's manipulative plan of redemption. As Ruth rests in Boaz and lies down until morning, Boaz will accomplish what can be gained by an appeal of faith and not by forcing someone to act according to the law. Boaz's plan gains Ruth the promise of redemption after they continue in rest until morning.

Both unbelievers and believers make attempts to manipulate their own provision and salvation. Unbelievers on one hand wish to demand that God conform to their liking, address the paradoxical questions of evil in this world to their liking, and jump at their beck and call to provide emergency healing for a dying relative before they will acknowledge him. Those are ways to engineer salvation by him or for unbelievers to remain masters of their own fates without needing to trust a God they cannot control.

On the other hand, unbelievers will present themselves as good or even religious people to others, hoping or assuming God will take their religious efforts as something more valuable than the death of his Son for their sins and his resurrection from the dead to offer life after death.

Similarly, they will try to regulate their adult single children's dating lives in order to secure a marriage and grandchildren, being no different from Naomi.

Believers will lobby in churches to like-minded, disgruntled members to turn the vision of a local congregation to their own liking. Instead, they should continue to give matters to prayer and wait on the leaders to give clarity and counsel. We have bought into the ideology that we are captains of our souls and that only by forcing our candidate into an office or getting our product or position more air time on social medial can we have any chance of maintaining the social values and community status we think we should have as Christians in the world— as if Jesus died so that we might make the world share our values and so that we might have status in our communities!

Jesus has a plan for rest that does not require us to manipulate plans, motives, intentions, goals, processes, or outcomes. We do not need to coerce, threaten to withhold love or inheritance, guilt-trip others into caring for us, or make all planning work to our level of detailed execution. Just as every unbeliever needs to trust the Lord for redemption by faith, believers need to trust the Lord for provision, sustenance, happiness, companionship, care in old age, change in the demeanor of a manager or pastor, and the full breadth of our redemption from beginning to end! We cannot manipulate present rest from God any more than we can manipulate final rest from God. We need to go back and ask him to make us encounter his presence through the Spirit so that we might drop our efforts to manipulate redemption from him.

Resting by Faith Incurs Abundant Blessings While Awaiting the Return of the Redeemer
RUTH 3:14-18

In case one might be tempted to think Ruth's deviation from Naomi's plan will be her undoing, the author gives us an insider's picture to what happens next. Ruth could end up with nothing because Boaz does not have to keep his word. Or Ruth could find redemption in the household of someone less noble, less compassionate, and of less integrity than Boaz. Ruth's identity could be exposed to others on the threshing floor, and she could go home empty-handed. Her plan to leave things at Boaz's discretion could have been her undoing.

The Blessing of an Honorable Name (3:14)

However, as Ruth obeys Boaz and rests until the morning, Boaz works to maintain an honorable reputation for Ruth. Losing her reputation would have made her less desirable for redemption in the eyes of another. It might have put her at risk to be harmed in a field if she needed to glean elsewhere.

The Blessing of Large Provision (3:15)

Boaz will send Ruth away with an unknown quantity of barley—simply "six measures." Even without knowing the size of the units, one sees the kindness of the act and the work of providing for the present need of Ruth and Naomi. The gesture certainly would have indicated the near-kinsman rest for which Naomi hoped.

The Blessing of Testifying about the Provider (3:16-17)

When Ruth returns to the city with the measure, however, her report of all Boaz did for her will reveal that the blessing has come by faith and not by planning. Ruth's testimony about Boaz will add words he said on the threshing floor that are only revealed in her report: Boaz expresses concern for the well-being of Naomi, Ruth's mother-in-law. The near kinsman's plan for redemption will do more than marry off Ruth; it will provide for Naomi.

The Blessing of Waiting for the Redeemer (3:18)

Naomi's final words in response to Ruth's report are significant. While the redemptive rest Ruth is seeking is promised, it is not immediate. The near kinsman has some work to do while she is back home. All Ruth can do is continue to trust that Boaz will be true to his word—as true and as merciful as he already has shown himself to be.

Ruth cannot run back to the threshing floor or be privy to the discussions of the men over the levirate marriage responsibilities. She cannot present herself as worthy of marriage or even valuable to a household. All she can do is wait until Boaz performs the acts of redemption.

Naomi has learned her lesson. She is trusting the redeemer rather than manipulating outcomes. Fanny Crosby's most famous hymn would state Naomi and Ruth's situation of trust and waiting with these lines:

> Perfect communion, perfect delight,
> visions of rapture now burst on my sight.
> Angels descending bring from above
> echoes of mercy, whispers of love.
> Perfect submission, all is at rest.
> I in my Savior am happy and bless'd,
> watching and waiting, looking above,
> filled with his goodness, lost in his love. (Fanny Crosby,
>   "Blessed Assurance")

We are a people who are watching and waiting for our Savior, Jesus, to provide final redemption for us. That same Jesus will provide all for us in this life as we rest by faith rather than trying to manipulate our own redemption.

Review and Discuss

1. When did you first learn that the Christian life is a walk of faith?
2. How should one understand the concept of "rest" in Scripture?
3. Why is resting a difficult discipline for believers to practice? What ideas in the culture contradict the biblical concept of resting?
4. What is good about Naomi's scheming? What is bad about Naomi's scheming?
5. Identify the four elements of Naomi's plan and the problems with them for Christians.
6. Why is matchmaking such a temptation even for believers? What might be the problem with third-party matchmaking?
7. How does Ruth alter Naomi's plan?
8. Name ways in which you have attempted to manipulate your own provision.
9. What would be the wrong way to understand the believer's need to rest for provision?
10. In what ways do Boaz's actions typify the work of Christ?

The Power of Legal Redemption

RUTH 4

Main Idea: Jesus's securing of Israel's redemption should bring praise and give us hope.

I. **Legal Redemption Exposes the Inability of False Redeemers (4:1-6).**
   A. The legal setting (4:1)
   B. The legal assembly (4:2)
   C. The legal case (4:3-4)
   D. The legal challenge (4:5-6)

II. **Legal Redemption Allows Witnesses to Affirm Redemption with Hope for Israel (4:7-12).**
   A. The legal custom (4:8)
   B. The legal witness (4:9-11a)
   C. The legal hope (4:11b-12)

III. **Legal Redemption Makes the Cosmic Marriage Complete with Glory for the Lord and David (4:13-22).**
   A. The legal consummation (4:13)
   B. The legal blessing (4:14-15)
   C. The legal lineage (4:16-22)

One amazing feat we occasionally witness at a high school graduation is a student who has completed school with perfect attendance. The achievement means that in the 2,340 school days from kindergarten through twelfth grade, the student never once missed a day. The accomplishment is even greater when you consider just some of the things involved in having a perfect attendance record. Perfect attendance means the student never took a sick day in thirteen years. Perfect attendance means the student did not let the weather ever deter her or him from being present. Perfect attendance means the student chose never to skip or hide out from school when he or she should have been in a seat; if the doors to the school were open, the student was there. The student did not miss class due to family vacation or by being a forced stand-in as a babysitter for younger siblings or an extra hand for the family business. Perfect attendance means the student could be counted on by his or her fellow students, coaches, music directors, and teachers to be on the campus at the start of each new school day.

Perfect attendance is a remarkable feat. But perfect attendance does not mean a perfect student. One could have perfect attendance but not perfect grades. One could have perfect attendance because he or she showed up in homeroom but actually skipped a class later in the day. Perfect attendance does not mean perfect attention because a student could be there but goofing off on a cell phone behind some books or daydreaming out a window. In fact, perfect attendance does not even imply perfect health, for we know from the COVID-19 pandemic experience that some parents are willing to send a student to school *sick*.

How about outside of school? Can we find perfection in our cities? Even the best citizens are not perfect citizens. Most law-abiding citizens are good people, but rare is the person who has never broken the speed limit, jaywalked, or had a parking violation—not even one for which you did not receive a fine. Uncommon is the person who never lived with an unknown housing code violation, always drove without even one day of an expired license plate, or never bent an HOA rule in order to have the house or amenities one desired in one's place of abode. Even more unusual is the person happily complying with every local law, every village fee, every additional tax, and every rule for every occupational, organizational, educational, or volunteer organization of which one is a part.

To be perfect in keeping the law is something only one human ever has done. That perfect law-keeping makes for us a perfect redeemer. Through a typological narrative in Ruth 4, Boaz is going to show us the power of a perfect redeemer and all it means for the greatness of our salvation in him.

Legal Redemption Exposes the Inability of False Redeemers
RUTH 4:1-6

The Legal Setting (4:1)

Having told Ruth that he would work to secure her redemption, Boaz now goes to the gate of the city—the place of legal transactions. That Boaz literally "went up" should not be lost on the reader of redemptive history, especially as much as Scripture runs an ascent-and-descent theme from the time of Moses's going up and down mountains, through David's going up and down hills and valleys, to Jesus's ascending the cross and descending into the grave—an idea most prevalent in the Fourth Gospel.

While in the gate, Boaz sees the nearer family guardian passing by. He invites this nameless person to take a seat with him, initiating what would be recognized as a discussion of business or legal affairs.

The Legal Assembly (4:2)

Additionally, Boaz calls ten elders from the village. They would act as witnesses to whatever discussion would now occur between Boaz and the nameless relative.

The Legal Case (4:3-4)

Before the elders, Boaz tells of Naomi's impending sale of the rights of her use of her clan's land until she is remarried or dies (Bush, *Ruth, Esther*, 202–4). He is legally informing the nearer relative so as to put before him the choice to acquire the land-use rights by redemption or make it known that the land is available for Boaz to redeem. Since it sounds like a way to gain more property, the nearer relative gladly agrees to redeem the land.

The Legal Challenge (4:5-6)

Yet the savvy Boaz has hidden the full picture from the eyes of the nearer relative. The land does not come as a simple cash cow. Instead, in comes with the responsibility of Ruth and of perpetuating the family name through the widow of the clan. This price is too much for the nearer relative to pay because it would mean he would have to split the inheritance for his children with any child born to Ruth. He rejects the offer to redeem Naomi's land and rights and offers to Boaz the prerogative to redeem Naomi, Ruth, and the land. In doing so, the man will expose himself as an unwilling redeemer due to his inherent inability to redeem the Israelite widow, the Moabite widow, and the land with its rights.

In redemptive history, Jesus's work to save the world redeems Israel legally where other would-be redeemers have failed—and that with the whole world watching. Like Boaz, Jesus must perform a legal action in order to redeem Israel and the Gentiles: he must keep the entirety of the law of God perfectly. Keeping the law perfectly will make Jesus perfectly righteous. In a sense different from Joseph, his earthly stepfather, who was known as a "righteous man," Jesus is righteous without a hint of unrighteousness. Whereas Joseph was righteous because he did what the law required of him when he sinned, Jesus never sinned and never had a need for making a guilt offering or any offering to atone for his sins.

Perfect righteousness means that Jesus could be a righteous substitutionary sacrifice to pay the price of complete righteousness on behalf of Israel and the Gentiles for their and our redemption. Having kept the legal code of God to perfection, Jesus could do what no one else could do. No other would-be savior of the human race could offer complete righteousness to God on behalf of sinful humanity. No other one claiming to be messiah or world ruler has met the legal requirement to rescue humanity from God's wrath against sinners.

Jesus's perfect keeping of the law allows him to be adjudicated legally on the cross by God the Father, and God remains "just" when he justifies sinners who have faith in Jesus's work on the cross (Rom 3:25-26). He shows that there is no other redeemer sufficient to provide what the peoples of Naomi and Ruth needed for redemption.

Legal Redemption Allows Witnesses to Affirm Redemption with Hope for Israel
RUTH 4:7-12

The writer continues with a note to help a generation removed from a custom in Israel to understand what they next will read. The inclusion of the note and the action also intend to portray that a legal transaction is taking place.

The Legal Custom (4:8)

The removing and giving of the sandal in ancient Israel was akin to signing a contract in contemporary society. The writer indicates the action was "legally binding," or "finalized" (NET), "attested" (ESV), and "confirmed" (ESV) in Israel. The nearer redeemer relinquishes his rights while removing his sandal to give it to Boaz, thus finalizing the transferring of redemption rights.

The Legal Witness (4:9-11a)

Wisely, Boaz is quick to solicit affirmation of the transaction from the witnesses present. The affirmation means the man cannot have a change of heart or mind on the transaction. It cannot be nullified by procedural error or a loophole in the law. Twice Boaz says to the onlookers, "You are witnesses today." Witnesses are the legal certifiers of a binding transaction.

Boaz solicits affirmation of their eyewitness testimony to two things. First, as the redeemer, he now has rights to the inheritance of Naomi left to her by Elimelech and her two sons, Chilion and Mahlon. He has the right to make sure Elimelech's name is not lost and his family's territory stays within the tribe in Israel.

Second, in his act of redemption, he gains Ruth as his wife. Boaz in detail describes her as Mahlon's widow, indicating he purposes to make sure Mahlon's name does not vanish from "among his relatives or from the gate of his hometown," which would be the court of his birthplace. Boaz is acting according to the law toward the widow in his clan, and his concern is for the legal perpetuation of the name of the deceased. In the history of Mahlon's hometown people, he wants Mahlon's name to be remembered for generations to come. Boaz gains the eyewitness affirmation from those present so that the transaction of redemption is both completed and sealed in perpetuity.

The Legal Hope (4:11b-12)

The response of the people is full of hope. They go well beyond the affirmation to express the hope of three blessings they look for the Lord to bring on Boaz for his actions as redeemer. First, *they wish for the home of Boaz and Ruth to be fruitful.* Rachel and Leah (and their maids) brought Jacob the twelve sons of Israel and a daughter, making up the nation of Israel. This happened despite the initial and intermittent barrenness of Rachel and Leah. They hope for Ruth, who appears to be barren (1:4), to have many descendants.

Second, *they hope for the strengthening of Boaz and for fame to come to his name.* The Hebrew phrase translated "powerful" might imply social power (CSB), financial prosperity (NET), worthy actions (ESV), or an additional statement on having children (NRSV). Wherever he and his posterity may be, whether Ephrathah or Bethlehem, their wish before the Lord for Boaz and Ruth is for his greatness and his fame.

Third, *they wish for a long line of male descendants.* They wish for this *despite the different beginnings for this child.* Perez, an ancestor of Boaz, was the offspring of Judah and Tamar after Tamar's widowhood. Perez then became the father of many generations of descendants. Knowing Perez's story, the witnesses wish the same for any child that comes from the union of the widowed and seemingly barren Ruth.

Each of these blessings grows out of the witnesses' reaction to the legal redemption by Boaz to secure Naomi. Seeing the legal course that will bring the wedding of Boaz and Ruth brings the celebratory wishes for the Lord's prosperous blessings to be on Boaz and Ruth.

When Jesus goes to the cross as the Lamb of God and Son, he goes as the legal sacrifice for Israel and as the price for redeeming Israel as the firstborn (Exod 4:22; 22:9; Lev 7:26). But his sacrifice is sufficient only if the Lord accepts it. The Father raises Christ from the dead, indicating his acceptance, and Paul tells us that more than five hundred people testified to his being alive after death (1 Cor 15:6)—that is, that the Father accepted the redemptive act of the Son and the Son certainly secured the redemption of Israel and the nations.

Legal Redemption Makes the Cosmic Marriage Complete with Glory for the Lord and David
RUTH 4:13-22

The remaining scenes of the Boaz redemption story all relate to marriage and the results of Boaz's marriage to Ruth. Yet one will notice that Naomi comes to the fore because the book of Ruth is a story about filling the emptiness of Naomi as much as it is a story about Ruth. The book carries the title of the Moabitess, but Naomi is the focus of this narrative.

- Naomi is the only character who remains from the opening scene when a family left Bethlehem for Moab to find food during a famine; she is left without husband and sons (so she is empty of family providers) in a land as a foreigner (1:5).
- Naomi is left with two daughters-in-law and no means of providing them with husbands (1:11-13).
- Naomi is welcomed back to Bethlehem as one "pleasant" although she felt "bitter" because the Almighty had struck her down (1:20-21).

- Naomi hatches a plan for Ruth's provision (2:1-2,22-23; 3:1-5,18).
- Naomi recognizes Boaz as her cousin and hopes in his goodness (2:20).
- Naomi is the one recognized for having a son, although Ruth bore the child (4:16-17).

The redemption-marriage of Boaz and Ruth results in everything that follows. While Boaz's redemption does secure land rights, the focus of this redemption story now becomes a male offspring who brings blessing to Boaz, Ruth, Naomi, and generations to come.

The Legal Consummation (4:13)

The writer is intentional in saying Boaz married Ruth, the two had a sexual consummation of the marriage, the Lord enabled the previously barren Ruth to become pregnant, and Ruth gave birth to a son. The development of Boaz as redeemer moves away from a direct discussion about land rights and building up the name of the dead to a focused discussion about the son born from the redemption-marriage and the acts that brought the birth of this seed.[97] Both land rights and building up the name of the dead now are tied into redemption-marriage yielding a son. The significance of the birth is evident in the details of the description, for the writer could have said more simply, "They bore a son." But the redemptive acts that would fulfill the emptiness of Naomi and Ruth involve marriage, sexual consummation, the divine opening of the womb, and the birth of a son in line with the ancient Genesis promise of the birth of a deliverer.

The Legal Blessing (4:14-15)

The women of the village once asked, "Can this be Naomi?" Now they are the ones heaping blessings of the Lord on the woman who once felt "Mara" within (see 1:19-20). They praise the Lord for his faithfulness, demonstrated in sending a redeemer. But the redeemer for Naomi is not Boaz. The women praise the Lord for sending the child born to Ruth, the offspring of the redemption-marriage, the seed the elders

---

[97] In Ruth 4:12, "offspring," or "seed," harks back to Gen 3:15 and the promise of a male offspring born to the woman who will conquer evil and evil's offspring.

hope to be full of the blessing of the line of Perez. It is the name of this son that they hope for the Lord to make great in Israel.

The son's significance for Naomi is that he will restore life to one who once had lost all hope, and he will sustain in old age the one who lost all her male, earthly providers to death. This son—this redemption-marriage son—is the kinsman redeemer of Naomi. He fills our understanding of the securer of land rights, rescuer of widows, and builder up of the name of the dead with the ideas of restorer of life and sustainer. Great indeed is the work of the kinsman redeemer!

Moreover, the women of the village recognize the blessing of Ruth to Naomi: she, the Moabitess daughter-in-law (and not genetic daughter), loves Naomi, is better to Ruth than seven sons, and has given the son-redeemer to Naomi. On the significance of these blessings, Daniel Block writes,

> But the women's last statement is the most remarkable of all. In the beginning Naomi had bitterly accused God of emptying her life by robbing her of her husband and her two sons. But now the women console her: she may have lost her sons, but she has gained a daughter-in-law. And what a daughter-in-law Ruth is! First, Ruth loves Naomi. . . . Second, Ruth has given birth to the *gō'ēl*. On the surface this may not seem so remarkable, but when one considers that she had been married to Mahlon for ten years but had borne no children for him, the significance of the statement becomes evident. The barren womb has been opened. Third, Ruth is better for Naomi than seven sons. The reference to "seven sons" is conventional, reflecting the ancient Israelite view that the ideal family consisted of seven sons. This is an amazing affirmation of the character of Ruth. All Bethlehem knew she was a noble woman (3:11), but these women place her value above seven sons; what extraordinary compensation for the two sons Naomi had lost! (*Judges, Ruth*, 728–29)

The Legal Lineage (4:16-22)

Naomi, apparently present at the birth of the child, becomes to the son a "mother" (CSB), "nurse" (ESV), or "caregiver" (NET).[98] The taking

---

[98] Naomi acts in the role of dry nurse. See footnote on "caregiver" in the NET Bible; see also Block, *Judges, Ruth*, 730.

of the son into her bosom overcomes the despair Naomi expressed as one who could not provide additional husbands for her daughters-in-law—as one who could not bear sons who would grow up to be the redeemers for the girls. The women again recognize that the son is given to Naomi even though he is born from Ruth. The writer intends for the reader to see that Naomi's hope for a full life did not rest in Moab, Elimelech, Chilion, Mahlon, Bethlehem, or even Boaz. Naomi's hope did not depend on her finding a means for keeping her family's lands within her family or even within her rights. Naomi's hope did not rest even on her being married again. Naomi's hope—that is, Naomi's *rest*—depended on a son from the redemption-marriage of Boaz and Ruth—a child they will name Obed.

This child is no small person in the history of redemption. First, in answer to the first prayer, this child would be for building the house of Israel. All Israel will prosper as a result of the birth of this son. Second, the son makes Boaz all the more powerful in Ephrathah by giving him an offspring to perpetuate his name. The name of Boaz is great in Bethlehem through this son, as the record of the genealogy shows.

Third, from this son comes a long line of male descendants in the vein of Perez who overcomes the sinful ways of their progenitor, Judah. Fourth, this son brings us the line of David, the original recipient of the Davidic covenant promises, the line through which a Son of David to rule the Lord's house forever will come. The double emphasis on David shows that the writer is identifying the redeemer-son of the redemptive marriage as *Davidic* to an audience who knew of David. The writer lives past the time of David, tying the great king after God's own heart to the Moabitess who loved Israel's God with her whole heart. The double emphasis invited the readers to consider the son's role in the redemptive plan of God.

Just as the final scenes of the book of Ruth all relate to the marriage of Boaz and Ruth, so the entirety of redemption is a story of marriage, of the cosmic marriage, the marriage between God and his people. In the plan of redemption, the Lord makes a marriage between himself and Israel when he covenants with them at Sinai (see Ezek 16:3; Jer 2:2; Hos 2:15). Israel is the wife of God—albeit the unfaithful wife whose idolatrous ways are adulterous acts against her Husband.

Yet from the Lord's choosing to make Israel his own, from them will come a promised Son. The Son of this union has rights to all the land allotted to ancient Israel, and he will claim them as Lord of all. This Son will build up the names of the dead by raising from the dead those who have placed their faith in him for eternal life.

This Son will be a restorer of life for his people and will sustain his people through all eternity. This Son is from the line that traces some of its origins to Boaz—this Son is a member of the Davidic line. This is the final Son of David who builds the house of God as one over the house and redeems the whole world as the greater Boaz and the greater Obed.

The Son of David, Son of Man, Son of Mary, Son of God is the promised Son who will bring glory to the house of David and redeem all those waiting for the redemption of Israel, and he is the redemption of everyone who has placed trust in him.

Review and Discuss

1. What are some common, false redeemers on whom people lean for their forms of redemption?
2. In what concrete ways are the above false redeemers unqualified to provide salvation?
3. In practice, what would it have meant for Jesus to be perfect as a child and teen?
4. In practice, what would perfection have meant for Jesus's thought life, speech, motives, intentions, and goals?
5. Why is eyewitness affirmation of Boaz's legal transaction important?
6. How does the Father reveal his acceptance of Jesus's legal atonement on behalf of Israel?
7. How does this chapter reveal the redemption of Ruth?
8. How does this chapter reveal the redemption of Naomi?
9. Based on Ruth 1–4, what is involved in the redemption of Israel?
10. How does Ruth 1–4 offer hope for a society that resembles Judges 1–21? (See Ruth 1:1.)

WORKS CITED

The 1689 Baptist Confession of Faith. https://www.the1689confession .com/1689/chapter-2. Accessed December 8, 2020.

Alexander, Paul. "Is Congregationalism a Democracy?" *9Marks Journal* (February 26, 2010). https://www.9marks.org/article /congregationalism-democracy. Accessed December 3, 2020.

Asmelash, Leah. "In the New Game of Monopoly, Women Make More Than Men." CNN.com, September 10, 2019. https://www.cnn.com /2019/09/10/us/hasbro-ms-monopoly-trnd/index.html. Accessed January 4, 2021.

The Baptist Faith and Message 2000. https://bfm.sbc.net/bfm2000. Accessed March 18, 2021.

Beldman, David J. H. *Deserting the King: The Book of Judges.* Transformative Word. Bellingham, WA: Lexham, 2017.

Block, Daniel. *Judges, Ruth.* New American Commentary. Nashville: B&H, 1999.

Boling, R. G. *Judges.* The Anchor Bible. New York: Doubleday, 1974.

Bowling, Andrew C. "Judges." Pages 158–78 in *Evangelical Commentary on the Bible.* Edited by Walter A. Elwell. Grand Rapids, MI: Baker Book House, 1995.

Bush, F. W. *Ruth, Esther.* Word Biblical Commentary. Waco: Word, 1996.

Butler, Trent C. *Judges.* Word Biblical Commentary. Nashville: Thomas Nelson, 2009.

Calvin, John. *Institutes of the Christian Religion.* Translated by Henry Beveridge. Christian Classics Ethereal Library. https://ccel.org /ccel/calvin/institutes/institutes.iii.xii.html. Accessed December 2, 2020.

Chase, Mitchell L. *40 Questions about Typology and Allegory.* Grand Rapids, MI: Kregel Academic, 2020.

Cornelius, Emmitt, Jr. "Anatomy of a Church Split." *Leadership,* December 10, 2012. https://www.christianitytoday.com/pastors/2012/december

-online-only/anatomy-of-church-split.html. Accessed December 22, 2020.

"Damned Lies—Nine Wars Started under False Pretexts." *Military History Now,* July 15, 2015. https://militaryhistorynow.com/2015/07/15 /damned-lies-nine-wars-started-under-false-pretexts. Accessed December 21, 2020.

Dates, Charlie. "'We Out': Charlie Dates on Why His Church Is Leaving the SBC over Rejection of Critical Race Theory." Religion News Service, December 18, 2020. https://religionnews.com/2020/12/18 /we-out-charlie-dates-on-why-his-church-is-leaving-the-sbc-over -rejection-of-critical-race-theory. Accessed December 21, 2020.

Davis, Dale Ralph. *Judges: Such a Great Salvation.* Ross-shire, UK: Christian Focus, 2000.

Diamant, Jeff. "Half of U.S. Christians Say Casual Sex Between Consenting Adults Is Sometimes or Always Acceptable." Pew Research Center, August 31, 2020. https://www.pewresearch.org/fact-tank/2020/08 /31/half-of-u-s-christians-say-casual-sex-between-consenting-adults -is-sometimes-or-always-acceptable. Accessed March 9, 2021.

Dueck, Ryan. "Angry at the God Who Isn't There: The New Atheism as Theodicy." *Direction* 40 (Spring 2011): 3–16.

Fausset, A. R. *A Critical and Expository Commentary on the Book of Judges.* London: James Nisbet and Company, 1885.

Gender Equality Funds. "Gender Equity in the Workplace." https:// genderequalityfunds.org/gender-equality-workplace. Accessed January 4, 2021.

Grisanti, Michael A. "Inspiration, Inerrancy, and the OT Canon: The Place of Textual Updating in an Inerrant View of Scripture." *JETS* 44 (2001): 577–98.

Gupta, Nijay. "Why Deborah Makes All the Difference." *CBE International.* https://www.cbeinternational.org/resource/article/mutuality -blog-magazine/why-deborah-makes-all-difference. Accessed March 17, 2021.

Gurnall, William. *The Christian in Complete Armour: A Treatise of the Saints' War against the Devil.* Christian Classics Ethereal Library. https:// www.ccel.org/ccel/gurnall/armour/files/armour1.pdf. Accessed December 17, 2021.

Hawk, Daniel L. *Ruth.* Apollos Old Testament Commentary. Downers Grove, IL: IVP Academic, 2015.

Hegewisch, Ariane, and Adiam Tesfaselassie. "The Gender Wage Gap: 2018; Earnings Differences by Gender, Race, and Ethnicity." IWPR #C484 (September 2019). https://iwpr.org/publications/annual -gender-wage gap 2018, Accessed January 4, 2021.

Hubbard, Robert L. *The Book of Ruth*. The New International Commentary on the Old Testament. Grand Rapids, MI: Eerdmans, 1988.

Jansen, Tanya. "How Societal Influences Affect the Gender Pay Gap." *HR Daily Advisor*, November 8, 2019. https://hrdailyadvisor.blr com/2019/11/08/how-societal-influences-affect-the-gender-pay -gap. Accessed January 4, 2021.

Kaufman, Joanne. "A Sign of 'Modern Society': More Multiracial Families in Commercials." *New York Times*, June 3, 2018. https:// www.nytimes.com/2018/06/03/business/media/advertising -multiracial-families.html. Accessed December 10, 2020.

Keach, Benjamin. *The 1677 Baptist Catechism*. http://baptiststudiesonline. com/wp-content/uploads/2007/02/keachs-catechism-of-1677.pdf. Accessed December 8, 2020.

_____. *Keach's Catechism*. Association of Reformed Baptist Churches of America. https://www.arbca.com/1689-confession. Accessed March 17, 2021.

Keely, Douglas F., and Philip B. Rollinson. *The Westminster Shorter Catechism in Modern English*. Phillipsburg, NJ: P&R, 1986.

Lewis, C. S. *The Screwtape Letters*. Toronto: Samizdat Ebooks, 2016.

_____. *Till We Have Faces: A Myth Retold*. New York: Houghton Mifflin Harcourt, 1980.

McKissic, Dwight. "From Boys to Men: My Response to the SBC Seminary Presidents' CRT Statement." *SBC Voices*, December 14, 2020. https://sbcvoices.com/from-boys-to-men-my-response-to-the-sbc -seminary-presidents-crt-statement. Accessed December 21, 2020.

Morin, Rebecca. "Vice President Kamala Harris Pushes Back on Criticism for Not Visiting the US-Mexico Border." *USA Today*, June 8, 2021. https://www.usatoday.com/story/news/politics/2021/06/08 /kamala-harris-lester-holt-interview-pushes-back-border-criticism /7600802002. Accessed June 24, 2021.

Nicholson, Bebe. "Hostility to Christianity Is Growing: Why This Is Dangerous and What Christians Can Do about It." *Medium*, September 24, 2019. https://medium.com/publishous/hostility-to -christianity-is-growing-ced4972e721a.

Nielson, Jon. "Why Youth Stay in Church When They Grow Up." *The Gospel Coalition*, July 29, 2011. https://www.thegospelcoalition.org/article/why-youth-stay-in-church-when-they-grow-up. Accessed November 27, 2020.

Noble, Alan. "The Evangelical Persecution Complex." *The Atlantic*. August 4, 2014. https://www.theatlantic.com/national/archive/2014/08/the-evangelical-persecution-complex/375506. Accessed November 27, 2020.

Peoples, Steve, and Jake Bleiberg. "'Obviously a Mistake': Cruz Returns from Cancun after Uproar." AP News, February 18, 2021. https://apnews.com/article/ted-cruz-mexico-vacation-amid-storm-b0cdc326db95bf25d93de9e877e05862. Accessed June 24, 2021.

Powell, Alvin. "McLean's Rosmarin Offers Perspective on the Pandemic's Raging Effects." *Harvard Gazette*. August 14, 2020. https://news.harvard.edu/gazette/story/2020/08/a-closer-look-at-americas-pandemic-fueled-anger. Accessed June 5, 2021.

Rivas, Jorge. "Cheerios Ad Starring Interracial Family Ignites Racist Hate Storm." Colorlines.com, May 31, 2013. https://www.colorlines.com/articles/cheerios-ad-starring-interracial-family-ignites-racist-hate-storm. Accessed December 10, 2020.

Ryken, Philip Graham. *Christian Worldview: A Student's Guide*. Wheaton, IL: Crossway, 2013.

Schatz, Elihu A. "The Length of the Rule of Joshua and the Periods of Subjugation in the Book of Judges." *Jewish Bible Quarterly* 41, no. 1 (2013): 32–34.

Sequeira, Aubrey, and Samuel C. Emadi. "Biblical-Theological Exegesis and the Nature of Typology." *SBJT* 21, no. 1 (Spring 2017): 11–34.

"The Simple Truth about the Gender Pay Gap." AAUW (Fall 2018). https://www.aauw.org/research/the-simple-truth-about-the-gender-pay-gap. Accessed January 4, 2021.

Smith, Mitzi J. "Reading the Story of the Levite's Concubine through the Lens of Modern-day Sex Trafficking." *Ashland Theological Journal* 41 (2009): 15–34.

Solzhenitsyn, Aleksandr. "A World Split Apart: Solzhenitsyn's Commencement Address, Harvard University, June 8, 1978." The Aleksandr Solzhenitsyn Center. https://www.solzhenitsyncenter.org/a-world-split-apart. Accessed March 9, 2021.

Spurgeon, Charles Haddon. "Chariots of Iron." *Metropolitan Tabernacle Pulpit Volume 28*. The Charles Spurgeon Center. https://www

.spurgeon.org/resource-library/sermons/chariots-of-iron /#flipbook. Accessed March 11, 2021.

Stankiewicz, Kevin. "Unruly Behavior from Plane Passengers Has Never Been This Bad, Says Flight Attendant Union Chief." CNBC, May 28, 2021. https://www.cnbc.com/2021/05/28/unruly-behavior-from -passengers-has-never-been-this-bad-union-chief.html. Accessed March 31, 2022.

Starke, Rachael. "Be a Boaz in Your Business." *The Gospel Coalition,* October 13, 2017. https://www.thegospelcoalition.org/article/be -a-boaz-in-your-business. Accessed January 7, 2021.

Stott, John R. W. *The Cross of Christ.* Downers Grove, IL: InterVarsity Press, 1986.

Tolkien, J. R. R. *The Fellowship of the Ring.* Boston: Houghton Mifflin Company, 1954.

Webb, Barry G. *The Book of the Judges: An Integrated Reading.* Journal for the Study of the Old Testament Supplement Series 46. Sheffield: Sheffield Academic Press, 1987.

West, Ralph D. "Commentary: Where I Stand on the Statement by SBC Seminary Presidents." *Baptist Standard.* https://www.baptiststandard .com/opinion/other-opinions/commentary-where-i-stand-on-the -statement-by-sbc-seminary-presidents. Accessed December 21, 2020.

Whitaker, Richard, ed. *The Abridged Brown-Driver-Briggs Hebrew-English Lexicon of the Old Testament: From a Hebrew and English Lexicon of the Old Testament by Francis Brown, S. R. Driver and Charles Briggs, Based on the Lexicon of Wilhelm Gesenius.* Boston: Houghton, Mifflin and Company, 1906.

"Women Are Paid Less than Men—and That Hits Harder in an Economic Crisis." *Lean In.* https://leanin.org/equal-pay-data-about -the-gender-pay-gap. Accessed December 17, 2021.

"World War I." History.com. https://www.history.com/topics/world-war -i/world-war-i-history. Accessed December 21, 2020.

Younger, K. Lawson *Judges–Ruth.* NIV Application Commentary. Grand Rapids, MI: Zondervan Academic, 2002.

SCRIPTURE INDEX

10:16 *128*
10:30,38 *76*
12:45 *76*
14:7-9 *76*
17:2,4 *100*
17:3-4 *76*
19:29-30 *278*

Acts
2:23-24 *137*
4:27-28 *137*
7:9-13 *129*
7:23-29,35-36
  129
17:31 *141*
20:17-35 *38*
20:28 *33*

Romans
3:25-26 *298*
5:9 *119*
6:4 *285*
8:4 *285*
9:14-18 *79*
10:21 *175*
13:4-5 *119*
13:13 *187, 285*
14:10-12 *99*

1 Corinthians
6:2-3 *98*
6:7 *34*
6:9-10 *187*
9:25 *186*
10:12-13 *182*
10:31 *186*
15 *100*
15:6 *300*
15:24-28 *100*

2 Corinthians
5:7 *285*
5:10 *99*
6:14–7:1 *217*
9:15 *139*
10:3 *285*
10:4-5 *85*
12:9 *89*

Galatians
3:28-39 *244*
5:16 *285*
5:16-23 *229*
5:23 *186*
6:16 *285*

Ephesians
1:3-5 *139*
1:19-23 *xi*
1:22 *99*
2:10 *285*
4:1,17 *285*
5:2,8,15 *285*
5:6 *120*
5:7,11 *217*
6:4 *160*
6:10-12 *35*
6:13-14 *182*

Philippians
2:3-4 *21*

Colossians
1:10 *285*
2:6 *285*
2:15 *85*
4:5 *285*

1 Thessalonians
2:21 *285*
4:1 *285*

4:12 *285*

2 Thessalonians
1:8 *96*
2:8 *96*
3:11 *285*

1 Timothy
1:17 *76*
2:9,15 *186*
2:12 *57*
3:2 *57*
3:3,8 *187*
5:17-20 *33*
6:16 *76*

2 Timothy
1:7 *186*
4:3 *33*
4:16-17 *267*

Titus
1:6 *57*
1:8 *186*
1:12 *187*
2:2,5-6,12 *186*

Hebrews
2:8 *99*
4:13 *99*
4:16 *188*
8:12 *188*
10:13 *99*
11:32 *184*
12:29 *96*
13:5 *77, 208*
13:17 *33, 99*

James
3:1 *xv*